COWBOY

In The Roundhouse

A Political Life

by BRUCE KING

as told to Charles Poling

SUNSTONE
PRESS

SANTA FE
New Mexico

Printed and bound in the United States of America. No part of this book may be reproduced in any form or by any electronic or mechanical means including information storage and retrieval systems, without permission in writing from the publisher, except by a reviewer who may quote brief passages in a review.

Sunstone books may be purchased for educational, business, or sales promotional use. For information please write: Special Markets Department, Sunstone Press, P.O. Box 2321, Santa Fe, New Mexico 87504-2321.

FIRST EDITION

10 9 8 7 6 5 4 3 2 1

Library of Congress Cataloging in Publication Data:

King, Bruce, 1924–
    Cowboy in the roundhouse : a political life / by Bruce King as told to Charles Poling.— 1st edition
        p. cm.
    Includes index.
    ISBN: 0-86534-280-6
    1. King, Bruce, 1924– . 2. Governors—New Mexico—Biography. 3. New Mexico—Politics and government—1951– 4. United States—Politics and government—1945–1989. 5. United States—Politics and government—1989–   I. Poling, Charles. II. Title.
F801. 4.K56K56   1998
978.9' 053'092—dc21
[B]   98-37896
                                   CIP

Published by SUNSTONE PRESS
              Post Office Box 2321
              Santa Fe, NM 87504-2321 / USA
              (505) 988-4418 / *orders only* (800) 243-5644
              FAX (505) 988-1025

Contents

Acknowledgements

Many people contributed their efforts and expertise to this book. I am particularly grateful to Virginia Sears and the late Paul Sears for their early interest in helping me write a book about my political life. I began this manuscript in the mid-1980s, when Paul started to tape my story. He also interviewed Jim Baca, Raymond Sanchez, Linda Kehoe, and Kay Marr while gathering background material on my early career. Melissa Howard helped organize and edit those early transcripts, which lay untouched until Charles Poling approached me in 1996 about writing a book on my political life.

We expanded on these earlier materials to include the events since my second administration. During writing this phase, others provided information to Charles and me, including Bill Garcia, Caroline Gaston, Gary King, John McKean, and Chuck Spath. John Garcia and Tony Hillerman deserve credit for urging Charles to pursue the project, while his father, The Rev. David Poling, provided advice and counsel as the manuscript developed. I am grateful to Charles for his help in crafting the manuscript into its present form. We both wish to thank all the State of New Mexico employees who helped, especially those at the State Library, the Secretary of State's office, and the Capitol.

Finally, I am eternally indebted to my wife, Alice King, for her ongoing support and her keen insights during the writing of this book. Her presence can be felt on every page.

—*Bruce King, Stanley, New Mexico, September 1998.*

Foreword

While I count myself among the many who wanted Bruce King to write an autobiography, I doubt if any of us had much hope he'd get around to doing it. Now he has and it's even better than we'd expected. We had feared Governor King's famous aversion to speaking ill of anyone (even during election campaigns) would cause him to gloss over interesting battles that marked his career in New Mexico politics. We should have known better. King presents his foes as reasonable people whose sole offense was having a different vision than he did on the issue in question. We should have remembered the Governor's unspoken motto: "Today's enemy, but tomorrow's friend."

I first became aware of Bruce King as someone special in politics about 45 years ago. Before coming to New Mexico, I had cut my teeth on political reporting in Texas, and sharpened them covering the Oklahoma Legislature. Otis Sullivan was the dean of the news room, where the operating philosophy of the capitol press corps divided the population into three classes: the taxpayers were sheep, the politicians were wolves, and we reporters were watchdogs. As Sullivan taught us, one told when a politician was being truthful by carefully watching his face. "If his lips move, he's lying."

This was the attitude I brought to Santa Fe in 1952 as United Press bureau manager. It prevailed when King had become Santa Fe County Commissioner and I was editing the *New Mexican*.

We crossed swords over a road project. The newspaper wanted the commission to revise its project priority list and pave Hyde Park, the access to

Santa Fe Ski Basin. King insisted on sticking to the priorities and paving a farm road to Moomey's Corner. As I remember the rhetoric I was using to lambaste King in my editorials, I argued that this road served only a handful of families, including the King Brothers Ranch, while the Hyde Park road would serve untold countless multitudes of taxpayers.

After a few such broadsides, King suggested we have a talk. His message: 1. The farm road project would be built no matter what I thought. 2. If I would get off his back, he would promise me that Hyde Park road would be promptly paved.

Where would he get the money? He would find a source for that. How? Well, he couldn't be specific.

Reading an early section of this book, I learned 45 years later why King was so reticent. He had persuaded U.S. Senator Dennis Chávez, chairman of the Public Works Committee, to use his clout with the Bureau of Public Roads to lend a helping hand. The senator had asked King to keep the arrangement quiet. King had pledged his silence, and he had kept that promise to the senator. In hindsight I'm impressed, but I shouldn't be surprised. That was the reputation King had established. I had asked about him among the old pols referenced by newsmen as those sources "who asked not to be identified." Yes, they had said, keeping his word was a peculiarity of the commissioner. The late Mike Gallegos (who claimed to be the only man fired three times by Governor Edwin L. Mechem) put it like this: "Bruce just won't make a promise unless he knows he can keep it, and that makes it hard to get votes lined up for him."

The next time King seriously impressed me was as a freshman member of the Agriculture Committee of the New Mexico House—a committee dominated by elderly farmers and ranchers where youngsters were expected to sit quietly and vote as advised. The committee was dealing with a proposal to require railroads to build sheep-proof fences along the right-of-way. Back in Oklahoma the press corps would have presumed this was a "Milnot," named after a company that manufactured a popular non-dairy condensed milk substitute. In defense of dairy farmers, legislators introduced anti-Milnot bills, giving Milnot lobbyists chances to persuade key lawmakers to be reasonable as the measures moved through various committees. Thus the bills would die forgotten in the final rush to adjournment. Milnot, Inc., finally tired of this expensive procedure, built a plant straddling the Oklahoma-Kansas border, and let it be known it was ready to produce only in the Kansas end of the factory. That ended the Milnot shakedowns but by then the Milnot tag stuck to all such bills.

The sheep fence proposal might be a New Mexico version of a Milnot. On the other hand, it might merely represent self-interests of the farmer-rancher committee, with a little element of revenge against the monopoly railroads that had exploited them for generations. Either way, it seemed the Agriculture Committee would pass the bill and start it on its way to the next committee. But it was not to be. Young Bruce King, a rancher himself, took the floor to say a word or two about it.

King told the committee that farm-ranch interests had the votes in this session to pass the bill. He reminded them of the days when the railroads controlled the legislature much as agriculture controlled it now. But rural political power was fading. Soon the cities would dominate. King argued it was unwise for agriculture to use its power to impose such punitive legislation on the state. I was surprised to hear that, and I was even more surprised by the respect the old timers had for this newcomer. They took King's advice and killed the bill.

King moved up another notch in my opinion. I already knew he kept his promises. Now I knew he would take the long view of things, even at the cost of alienating key people in his rural political base. The next decades provided a multitude of other illustrations of Bruce King's character, and why we New Mexicans can count ourselves lucky he dominated our state's development during the last half of the Twentieth Century.

I should end this introduction and start you reading an honest autobiography that will help restore your confidence in our political process. But first a final anecdote. The late Jesse Price, then information director of the University of New Mexico, shared my admiration of King. We wanted to help him in his first run for governor. King, a cowboy all his life, sounded like one. Since radio and television were becoming politically important, we thought King's weakness as an orator would hurt him in the huge city precincts full of newcomers. We called a University of New Mexico speech professor who remembered King folly from his student days. Yes, he'd be pleased to work with King to improve his rhetoric and delivery. Jesse and I met King for lunch and made our proposal. It was the closest to anger I've ever seen in the man.

He was polite about it, knowing we meant well. But he let us know he wouldn't try to persuade voters he was something he wasn't. If they didn't want a Stanley rancher for Governor, they should vote for someone else.

That's Bruce King. What you see is what you get. And we New Mexicans have been smart enough to show, election after election, that we liked what we saw.

—*Tony Hillerman*

1

A New Day In Politics

The idea of being governor first entered my head when I was in the seventh grade. On a sunny winter day in 1936, Governor Clyde Tingley came out to dedicate our new school at Stanley, New Mexico, about 40 miles south of Santa Fe. Us kids were all excited about the new building, which had been a community project—the Works Progress Administration had furnished the labor and the community had provided the materials. Now Governor Tingley was standing in front of us, saying, "I hope I'll live to see one of you students sitting in the governor's chair." Well, I got to thinking, if it was going to be one of us, it might as well be me.

I like to tell that story to students today, and I always add, "Perhaps one of you girls is someday going to be the first woman governor of New Mexico." I get more applause for that remark than anything else I say in the schools.

Governor Tingley and my dad, Bill King, were very good friends. Dad had been a staunch and active Democrat at a time when that was a rare breed in Santa Fe County, although everything changed after the New Deal. He had known Governor Tingley for years, helping on his successful campaigns for mayor of Albuquerque and for governor.

I learned something about politics from my dad, but first he taught me about farming and ranching. In 1918 he and my mother, Molly King, drove their Ford Model T roadster out from Robert Lee, Texas, to visit some friends at Stanley. They were looking for a quarter-section homestead, but discovered that other farmers had already staked claims to all the available free land. Undaunted, they asked around and found some folks four miles west of

Stanley who hadn't lived on their homestead long enough to satisfy the requirements for ownership and wanted out. My parents struck a deal with them, trading that Model T for the rights to the homestead. If they could meet the requirements of the Homestead Act, the land would be theirs. They got 160 acres and all the improvements: a dugout to live in, a milk cow or two, a couple of horses, and an old circus mule that kicked whenever you took off the bridle. As part of the deal, the original homesteaders hauled out of the dugout whatever furnishings they could squeeze into the Model T and drove off. That left my parents with just the horses and an ornery mule for transportation. They were true pioneers.

Governor Clyde Tingley inspired me to run for governor. Shown here standing outside the old Governor's Mansion in downtown Santa Fe, Governor Tingley visited our school at Stanley the same year this picture was taken in 1936. He even drove the same car. (Photograph courtesy Museum of New Mexico, #50497)

Stanley sits out on the plains toward the northern end of New Mexico's 60-mile-long Estancia Valley, an ancient lake bed that long ago went dry. The land lies very flat right around here without many trees, but from our ranch you can see mountains in three directions. The Sangre de Cristo range spreads in an arc across the northern horizon from above Santa Fe eastward clear to Las Vegas. Snow covers those high peaks about half the year. Close by Stanley to the northwest are the San Pedro Mountains, which have been mined for gold, lead, and coal. Farther west—about 20 miles—the Sandia Mountains rise to a long ridgeline above 10,000 feet. Out of sight beyond them lie the Rio Grande valley and Albuquerque, the state's largest city, which is about 35 miles or so due west of Stanley through the pass at Tijeras Canyon. Just south of the canyon, the Manzano Mountains pick up and stretch far into the southwest.

At over 6,000 feet elevation, Stanley often gets cold and snowy winters by Southwest standards, but spotty rainfall makes dryland farming risky without deep-well irrigation. However, this climate didn't frighten off the early homesteaders, who made a go of it with crops like pinto beans and corn during some fairly rainy years. Unlike today, Stanley was a bustling farm town in the early twentieth century. With every 160-acre homestead taken by the time my parents came, the entire Estancia Valley was much more populated back then and for a while it was prosperous. It's hard to believe now, but Stanley had two hotels, a couple of restaurants, several businesses, its own newspaper, and stock pens to hold animals for shipping. Miners hauled lead and gold ore down from the San Pedro Mountains by wagon to the Stanley depot of the New Mexico Central Railroad. The road they took from the mountains to town passed right by our homestead, so people often stopped to rest and water their stock. If travelers needed to put up overnight, my folks gave them a place to sleep and my mother made sure no one went hungry.

The drought of the 1920s and the Great Depression brought a change in fortunes for many folks in our area. Farmers found it harder to make a living with dryland crops and credit was getting tight. We didn't have much money, ourselves. By then, my parents had four children. The oldest two—my sister Leota and my brother Sam—were born in the dugout and lived there a few years. By the time I came along in 1924, we lived in a house. My younger brother, Don, was born six years after me in an Albuquerque hospital. To support the family in those early days, my dad did all kinds of things.

He was a good mechanic, and during my folks' first winter here he worked in a Santa Fe garage. He also took winter jobs in Albuquerque. Later he would sell milk and meat door to door all around the Estancia Valley.

My parents were compassionate people. During the hard years of the Depression, they gave food to those who couldn't pay. People learned if they were really hurting to come to my dad and he would help them some way. If they needed a place to stay for a couple days or a couple months, he would put them up. I grew up thinking that this kind of hospitality and generosity were a way of life. You shared what you had, and you helped people who didn't have as much as you.

From early on, Bill King showed an entrepreneurial streak. In 1920, he got a tractor and farmed another 320 acres with a neighbor. Then 1922 and 1923 were dry years here, so he couldn't plant, but from the weeds and whatever else grew, he managed to cut feed for livestock. Those drought years were hard on farmers, and people were moving out. Santa Fe banker and future Governor Arthur Seligman was a major lender to farmers in the 1920s, and with so many people defaulting on their loans, he had to repossess their livestock. Seligman asked Dad to gather and keep the stock—mostly Holsteins, or dairy cows—until the bank could sell the animals to cover the debt. My dad bought some of those cows and sold the cream and milk, which gave him another source of income. The W.S. King and Sons Ranch was now a growing, diversified outfit.

Bill and Molly King's homestead looked something like this rustic home of Fred and Glenna Myers, six miles west of Stanley, New Mexico, in the early Twentieth Century. When I was growing up, we called this place the Mort Dunning house. The site is now on the King Brothers Ranch, though the building was torn down long ago. (Photograph courtesy Museum of New Mexico, #85886)

All us kids worked on the ranch from the time we could heft a half-bucket of grain. We learned to ride about as soon as we could walk. Our parents drilled into us the belief that success comes from elbow grease and the sweat of your brow. It was a rewarding way of life and even as a young man I never had any doubts I would be a farmer and a rancher. I did attend the University of New Mexico in Albuquerque in 1942, where I played a little football. Pretty soon, though, I went back to work on the ranch. These were war years, of course, and while my older brother had a deferment to work on the farm, I was drafted in 1945. At first I was going into the field artillery, but the war ended and we didn't have much need for artillery men, so I was assigned to the military police and served about a year in Kyoto, Japan.

When I was mustered out of the Army in the spring of 1946, I came back to New Mexico and again took my place alongside Dad and my brothers running the family ranch. I had already invested my life savings in expanding our holdings. While I was a soldier, I had saved my salary in a special account, which I used after I got out of the Army to buy even more farm land. Pretty soon, my brothers and I owned about half the W.S. King and Sons Ranch, although it was still pretty small back then and we didn't have much hired help. I always handled the cattle, my older brother Sam took care of the farming, and my younger brother Don ran the trucking operation—we hauled cattle, feed, beans, all kinds of things. Leota had gone off to college in Texas, then married and moved to Montana, so she wasn't involved in the ranch.

I hadn't been back in Stanley long after the Army when George Blackwell, a friend of mine just out of the Marine Corps, came by one Sunday and asked me to go with him to the Moriarty Baptist Church, a dozen or so miles south on highway 41. I knew most of the kids there, so I stayed on after the service for punch and cookies. One fine-looking young lady caught my eye. Her name was Alice Martin. I went up to her and we started talking. We found we had a lot in common. Like me, she came from a pioneer Estancia Valley family. Her great-grandfather had come from Scotland and settled around Moriarty. Her dad had a small dairy operation. I liked her a lot, and I guess she liked me, so we started seeing each other regularly after that. Things went pretty well and in 1947 Alice and I got married. Since then, we have been lifelong partners in everything, both the ranch and politics.

Alice and I moved into a house that was really just a couple homestead shacks nailed together, four miles north of our current house. It was rustic. We didn't have any electricity or a telephone, we burned wood for cooking and heating, and we had to carry water from a well to the house. That was pretty much how everybody lived at that time. When winter came, sometimes I could barely fight my way home through the snow. The weather was just terrible. It's a wonder nobody froze to death in those years. After we lived about six months in those little shacks, Dad built us a house, as he did for all of us when we got married. They finished one room so we could move in out of our cold homesteader place, then they continued working with us in it. Alice and I lived in that house for 28 years, until 1975.

Alice Martin became my wife in 1947. After the ceremony, we posed outside behind our wedding cake on the ranch at Stanley.

One day in 1949, my dad and I went out to check our first crop of wheat grown with water from our new irrigation well. Afterwards, I dropped him off at the house to have lunch. He went in, sat down on the divan, and fell over. He was having one of his spells, as we called them. It was a cerebral hemorrhage. My brother Don ran out to get me, but when I got back there, he was dead. The nearest phone was in town at Stanley, so calling a doctor wasn't any help. My brothers and I tried to revive him, but we were too late. He died just that quick, at age 57. Though he was still young, at least he lived to see the benefits of all our labor putting in that irrigation system.

My dad's death was a hard loss, but we knew we had to keep the ranch going. My brothers and I took the whole outfit over, and we eventually changed the name to King Brothers Ranch. My mother continued keeping the books and otherwise working with the business. The 1950s were hard drought years, almost another Dust Bowl in the Estancia Valley. When the wind got to blowing, Alice would hang sheets over the windows to keep the dust out. You felt like you ate a dose of grit with every meal. As these dry years put the squeeze on farmers, many of them just gave up and moved away. We were able to acquire their land and by sinking more irrigation wells so we weren't so dependent on the weather to raise a crop, we managed to survive those challenging times.

≈≈

Besides running the ranch, Dad was active in county politics until he passed away in 1949, so politics seemed as natural a part of my life as plowing a field or mending fence. He knew just about everybody and was friendly with a few governors, including Clyde Tingley, John Miles, and Arthur Seligman, who had been my dad's banker. Bill King had been precinct chairman in Stanley and one of the four Democratic Party committeemen for Santa Fe County. When the position of foreman came up in 1932 for the highway district that ran from Santa Fe southeast 90 miles to Encino on highway 285, my dad went up to talk to Governor Seligman about it and he got the job. That's how close-knit New Mexico was in those days—you had to talk to the governor just to be the road foreman of a highway district. When I was growing up, it seemed like everybody knew the governor. The system worked because it kept close ties between politicians and the farmers and the truck drivers and mechanics and all the other ordinary people doing ordinary jobs. My ideas of how one goes about being a governor—of being accessible and relating personally to the citizens of the state—were influenced by that kind of relationship.

Although I was aware of politics throughout my youth, leaving New Mexico to serve in the Army in Japan at the end of World War II broadened my views on the subject and expanded my values, helping me think more clearly about the true purpose of public service. When I was at Fort Sill, Oklahoma, we had a weekly orientation with an officer who talked about how important it was to be involved in politics, either as a candidate or promoting one. He used to say that all you needed for evil to prevail in politics was for good people to do nothing. I took that to heart and decided to get myself into the position where I could do good work.

I saw that it's very, very important at the grassroots level for citizens to exercise their influence on government. They must realize that all government starts at the grassroots, then works its way up. If the honest and decent people don't get involved, then the others will figure out how to make government work for them personally and serve only a small segment of the population.

As a rancher, I became quite active in agricultural organizations after the war, including the New Mexico Farm and Livestock Bureau, the Soil Conservation Service, and the New Mexico Cattle Growers Association. Working with these groups gave me the opportunity to support their efforts to improve conditions for farmers and ranchers like myself. Through my involvement, I developed a broader view of what those problems were. And it started me on a path toward politics, though I didn't see it that way at the time.

By the time I was 24 or 25 years old, I was getting more involved in the Democratic party, too. My first practical experience came about when we needed road work in southern Santa Fe county. To call attention to our road needs, I backed certain candidates for the Santa Fe County Commission. Then later on, U.S. Senator Dennis Chávez, another friend of my dad's and a great fella, assigned me as his liaison in southern Santa Fe County, around Edgewood and Stanley, and in Torrance County to the south—he had a lot of friends over in Chilili and always wanted me to go see them. If anyone from that area wrote him a letter, he would refer it to me, then I would personally inspect the problem and pass the information back to the senator. Many of us in politics could still use that approach—in creating more sophisticated processes we often get too far removed from the basic needs and interests of the people we serve. Senator Chávez had a good feel for the human side of public service. He always wanted to know what had happened to this person and that, and he would make sure his staff followed up.

In 1954 when I was 29, an old friend of mine and my dad's, Mike Leyba, encouraged me to run for county commission. I hadn't seriously considered public office before. Mike was Santa Fe County Democratic chairman and he, too, had been highway foreman. After my dad passed away, Mike acted much like a father to me, giving me advice during my early political career. Well, this time he said he knew I would enjoy campaigning and the whole thing would be a great experience, even though I wouldn't get elected. They just needed someone to fill a hole in the Democratic ticket.

At the time, Alice was expecting a baby. It would be our second son, Gary. Our first boy, Bill, was born in 1951. When Mike started urging me to run for county commission, Alice resisted. The ranch was small and we didn't have a lot of money. I was still investing whatever I could into farm and ranch land around Stanley. Since we couldn't afford to hire much help and there was always a lot of work to do, Sam, Don, and I did almost all the labor. I had to admit it didn't seem like the best time to get into politics, so on the day Mike wanted my decision, I promised Alice I wouldn't run. When I met with Mike and the others, however, they were pretty convincing. They told me they already had the signatures on the petition and it wouldn't take long for me to campaign. It seemed like a done deal and I couldn't see the harm, so I said yes.

When I got home Alice said, "Did you let them talk you into it?"

I said, "Well, kinda, but they promised me I wouldn't win!"

It didn't quite turn out that way.

With Mike spurring me on, I began my first-ever run for office in the 1954 primary election for one of the three county commission seats. They were all currently held by Republicans, the minority party in New Mexico. Even though I was unopposed in the primary, I campaigned in Santa Fe and farther north with a few old timers in the party who had a lot to say about what went on around the county.

Without an opponent, I found it pretty easy to win the primary. Now I was in the general election race for county commission. Right in the midst of it all, Alice gave birth to Gary in Albuquerque in late September. Joe Montoya, who later became U.S. senator from New Mexico, was running for lieutenant governor and beat Mike Leyba's son, Sixto, in the primary. Sixto had been in the legislature, and although he ran strong in Santa Fe and Rio Arriba counties, he lost out elsewhere in the state. Mike was disappointed Sixto didn't do better. Despite his active role with the state Democratic party, Mike at first said he was going to resign as county chairman. Then he thought for a minute and said, "Oh, well, I've got to stay and help Bruce get elected."

In the general election campaign, John Simms was the Democratic candidate for governor, and of course he went everywhere to drum up votes. When he came to our area, we'd get up to Santa Fe and meet with all the county Democratic officials. There was a good deal of jockeying when everyone got together. People would come to the meetings and ask Simms how he was going to take care of this and that, and whether he was going to recognize his friends. My brother, Sam King, was our precinct chairman. We were the new guys at those meetings, but many of the people in the Hispanic communities of Santa Fe County knew us through my dad. They had confidence in him. Some of them remembered those days during the Depression when people didn't have much money, and they would come out to our farm to get food. My family believed in that kind of generosity and charity, which meant a lot of people knew the Kings and I had friends all over Santa Fe County when I entered politics. My friend and longtime ally Fabian Chávez used to say, "They elected us the first time because they liked our dads. But from now on, we're on our own." That might have been the case, but regardless, when the November election came around I won a seat on the Santa Fe County Commission.

≈

Along with Jess Kornegay and Juan Medina, I was sworn in as county commissioner on January 1, 1955. We were all Democrats, and we were taking over from a Republican county commission. That changing of the guard turned out to cause an immediate problem.

To my surprise, on the first day after we took over, not a single county employee who had a job under our predecessors reported to work. They just didn't show up. They all assumed they were discharged, even though some of them were good friends of mine. Then after a few days, some of them came by and wondered if we wouldn't help them fill out the forms to get back their contributions to the employment fund. They weren't mad or anything. That's just how it worked back then. Every last job was based on political spoils. You had to vote the right way in the primary and the general election or you were going to be unemployed in January. A similar situation made property taxes unfair, since they rose and fell depending on who was in power. People accepted the situation, because whichever party won did the same thing. I struggled against it for nearly 20 years before I was able to bring about lasting reforms.

Because of this political spoils system, we didn't have anyone around telling us what items of business were pending before the commission or anything about the operation. It would have been nice if at least a few key professional employees had told us things like, "Here, this road grader usually works in the southern end of the county and it's been overhauled in the last six months," and so on—just some of the details of running the county. But we had no way of knowing any of that information. So we had to start from scratch. We went and looked around, and whatever was there, was there.

It seems strange now, but every level of government in New Mexico worked that way back then. For instance, when Democrat John Simms defeated a Republican for governor in 1954, the Republican administration of incumbent Edwin Mechem moved out in a complete turnover of all state employees. Then just two years later, Simms lost to Mechem in the next election, and again the same thing happened. It was the platoon system. People moved out, and their replacements moved in. Then two years later, Democrat John Burroughs defeated Governor Mechem and sure enough, they immediately ran in a Democratic platoon. Then Mechem defeated him the next time, and they did it again.

I felt from the start we needed to correct that situation with the personnel system at the county level so we could keep competent, experienced people in their jobs. Later, when I reached the state legislature in 1959, I began to work for a state merit system to replace the political spoils system. It took us a couple of years, but in 1961 we passed the first state personnel laws, even though they were weak. But at least in the lower ranks of state government, if you were competent you stayed in your job. The 1961 laws didn't apply to county government, but we passed enabling legislation to encourage county personnel systems and by now most counties have adopted the merit system. Today, at least new county commissioners know where their road equipment is. When I was governor in the early 1970s, I was able to professionalize the state-level personnel policies and completely toss out the old patronage system. Although reducing the number of jobs subject to political patronage changed the very nature of two-party politics in New Mexico, it has made for better government. As governing grew more complex in the 1950s and 1960s, we needed more professional staff. Marching the platoons in and out with every change of regime became a luxury we could no longer afford.

In November 1954, however, all those personnel system reforms lay in the future. So between the election and the day we took office in January, we had to name appointees to each and every position in county government, from the county manager on down to the secretaries in the county manager's office. I realized that the key to good government was to surround yourself with excellent people. Through the concern of the other commissioners and Mike Leyba, we were able to assemble a competent county crew. We also worked closely with the other elected county officials. We probably had 75 employees in all aspects of county government. As our top three people— those who would work most closely with us—we named county manager A.B. Martinez, road foreman Ramon Gomez, and bridge foreman Richard C de Baca, who was also in charge of personnel in the road department.

The three of us commissioners were pretty compatible. We agreed on how things should be done, so we began putting together a strong operating procedure, a manual, so to speak. For instance, we expected everyone to put in an eight-hour day. Furthermore, we began accounting for the different pieces of county equipment, an inventory that took us several days to complete. As we looked over the operation, we realized we had too many employees around the courthouse. One day, after we had elected Jess Kornegay chairman, we asked our county manager and our two road foremen to assemble all the employees at the new county road office south of Santa Fe, except for a skeleton crew to keep the courthouse open. Jess made a brief talk, then it was my turn.

Considering the political realities of those days, I said, "Admittedly, the reason you all are employed, in addition to your ability to fill the position, is the fact that you're good Democrats and you helped get us elected. But I want to make one thing clear to each of you. The only thing that most of the people who voted for us will ever get in return is good government. You're here in a job, and you have an opportunity, but you're going to have to perform and provide the people of Santa Fe County with good government, or I'm going to insist that we make changes. We will terminate anyone who doesn't measure up to those standards or who doesn't do a good job."

Things got very quiet. We went on through the rest of the business at hand and tried to figure out where all the equipment was. As we began to leave, several people came by and said, "That was a nice presentation, Bruce, but you can't be laying off these people, just on whether they do a good job or not. That just isn't the way the system works."

"That's the way I am going to work," I said. "The first ones who don't do a good job, we're going to change."

"That's not the way politics works," they insisted.

"Well, we'll see," I answered. And sure enough, it wasn't a month until some of the road crew weren't working the way I felt they should. We fired one or two. As a result, some of the strong Democratic families became disenchanted with my approach to running county government, but for the time being I went about my business without much open conflict.

I also felt strongly, as did Jess and Juan, that we should equalize property taxes across the county. That was one of the major reasons I had agreed to run for a seat on the commission. In those days, your tax evaluation fluctuated along with who might be in power. If your political party was in, that was one thing. If not, that was another. Your assessment was strictly up to the tax equalization board, which consisted of the county commissioners, the county assessor, an at-large Democrat, and an at-large Republican. If they wanted to assess a building at 10 percent of its value, that was what they used. If they wanted 50 percent, that was it. In some counties, the assessments ran all the way up to 90 percent. Since then, the state has passed mandatory equal assessment laws, and most counties use 33.33 percent.

In my first term as a commissioner, we decided to stabilize the tax system in the county by assessing everyone on 33.33 percent of the actual value of the property. However, knowing it would be impossible to evaluate all the properties at once, we appealed to the fairness of the people. For most of

February 1955, we asked them to come in and meet with the tax equalization board so we could determine their new tax. Pretty soon after convening the board, I found myself sitting as the sole hearing officer from the commission, along with county employees a great deal of the time. Juan and Jess both had permanent jobs, and since I was my own employer, I could get away for this county business. Besides, February was a slow month on the ranch. The hearings went well, and overall I was impressed with the fairness of the people coming in. Some had been assessed extraordinarily high and we would try to adjust it back, and some hadn't been assessed high enough, so we tried to work that up. We also began getting the building permits and assessing a one-third valuation outright on those new improvements. That was contested at first, but soon became accepted.

By doing things differently with tax assessments and the personnel system, I was trying to show a new, nonpartisan approach to county government. It seemed to me that we should act in the best interests of all taxpayers and be fair to everyone. That was always my approach: everyone pays taxes, so everyone is entitled to basic good government.

≈

The Santa Fe County Democratic party was divided into factions in the 1940s and 1950s. I was considered a member of the Mike Leyba camp. A strong faction of Young Turks followed Santos Quintana, who was a protégé of Johnny Walker, the state land commissioner who later went on to represent New Mexico in the U.S. Congress. Because of the in-fighting between these factions, the Democrats hadn't held any county offices for a decade or so before 1954. The county commission had been in Republican hands most of the 16 years before I was elected, except for one two-year term when Quintana did manage to elect some Democratic commissioners.

These factions each kept a close watch on the activities of county government. Jess Kornegay held weekly if not daily breakfasts and other organizational meetings with the Santos Quintana faction. For my part, I had less frequent meetings with Mike Leyba, Richard C de Baca, and a few other key people from Mike's group. So when it came to issues of a political nature, Jess and I were divided, based on the political implications between our factions. It was extremely difficult to persuade either of us to move from our positions. At commission meetings we would engage in a great deal of heated discussion on political matters, never resolving any particular issue. Finally, I would say, "Well, let's vote." That always left Jess voting one way on a political matter, me voting the other, and Juan Medina caught in the middle. The least talkative of the three of us, Juan would say, "Both of you guys, you argue here a long time and then you always want me to make the decision." He tried to work both groups, which helped a great deal in pulling us together politically. When we moved away from politics, Jess and I usually saw eye to eye on such issues as roads and land-use planning, and Juan worked closely with us. Over the years, Jess and I became good friends. Several years later, I worked hard as one of the coordinators and chairman for Jack Campbell's 1960 campaign for governor. I talked Jack into appointing Jess as the chief state tax commissioner, and he did a good job. Years later, Jess reciprocated by supporting me for governor.

≋

Building, improving, and maintaining roads was a big deal in county politics. Juan, Jess, and I made a point of maintaining the roads quite well. We bought some of the first equipment to hard-surface and gravel the roads in Santa Fe County. We had the first loader, dump truck, and modern graders, so up north we were able to build the road straight through from Chimayó to Nambé. Most of the credit goes to our road foremen, Ramon Gomez and Richard C de Baca, who stretched the money a long ways.

By improving roads throughout Santa Fe County, I made many friends who later helped elect me to the state House of Representatives, but I also nearly got myself in a whole bunch of trouble. In 1956, I found myself crosswise with a crowd that included Tony Hillerman, the now-famous mystery-novel writer who was then editor of the *New Mexican*, over paving the Hyde Park road, which was a dirt track from the city of Santa Fe to the nearby recreational areas in the Sangre de Cristo Mountains. This whole flap started with a promise of confidentiality I made to Senator Chávez, who had offered to help us with our county road projects.

When I came onto the commission, we inherited a county land-use plan. Already in place, it was part of a national rural planning effort that included farms and roads. Our plan, which had been developed by about a dozen community leaders from all around the county, set priorities for road work. Ranked first on the list at that time was the Stanley-to-Edgewood road connecting the southern part of the county to the capital city. It also ran right by King Brothers Ranch. Though it was a school bus route, that road was just a bladed-out track without any road base on it. The plan was to make it an all-weather road with gravel and proper grading.

Despite the merits of this road and its place at the top of the priority list, Jess Kornegay and many other people who lived around the city of Santa Fe—including Hillerman—had concluded there wasn't sufficient funding for the southern road. Instead, they wanted to take the available money and pave the road to Hyde Park. I objected. I felt we should stick to the priority list—once you broke from that land-use plan, the whole thing would go out the window. But the heavy pressure from the Hyde Park advocates continued, even though it was only fourth or fifth among the plan's priorities, and the disagreement turned a little nasty. At one point, Hillerman wrote that three burros could pack out everything of value that southern Santa Fe County ever produced. In reality, that part of the county grew a lot of corn, alfalfa, and cattle, and it still does. We got pretty hot about it.

Along about that time, Mike Leyba was co-chairman of Senator Chávez's campaigns in New Mexico. Soon after I was elected to the commission, he told me, "You'll want to meet with Senator Chávez and go over some of the problems he might be able to help you with." I continued to support him as his liaison in southern Santa Fe County. When I met with him one day, we discussed two or three of the letters he had received from constituents in my area. Then I brought up the Hyde Park road, explaining the problem to him. He heard me out, then said, "Well, you know, Bruce, isn't that a state road?" He always smoked a cigar and he talked down real low.

"Yes," I told him, "but they don't ever spend any money."

"That shouldn't be too difficult," he answered. "Why don't you contact Spike Keleher." He was the representative for the federal bureau of public roads in New Mexico, so he oversaw all the federal funds that came into the state highway department. "And why don't you talk with Pete Irwin," the chief highway engineer, "and we'll see if we can't get the highway department to designate work needed in that area. Then I'll get the Senate Public Works Committee"—he was chairman—"to make some money available to build the Hyde Park road."

"That would be wonderful," I said. Senator Chávez's strategy meant we could do the Stanley road with county funds and still do Hyde Park with federal funds, which solved all my problems.

"Well, don't mention this funding to anybody but Spike Keleher. You just talk to your fellow county commissioners and tell them and Pete Irwin you think there is funding, but don't mention it to anyone else, or it will jimmy the whole deal and we won't be able to get it." He didn't go into a lot of detail, but he made it crystal clear to me that I should keep quiet about the funding. I guess he still had to work out the details with the Senate committee, so he didn't want to make the deal public just yet.

At the next county commission meeting, I repeated my stand about sticking to our priorities for road improvement and doing the Stanley road, but I added that we could find money for the Hyde Park project, too. Of course I didn't mention the federal funds that Senator Chávez was working out for the state Highway Department to build the road. People didn't seem to listen, and the press blasted me in front-page headlines: "KING OPPOSES HYDE PARK ROAD." But I didn't oppose it, and I wasn't trying to use my influence to get a road in my neighborhood before its time. We discussed the issue at great length and held many county land-use plan meetings and public meetings. I kept insisting that we shouldn't deviate from the land-use plan and that we could still put together funds to pave the Hyde Park road as well, and I got all the bad press. Hillerman and the *New Mexican* suggested I came from too far back in the country to understand all this financing. On its front page, the newspaper explained in detail the great needs for Hyde Park and what all it would do for the economy of Santa Fe. It noted that the other commissioners were strong for it while I was the sole opponent.

Despite that pressure, the other commissioners felt they couldn't take any action unless they persuaded me. Even though he favored the Hyde Park road, Juan backed me in sticking to the land-use plan and refused to budge. "I think Bruce is right, we have the plan," he said. Right after the Stanley road on the priority list was one that would go by Chimayó, which was Juan's home base. He could see that was coming up pretty quick.

This went on for a couple months, until Senator Chávez got back to New Mexico. He had been getting all the press clippings. He called me in and, taking his cigar and biting it, said, "Well, Bruce, what's going on here? Here's these guys trying to say you're not for the Hyde Park road, but you've already made arrangements with me to build it. Why do they say that? If they're going to keep it up, we're not going to build that road!"

"Oh, no, Senator!" I said. "We have to build the Hyde Park road now, or I really will be in trouble, after saying we're going to build it."

He thought a minute and said, "That's right. But why didn't you tell them the Public Works Committee was going to fund that road?"

"You told me not to."

"But I didn't realize it was going to get into this much controversy," he said. "I meant, basically, don't say too much."

So before he left Santa Fe that day, he went down and told the *New Mexican* how we were going to build the Hyde Park road.

Later, Tony Hillerman came in and said, "Bruce, why didn't you tell us what you'd worked out and what you were planning?"

"The senator told me not to say anything," I said. "I kept trying to tell you guys there was money and that we could get it worked out, but it would take a little time."

"Yes," Tony said, "but we've heard that so many times we didn't believe it."

Pretty soon, the contract was let to build the road and construction started. It didn't take near as long to process road work in those days as it does now, so the project went quickly.

Later Tony said to me, "Well, I'm never going to be against Bruce King again. I understand more about how you work. From now on, if you tell me something will be a certain way, I'll have confidence in you." That began another lifelong friendship. When I ran for the legislature in 1958 as representative from Santa Fe County, Tony and the *New Mexican* endorsed my candidacy.

I learned several lessons in politics early in my career from U.S. Senator Dennis Chávez.
(Photograph by John LeRouge Martinez, courtesy Museum of New Mexico, #57271)

≋

I continued to struggle against Santa Fe County Democratic politics when I ran for my second term on the commission in 1956. Mike Leyba retired as county Democratic chairman that year. To fill the job, the party elected Johnny Vigil, a young man about my age. His position caused immediate problems for my candidacy.

Johnny had been involved in politics for years. It was in his blood. His deceased father had been county Democratic chairman, and his mother remained active in Democratic interests. Johnny took the office of chairman as a conciliator among the various factions that were dividing the party. He was from the old school of politics, and I'm sure under a great deal of influence from the Santos Quintana group. They decided that my way of doing business wasn't in the best interests of Santa Fe County, pointing out to me along the way that politics didn't work as I had explained it to the county employees. The fact that I had followed my words with action by firing a couple road workers made matters worse in their eyes. They said we couldn't go on that way.

When the 1956 primary came around, I had a fight on my hands with a gentleman named Clay Hughes, who filed against me. Clay had recently moved into the Cerrillos area. Like me, he was a rancher. In later years we became good friends, but that year he was my opponent. I think I was the only county official who had opposition in the primary, which I felt wasn't quite fair, but I didn't let it bother me. I said as long as I was in office, I was going to operate county government like I thought it ought to be run, and if I got beat I wouldn't feel bad. On the other hand, if I bowed to the wishes of that faction whose political philosophy I didn't agree with, then I would always feel bad whether I won or lost.

As part of the primary process, we held Democratic precinct meetings around Santa Fe County. One night, Johnny Vigil got together several of the key county politicians, the ones who could sway many votes, and told them, "Now look, guys, we're not going to help Bruce this time, are we? We're going to support Clay Hughes." To me he said something like, "Because you didn't carry out this and that of our political requests, and you laid this guy off because you didn't think he was doing the work he should, and he is a great friend of ours, we aren't supporting you this time. We're going to support your opponent."

I thought about it for a minute, then I said, "All of you?"

"Yes, all of us," Johnny said.

I turned to the others. "Well, what about the rest of you?"

Augustine Garcia said, "Well, I'm going to help Bruce." Augustine had been capitol custodian and was along in his late 60s then. He was one of the best politicians in Santa Fe County.

Then another old timer, said, "I'm going to help Bruce, too." And the others joined him, leaving Johnny with only one or two of the newer guys who said they weren't going to help.

After that, my campaign went along pretty well. The *New Mexican* endorsed me, mentioning the many things I had done for good government in the county. When it came to the primary vote, I was surprised to get far more votes than I'd expected and I beat Clay Hughes without any trouble.

The day after the election, Johnny Vigil came by. "Bruce," he said, "I want you to know I didn't work very hard against you. We always had second thoughts about it. From now on, whatever you run for, we're going to be for Bruce King." So right there I established a lifelong friendship. Johnny has always helped me in anything to this day, whatever position he was in.

In the general election, I fought a tight race. President Eisenhower was running for re-election and he was popular in Santa Fe County. I was worried I might lose the election to a Republican riding his coattails, but I won by a small margin. Jess Kornegay and Juan Medina also won re-election. I served the next two years as chairman of the county commission.

One thing us commissioners all agreed on was that Santa Fe County needed an airport as part of our plans to modernize the transportation system. While we were working hard to get a bond issue passed to build the airport, people in Santa Fe would say, "Oh, folks in Santa Fe county don't have many airplanes. They're not interested in an airport." We had to convince them to stay up with the times. A thriving community—especially a capital city—needed access by air. Apparently we made a good case. Voters approved the bond issue in the second year of my first term and the airport was completed west of town in my second term. Santa Fe hadn't yet built-up much out that way, so the airport was the only thing in the middle of a great big cow pasture.

I was the speaker and master of ceremonies at the airport dedication. When were driving to the dedication—as usual, about 30 minutes ahead of time—we turned onto that airport road and found a string of cars stretching all four miles from highway 85 to the airport, and they weren't moving. The dirt road was jam-packed. No one had made any preparation for such a large number of people, five times what we had expected. We waited in line about an hour and still hadn't moved any closer to the airport. Finally, someone sent the police to escort us in, because I was supposed to open the ceremony. We pulled onto the grounds, got out of the car, and hurried up to the top of the building with a big loudspeaker to join the mayor and the Federal Aviation Authority people.

Below me was the largest crowd I had yet spoken to, and one of the largest I ever addressed. Hundreds of people were walking around looking at the airplanes, and paying little attention to the speakers before me, which was typical at those open-air functions. So when my turn came to speak, everyone was going merrily about their business, but as I talked about the importance of the airport and what we were trying to do, everyone began to stop and listen and look around to see what I was telling them. I was impressed. Just by the tone of my voice through the PA system and the approach I took, people stopped to reflect on my words. It was gratifying to see their warm response.

〰

I began to realize that many of our problems with things like maintaining the road system, making taxes fair, and getting our share of the state's general revenues were not unique to Santa Fe County—they were common to other counties statewide. Jess and I, and others, too, felt the need for a strong organization of New Mexico county officials to work on solving some of these concerns. The existing county group had faltered along the line, so in 1956 we held a meeting in Ruidoso to try to revitalize the organization. Then we agreed to hold a convention of county officials in Santa Fe County in 1957.

Jess wanted to be chairman. We worked hard and got him elected. Since I had managed his campaign, they insisted I take one of the vice-chairman positions, so I chaired the county commissioners division. At that point I became reacquainted with Harry Kinney, a Bernalillo County Commissioner who later became mayor of Albuquerque. He and I had attended the University of New Mexico together in the 1940s. We discussed various problems that required legislative action. I worked along and became acquainted with those needs, which helped me gain a statewide perspective that I could draw upon when I ran for the House of Representatives in 1958.

Several of my supporters urged me to seek a seat in the state House of Representatives. Chief among them was my old friend, Fabian Chávez. His dad, Fabian Chávez, Sr., and my dad had worked together in county politics and always encouraged us to get involved. So from the time we were both 16 or 17 years old we were attending conventions and showing interest. By the late 1950s, Fabian had already served in the House, but then he had lost a race for state senator to the incumbent. When 1958 came around, Fabian was again seeking the Senate position and he felt it would be nice if I ran for the House seat. Others urged me to run, including the mayor of Santa Fe, Leo Murphy, who was also president of the New Mexico Municipal League and interested in city legislation. Later I worked with Leo to accomplish many of the things we both wanted. So Alice and I talked it over and I decided to run for the House. Once again, I was one of the few with opposition in the primary, but I beat my fellow Democrat, Jimmy Garcia.

In the general election, although the incumbent Republican had decided not to seek office again, I drew a strong new Republican opponent, Eppie Chávez. I had to campaign hard. A well-known furniture store owner in Santa Fe, Eppie had several children and on election day, every one of them passed out cards in front of a precinct, saying, "Won't you vote for my dad?"

My brother, Don, was going around with me and he said, "Golly, Bruce, there isn't anyone who is going to vote against that kind of campaign!" But it didn't turn out to make much difference, since I won the race. Both of those 1958 opponents—Jimmy Garcia and Eppie Chávez—later became my supporters.

☵

Political campaigns were a lot more relaxed and personal in those days, with a warmth that's gone today. It was a pleasant endeavor, because I had so many friends and they looked forward to seeing someone they thought would relate to them and their interests. They knew they would have a dedicated friend they could always reach if they had a problem, or if they couldn't get me, they could always find Alice and have an opportunity to be heard. I guess they felt I had established my credibility. From all the work I had done getting roads built or improved, I had earned strong support throughout the county. Even many lifelong Republicans and some who had been Republican officials said that Bruce King did more to build roads in northern Santa Fe County than all the commissioners we had in the past, put together. They liked the way we acquired access and easements and looked after their communities. The feeling was I had done my groundwork and was entitled to move up.

There were two keys to getting elected back then. One was a lot of people-to-people contact. The other was always attending the county political meetings, which were held in all thirty-one precincts before the election. You needed to attend as many of those as you could. Alice and I would always try to get there thirty minutes early—most people would, because that's when you got to do your electioneering. During my campaign for the legislature in 1958, I would work all day in the farm fields driving a tractor, irrigating, putting out feed for the cattle, cutting hay, and so on, then get home with barely enough time to change clothes and drive wherever we were going. Alice would fix me a sack lunch, maybe something easy to carry like a sandwich and a can of pop, so I could eat while she drove. We went to thirty meetings in thirty straight nights that month. Our travels took us to every community in the county, including the little villages up in the north and down around Stanley—there were a lot of small settlements in those days. It was great fun to go out and meet the people and see their customs. We always had large crowds, since political rallies were social events, too. Nearly everyone came, not just to listen to the politicians but to visit with each other. You really got to know the people in a different way than you do now.

Each meeting started with a potluck supper at 6:30 P.M. That was followed by the speeches, which were supposed to end at 10:30 so the dance could start at 11, but we hardly ever did. The speeches would sometimes go on until midnight, then everyone would dance until four o'clock in the morning. In those days things could get pretty rough. People would dance and drink and they would get to fighting. Mike Leyba once told Alice and me that the way to stay out of all this was to get our business done and tell them, "Well, we got to get all the way back to Stanley tonight, so let me speak first." And no one worried about that, since they knew we had to drive the farthest. Sometimes we stayed for the dance, too.

The speeches went on so long because every political leader in the community talked, along with the candidates and any other visiting politicians. Sometimes even the candidates for governor and senator would come into these little villages. So people had to sit for a long time, and they were willing. We were part of the entertainment, and we had some politicians who were real entertaining. In northern New Mexico, all the speeches were done in Spanish except for mine, even though I had picked up a working knowledge of the language around the ranch. I addressed these groups in English with a translator, and we added a little bit of color to that. One time I was listening and the translator didn't get what I'd said quite right, so I interrupted him with my correction—in Spanish. The crowd went wild over that. I worked it into my presentation as a regular feature. My routine still didn't stack up against some of the old timers, like Emilio Trujillo, who could tell the funniest stories and the crowd would just howl, as much as they would for any entertainer in the world. Even as he was cutting up the crowd, he would always make his political points, too.

Sometimes tensions between the speakers heated up. I remember when things got a little out of hand at the big county rally at Seth Hall in Santa Fe the Sunday night before the election. Land Commissioner Johnny Walker was running for the U.S. Senate against Dennis Chávez. He got up for his speech and he just started right in on Senator Chávez, saying this guy doesn't represent us and hasn't done any kind of job at all. The senator just sat there and didn't say anything until Walker said, "Senator Chávez employed all his kinfolks and he even had his brother appointed judge advocate in the Army."

U.S. Representative E. S. "Johnny" Walker was a colorful figure on the campaign trail. (Photograph courtesy Museum of New Mexico, #30255)

Senator Chávez leaped to his feet and yelled, "That's a damn lie!" Only he said it a lot stronger than that. They started yelling and shouting at each other and the people were getting all excited. Alice told me that if politics was going to be like that, she didn't want any. She thought she was going to have to leave the building.

Finally Johnny Walker said, "If you don't want to hear about his family, I guess I'll just quit talking," and he sat down. Then after Johnny lost in the primary election, he said, "I guess the old senator is tougher than I thought" and he was back helping Dennis again.

I think I probably spent $65 on that 1958 campaign, just to have some cards printed up. Other than gas, that was all our expenses amounted to. Those days of local rallies are long gone now, at least with that kind of personal quality. They began to taper off during the early 1960s. In the 1950s, we didn't do any advertisements or anything like that. What got you elected was going to every community and getting to know the people. These days, you have to try anything you can think of to get crowds out. Back then, people came out to see who the candidates were—*they* wanted to know *you*. Since then, harsh, impersonal campaigns have replaced a series of warm, fun community events. New Mexico is just too big now for the old grapevine to work, which has completely transformed our politics. The old person-to-person encounters have yielded to a media-based approach built on the recommendations of political consultants. Maybe that's due in part to TV, but it's also because people just don't have confidence in their government—they don't feel part of it, anymore. They used to think you couldn't get elected unless they helped you. Nowadays, a lot of people really don't care, and they don't think their vote counts.

Political rallies in rural New Mexico were informal affairs, often barbecues at the ranch of a party stalwart. In the 1950s and 1960s, my campaigns involved traveling to every small town and meeting as many people as I could. (Photograph courtesy Museum of New Mexico, #29823)

⩳

I ran for office countywide five times, twice for the county commission and three times for the legislature. When the district was changed in a legislative reapportionment, I won two more times, but it wasn't countywide. Representing a county as big and diverse as Santa Fe gave me a good grounding in the perspective required to represent a wide range of constituents. I learned that your views have to go beyond the needs of any small locality. Santa Fe County is about 80 miles from north to south, the size of a small eastern state. The county includes many predominantly Hispanic communities in the north, the city of Santa Fe, several Indian pueblos, and farming and ranching communities like Stanley in the south.

Being the only Anglo candidate gave me good insight into working with the Hispanic population, which was always supportive of me. In the 1958 election, the Hispanic communities worried I might get beat, so everyone made an extra effort to drum up votes for me. I ended up not only winning my election but leading the ticket. It was an honor, and I accepted the responsibility of representing predominately Hispanic constituents. New Mexico has a large Hispanic population, mostly concentrated in the Rio Grande valley and in the north-central mountain areas. They have a long history here, having come to New Mexico before the first Pilgrim set foot on Plymouth Rock. Santa Fe is the oldest capital in the United States, and many New Mexico families can trace their roots in this area back to the days of the Spanish conquistadors, 400 years ago. A large number of these voters became Democrats during the New Deal, and their old system of local politics led by *patrónes*, or bosses, has influenced Democratic politics until very recently.

Working as a county commissioner and campaigning for the House opened my eyes to the way politics works in New Mexico. I guess you could say I started to develop my own political style, and I gained supporters who would help me take the next step into the politics of the legislature. Looking back on those early years of my political career in the 1950s, I can see a number of challenges and issues that set me up for my future terms in office. Keeping up roads and building new ones was important because they addressed a basic need for people living in the scattered communities of New Mexico. Like the airport we got built, roads are part of the transportation system that helps people go about their business. Other issues, like overhauling the personnel system and taxing everyone fairly, applied to both the local level and statewide.

Even during these early years, I began to set my sights on bigger goals in politics. I was encouraged by Senator Chávez. Along about the 1958 election, he wanted me to make contacts with the Chávez and King friends all around Santa Fe County, and farther north, in Taos and Rio Arriba counties, which I did, and again I made many friends. Senator Chávez then said to me, "I want you to know our friends, Bruce, because we'd like to see you seek higher office than House of Representatives sometime." I appreciated his words, but I was focused on beginning my service in the legislature, where I would spend five two-year terms for a total of ten years, honing my leadership skills and building my base of support in preparation for my first run for governor. During the 1960s, I gained a lot of political ground, but I also suffered a few disappointing setbacks and even considered quitting politics before I finally achieved that seventh-grade dream.

2

You Don't Vote 'Maybe'

Something like 50 or 60 percent of the House of Representatives were new members in 1959. This tremendous turnover meant the House had more freshman members than veterans, which created vacancies on all the committees and gave me excellent opportunities. Everyone was elected countywide in those days. Even the least populated county had at least one representative, a situation that would change under later reapportionments when we redrew district lines. Bernalillo County, which was and remains the most populous, had nine representatives, Santa Fe County and a few others had three, and the rest had just one or two.

New Mexico has what we call a "citizen" rather than a professional legislature—ours is made up of unpaid representatives and senators who receive only per diem and mileage reimbursements for their trouble. This system means everyone has to work a regular job and take time off for their legislative duty, which can include serving on an interim committee—these days, either the Legislative Council Service, the Legislative Finance Committee, or the Legislative Education Study Committee.

I enjoyed the legislature from my first day there. Having grown up in the homestead days, I was impressed with my new position. As I approached my first legislative session, I believed I could exert a great deal of influence in the House of Representatives, but I quickly found it was a highly competitive place, with its own brand of internal politicking and maneuvering for position, and its own unwritten rules about how you got things done. I soon learned that all 65 other House members had a constituency to represent, too. Naturally, the folks at home expected us to perform in a way that enhanced our own counties, and my fellow legislators from other regions didn't necessarily share my goals.

So despite my great visions of rapidly enacting bills that were obviously needed—at least in my estimation—working in the House wasn't as simple as it seemed. Nothing was black or white. Every other legislator sincerely believed *his* ideas were right. We all felt that if the others would just listen to our presentations and follow our recommendations to the letter, things would turn out just fine. Of course, it rarely worked like that, which was a lesson I had to learn the hard way. I was a go-getter, but even though I managed to lock horns with the House leadership once or twice, those fights weren't fatal. In the process I saw it took more than just thinking you're right to get legislation passed. I also learned the importance of voting my convictions. It seemed like every action you took in the House had consequences somewhere down the road.

When I first went to the House, we convened in the old capitol on Don Gaspar Street in downtown Santa Fe. In the 1950s, the legislature met for just 60 days in January of every odd-numbered year, although the governor could call a special session any time, or the legislature could call one by a three-fifths vote in both houses, something that never happened. We later added a 30-day session on even-numbered years in 1966 to handle the increasingly complex business of state government, especially in the area of finances—only money-related bills can be considered in the short session. Unlike today, when the elections for officers are held a month ahead of the mid-January opening day of the legislature and the factions have time to organize, the politics of the House used to start the night before the session convened, when each party caucused to elect the officers of the legislature. In 1959, the House had only four Republicans, so all the action was in the Democratic party. The campaigns were hard-fought for the positions of House speaker, majority leader, chief clerk, and sergeant-at-arms. Each member would back those leaders he thought would be favorable to him. I was no different. In 1959, Mack Easley of Lea County wanted to be speaker, which was certainly one of the two or three most influential and prestigious positions in the legislature. I had visited with him about the legislative process, and along with the other two Santa Fe County legislators, Ralph

Gallegos and Armando Larragoite, I had decided to support Easley for speaker. Both Ralph and Armando had had previous experience in the legislature. We were working pretty much as a three-member unit and were also pushing Ralph as candidate for majority leader.

Like all good politicians seeking office, Mack acted like he had no other interests except mine. "Bruce," he said, "What committees would you like to serve on?" Making committee assignments is one of the most important responsibilities of the speaker. I knew that the committees I ended up serving on would greatly influence my impact in the legislature. Since I was quite focused on farming and ranching, I told him I wanted to serve on the agriculture committee and, having had experience with county roads and the Santa Fe airport, maybe on the transportation committee. I gave him another choice or two, and he said, "Fine, we'll see what I can do. You ought not to have any problems getting on those, if you'll support me for speaker." Of course, I agreed, since we had already decided to, anyway.

Pretty soon, the acting state Democratic chairman called the party caucus to order, as was customary. Mack Easley won speaker without much opposition. The next position up was majority leader. I nominated Ralph Gallegos and others nominated W. O. Culbertson, who was a livestock man and a friend of mine. W.O. won by a good margin. He knew that Ralph was a good friend of mine, so as a favor to me he immediately jumped up and moved that we have an assistant floor leader, and he further moved that we elect Ralph into that position. We did that by acclamation. Next came chief clerk. We elected Al Romero, who served throughout all my tenure in the legislature and my years as governor into the 1980s. After the group elected Romero, I nominated David Branch for sergeant-at-arms. That turned out to be a minor blunder. Because I was new and unacquainted with the system—as were so many other new House members—I didn't realize that I had snubbed the former sergeant-at-arms of several years' standing. Dave Branch won. The next morning, the other fellow was waiting for me in the hall and he was none too friendly. "Boy, you sure did me in!" he said. "You've cost me the job I've had for the last several years and you don't even know me!" He carried a grudge for a few years, but he finally got over it.

With this organizing activity behind us, we convened the legislature the next day, when we all signed the roster and the secretary of state swore us in.

〰

Mack Easley pulled together the inside group that got him elected speaker and they started naming people to committees. I had friends putting in a plug for me on agriculture. Because there were so many rural legislators then, it was a coveted committee and half the legislators in 1959 named it as their first choice. Although getting on the agriculture committee would be something of a feat, when the speaker announced the committee assignments, I found myself a member. Despite the odds, I could see why it happened, since I had a farming and ranching background and some influential supporters. But I was greatly surprised to be named to the labor committee, which I hadn't even listed as a choice. Wondering why I was tapped for that committee, I asked around and was told the friends I had made among the working people of northern New Mexico felt I should serve on labor to look after their interests and concerns. So I agreed, and the labor committee proved to be an excellent place to widen my knowledge of issues affecting the state.

I still had one more surprise coming: along with another rookie I was assigned co-chairman of the enrolling and engrossing committee, which was responsible for proofreading all the bills for clarity, grammar, misspellings, and so on. I soon learned that the House leadership always picked two industrious and knowledgeable freshman members for this position. Then they assigned all the freshmen to that committee. I broke down my committee into several groups and we got the job done. As co-chair, I always moved for the adoption of the enrolled and engrossed committee report, and that gave me a great deal of additional confidence on the floor of the House. Although this assignment gave me a leg up, I later suggested that professional proofreaders ought to handle this task, since they had the skills needed to carry it out effectively. As a result, proofreading did become a staff responsibility.

The agriculture committee was large and influenced quite a lot of legislation. We were a knowledgeable group and we began some of the first work on equalizing taxes and on creating greenbelts, along with some wildlife issues. When the committee met, I had little problem relating to whatever they were discussing. Farm and ranch issues were one of my basic interests and I enjoyed working on them. Hy Overton, a long-time friend of mine, was chairman and Albert Matlock was vice chairman. I had worked with them on the boards of the Farm Bureau and the Cattle Growers Association and we had all been involved with the Soil Conservation Service. I had gotten involved in those organizations in the late 1940s and early 1950s because I wanted to improve conditions in farming and ranching. It also gave me good ties with the agricultural interests on the east side of New Mexico. As we went about the state to Farm Bureau and Cattle Growers meetings, the chairman of the agriculture committee in those days was the most sought-after speaker because people considered him the most knowledgeable individual in agricultural circles. I thought it would be nice if someday I could be chairman, expounding about the legislative process and how legislation would affect farmers and ranchers.

One bill that came before the agriculture committee my first session would have required fruit vendors to have licenses and fruit peddlers to have permits. It would apply to the people up and down the Rio Grande valley in northern Santa Fe County and Rio Arriba County who had little orchards and irrigated tracts. They grew fruit and vegetables, then loaded their trucks with the produce and peddled it door to door all over the area. This was a controversial activity. Many larger farmers from around Las Cruces, the lower Rio Grande valley, and the Deming area wanted to tighten up the regulations, forcing these peddlers either to sell to them, as middlemen, or go out of business altogether. To achieve their goal, these larger farmers lobbied for much more stringent requirements on processing sheds and related matters. This issue became very political. The farm organizations decided they would resolve it by proposing to license only the larger producers. They also wanted to require bonding for produce companies to prevent fly-by-night operators from coming in, buying up produce on credit, then skipping the country with the goods and leaving the farmers empty-handed.

The fruit growers and vegetable growers in northern Santa Fe County were good friends of mine—they had supported me in the election—and their Rio Arriba counterparts were rapidly becoming my allies, too. They all came to the capitol when the committee considered the bill—so many came, in fact, that we had to move to a larger room. This bill was a big deal to the small farmers from the north. I sat back and listened as everyone made their presentations, and I tried to clarify different points as they came up. Hy Overton and many others on the agriculture committee supported the bill. The groups opposing licensing didn't have much of a spokesman. After making their presentation, they caucused in the room off to the side and wondered if I wouldn't come join them. "Sure," I said. These gentlemen conversed mostly in Spanish, which I understood sufficiently to follow the conversation. Finally they said, "We haven't had a lot of training or background in the legislative process and we can't decide how this is going to affect us. So let's just let Bruce decide what will be best for us, and that will be our position." They were mostly concerned that there was something hidden in the fine print that would turn out to hurt their business.

I mulled this over for just a second and I thought, if these fine people—mostly gentlemen in their 50s and 60s who have devoted their lives to farming and peddling their produce—have that much confidence in me, I wouldn't want to do anything to cause them trouble. So I told them, "Well, fellows, if you're going to leave it up to me, I think we better go back there and try to kill that bill." They all agreed, so they went back and said, "After discussing this among ourselves at great length, and discussing it with Representative King, we've decided this wouldn't be a good bill."

After that, we didn't hear much more testimony, and I moved that we give that bill a "do not pass." I had developed a nice following among members of the committee, and we managed to kill the bill. However, many of my other friends on the committee were unhappy about my performance, since the Farm Bureau and others had endorsed it. But I never worried about that. I felt like we'd taken a step in the right direction.

≋

I found controversy on the labor committee, too. As we listened to presentations and considered various bills, I learned more about the issues affecting labor. About that time, right-to-work came into play as a major issue, one that would keep resurfacing throughout my political career. Right-to-work was basically anti-union. I had been working with the agricultural groups who felt we really needed a right-to-work bill, and with the working people in the Santa Fe and Los Alamos area who felt we certainly did not. The issue was becoming more and more complicated and divisive. I finally decided to oppose right-to-work, a position I held for many years. That decision brought me many followers, but I also found people who would have supported me except for my stand on that one issue.

We also discussed at length a bill to raise the minimum wage from 50 cents to 65 cents. I sat and listened. The discussion went around and I became the pivotal vote in that committee. The restaurant owners and many other opponents to raising the minimum wage felt I would probably be their ally, being in agriculture and all, but I knew how little money some people made, and I felt sorry for them. When it came to the committee vote, I said "yes" to raising the minimum wage. That didn't set too well with the opponents of the bill. Someone representing the restaurant owners got up and said, "I'd like to know what Representative King pays those farm workers down on the King Brothers Ranch."

I said, "If we couldn't afford to pay them 65 cents an hour, I would just tell them they ought to go on and look for a job where they could make a living, and I'm not going to worry about how that affects us." From then on I was considered a friend of the working people, which I certainly was. The people had supported me, and we had discussed things, even though I had made no commitment to them on the minimum wage or right-to-work, either one.

Even in the middle of all this controversy, we found a little humor. When the bill came to the House floor, those presenters in support of the 65-cent minimum wage were saying how difficult it was on the current wage to maintain a household and try to have the standard of living they felt entitled to. Countering that perspective, Representative Finis Heidel of Lea County showed off a stack of telegrams and said, "I've gotten all these telegrams from my constituents, and they're all against any increase in the minimum wage. A lot of these telegrams come from people with names like Mr. Sanchez, and Chávez, and Naranjo, and Marquez—our people who are working in the jobs we're talking about today, and they feel the increase would be harmful to them."

He finally yielded the floor to Representative Al Serrano of Bernalillo County, who had a great sense of humor. "Mr. Speaker," he said, "I, too, have gotten many telegrams from people throughout New Mexico, strongly favoring *increasing* the minimum wage, and these telegrams come from names like Smith, and Jones. . . ."

The House broke up over that comment, and later went on to pass the bill raising the wage.

∭

In my first legislative session, the issue that I put the most effort into—and probably learned the most from—was anti-billboard legislation. As I drove the scenic roads around Santa Fe and Albuquerque, I would see new billboards springing up like weeds. I wasn't alone in feeling strongly they were an unsightly nuisance. Someone in Santa Fe made the point forcefully by cutting billboards down after dark. I thought it would be more useful to have the Legislative Council Service draft a long, drawn-out bill to prohibit billboards in scenic areas, a position I think most of the people of New Mexico would have gone along with. Tony Hillerman at the *New Mexican* agreed and did his part with the media. Unfortunately, I was unaware of one crucial detail that doomed my bill right from the start.

During the first week or so of the session, I got around and collected enough signatures on the bill to pass it through the House before I introduced it. I thought that was quite clever. To my surprise, however, the morning I introduced my bill, the speaker referred it to four different committees, even though it had enough signatures to pass. I realized I had some problems.

I tried to get my bill heard in Representative Fred Cole's committee on natural resources—I still don't know how it happened to be assigned there. Every day I would ask Representative Cole, "Well, when are you going to hear my bill?" As this went on and on, I began to realize they weren't going to let my bill out.

Finally someone told me, "Gordon Melody probably doesn't like that bill. Maybe you better go over and talk to him." Gordon chaired the Senate finance committee, and he was the most powerful man in the legislature. His contributions to New Mexico were of enormous value and he became a strong ally of mine in later years. But at this time, I couldn't see what a senator had to do with our House legislation. Then I discovered he just happened to own the Melody Billboard Company over in Las Vegas, New Mexico. Obviously Gordon wasn't interested in legislation that would restrict his signs. To represent the billboard industry, he had brought in Waldo

Spiess, a leading attorney and former state Democratic chairman who later became a judge on the Court of Appeals. I was stepping into the ring against the heavyweights on this one.

Undaunted, I went on over and visited with Gordon Melody. For some reason I couldn't fathom at the time, he got to calling me Rufus instead of Bruce. Only many years later did I realize that he must have been confusing me with Senator Buddy Wamel, who was big like me and came from an agricultural background. Buddy's real name was Rufus. Anyhow, on this particular occasion, Gordon said, "Rufus, it looks like a pretty good bill. You know, we're not against billboard legislation, but we want to have more input into it and we want to be sure its workable."

That made sense to me. I said, "Well, mine's workable."

"Work something out with Waldo," he said, "and that'll be all right with me."

So I kept at Fred Cole to set up a hearing on my bill, then finally my fellow Santa Fe County Representative Armando Larragoite set it up in the natural resources committee, where he was vice chairman. That probably never would have happened without his help. I worked hard and made my presentation, and found I had enough votes to get it out of committee with a number of amendments. It was the same with the other three committees where it was assigned—I got it out of all of them. I thought to myself, "I'm about to get this billboard bill out on the floor!"

Lo and behold, the day it was on the calendar and started to come up on the House floor, judiciary committee chairman Jack Campbell said, "This bill obviously has serious constitutional questions, and I'd like to see it over in the judiciary committee." So there goes my bill.

Despite my determination, I was beginning to realize just how hard it is to pass legislation from a single viewpoint. Even though I think the vast majority of citizens would have strongly supported a law to keep billboards out of scenic areas, my opponents raised questions about how you compensate someone if you are preventing their financial gain by using their property for a billboard. I hadn't thought of that.

I went over to judiciary and I said, "Look, you guys, this is a good bill." Jack Campbell, who later was elected governor, told me, "We'll try to correct these constitutional problems." He and I became friends and I kept going to his committee, pointing out that we had enough signatures to pass the bill. Nonetheless, it was obvious these stalling tactics were going to kill it. Finally, Campbell said, "Bruce, as a courtesy to you and the dedicated manner in which you have worked at it"—and, I'm sure, partly because of the widespread publicity it had attracted—"we're going to put your bill out, but I have to tell you, I am going to have to oppose your bill on the floor."

"Okay," I agreed, "let's put it on the floor and we'll see what happens."

So the committee reported the bill out. I was well prepared, and I got up and put the bill on passage before the full House. We debated it for some two hours. But unknown to me, Majority Leader W. O. Culbertson, who came from San Miguel County along with Gordon Melody, was carrying the opposition, which included other prestigious legislators in addition to Culbertson and Campbell. I'm sure much of that support came about because Gordon Melody had bills of theirs over in the Senate. So I put up what I thought was a gallant fight, and we lost by about five votes. Even some of the legislators who had signed it voted against it. My friend Hy Overton didn't say much beforehand. Then immediately after we voted, he rushed right over to my desk and said, "Bruce, I never hated to vote against a bill so bad in my life, but the key politico in my county, who has worked hard to keep me up here, has got billboards all up and down the road, and I just wouldn't be back if I voted for that bill."

I understood that and appreciated his forthrightness in explaining why he had voted against it. I realized frankness was the best course to take if you really couldn't support a bill. Some of those people who had said they would vote for it and didn't, I didn't see for about a week. I wasn't happy about that.

In reflecting on my legislative years, I realize that compared to the billboard bill, no other experience gave me the working knowledge of how many sides make up any piece of legislation and how difficult passing a controversial bill can become. Right there, I learned many of the tricks for getting a bill all the way through the House. I saw that it was important to remain always congenial—which was my nature, anyway—and I tried to make as many friends as I could. You have to understand what you're trying to accomplish, and when you explain it, be explicit but not *too* detailed. One-on-one contact is the best. I guess I've got a great knack for that. I'd see a guy just standing in the hall and I'd go up to him and explain my position by being sincere and giving him all the facts. I would tell him what problem I was trying to cure.

I knew that even if, for any reason, he couldn't vote for my bill, maybe next time he would.

During that first term I also noticed that when someone wanted to kill a bill, one of the senior, learned attorneys in the House would get up and say, "Look, we're just about to pass a bill here that's obviously unconstitutional. I hate to see us do that because it's not going to work." At first, I'd sit back and let it go. After a few times, I told Alice, "I'm going to study the law books and make *my* determination of what's constitutional and unconstitutional." And I'd study at night and try to figure out what the unconstitutional part was. I finally concluded it was just something that didn't work to their advantage.

By the time we went back into the next session I had substantially enlarged my knowledge of the statutes and constitution of New Mexico. From that time on, I would get up and say, "In studying the constitution at great length, I've concluded that it is up to the courts to decide what's constitutional and what isn't. I would advise those who think this is a good piece of legislation to vote for it." The first three or four times I did that, I lost. But after a while, I began picking up votes. Terry Boucher, a lawyer from Valencia County who now chaired the judiciary committee, said to me, "We're going to get you a law degree if you keep practicing law" and they put a set of law books on my desk. Finally in the 1961 session we got together a group strong enough to pass bills despite claims of unconstitutionality. And frankly, few of them ever turned out to be unconstitutional. Most of them were never even challenged in the courts.

⋙

During my freshman legislative session, I made many friends who stayed with me throughout my political career. Some—like Hy Overton (who died in a tragic 1971 plane crash), Louie Trujillo of Taos, Louie Page of Guadalupe County, Lilburn Holman, and Earl Parker—were valued advisors to me. I still got support from some of my earlier mentors, like Senator Dennis Chávez and former speaker Calvin Horn, who was no longer in the legislature at that time. Holman was a Republican representative, while Parker was a Democratic senator, both from Torrance County. They advised me on committee assignments and with their help, I drafted some legislation based on my experience as a county commissioner. These more experienced legislators would help me work a bill through the various committees, suggesting tactics and giving me tips on House politics. Others helped me think about the issues around a bill or the impact of a certain vote. I also won allies among my fellow freshman legislators and continued to build friendships with Tony Hillerman, the syndicated columnist Will Harrison, and others in the press.

Some of the older House members were quite colorful. Representative H.C. Gilliland, who had lived in Clayton all his life, was a gentleman along in his seventies then. Because his health was poor, he took medication that tended to make him doze. Realizing that we had similar philosophies and interests, he told me, "Now Bruce, when we get ready to vote, and particularly on legislation you're interested in, you just run down and tell me." He sat in the second row from the front and I was back in about the last row.

At first I would go down and say, "Mr. Gilliland, this bill does such and such, and I think we should vote this way."

He'd quickly say, "Don't go into particulars. Just tell me 'yes' or 'no.'"

It got to be a big joke around the House. One day even Mack Easley mentioned it from the speaker's chair when he saw me walk down to visit with Representative Gilliland: "There goes Bruce to get his second vote." H.C. Gilliland later worked hard on my candidacy for governor.

Fred Foster and Bob Martin, both of Grant County, were two of the more senior House members who also later supported my ambitions to be governor. They gave me guidance of a more philosophical, but humorous nature. One night at dinner they told a story for my benefit, to make sure I didn't get too carried away with being a legislator and with the powers that went along with the office.

It seems that Bob and Fred were driving with their wives from Silver City to Deming to make a presentation about the legislative session at a banquet. They got a late start. While Fred drove, they soon became absorbed in their conversation and he got going a little beyond the speed limit. A state policeman pulled them over. Fred and Bob got out and went back to see the officer.

"You guys were going fifteen miles over the speed limit," he said.

They said, yeah, they were kinda in a hurry to get to a function.

By this time the young officer had his citation book out and was beginning to write. He wanted to see Fred's driver's license, to which Fred said,

"Officer, you must not know who we are."

The state trooper looked at them and said, "Yes, I know who you are. You're Representative Foster, and he's Representative Martin. You guys make those laws up in Santa Fe, and down here we enforce them." Then he finished writing the ticket.

≋

I had already developed a pretty thick hide where the press was concerned. Incidents like the Hyde Park road controversy during my two terms on the county commission had toughened me up. So when the veteran newspaper columnist Will Harrison took aim my way, I didn't let his needling get to me.

Will loved to pick on legislators with agricultural interests because they would get so indignant. He would write those articles about Hy Overton, and old Hy would threaten to mop up the floor with him. And Tony Heimann had been involved in politics and had been highway commissioner. Will would write derogatory columns about him, and Tony would threaten to really maul Will, then Will would write, "Heimann said he was going to really maul me." Naturally, when Will saw me, he must have thought, "I've got another good one here in old Bruce King." When I introduced a bill that would outlaw smut literature, he let me have it.

I had worked with the Catholic church, which was the majority religious group in Santa Fe County, to develop legislation restricting indecent literature. I didn't realize they introduced this bill every year. They thought since I was a Protestant with a different following than past sponsors and with support in agriculture and so on, the bill might go pretty well if I introduced it. We had discussed the issue during the campaign so I wasn't a surprised when they brought around the bill. Thinking everybody was against indecent literature, I put my name on the bill and turned it in. I thought I had a good piece of legislation here that should go easy.

The next day I read Will Harrison's column. "That figures," he said. "They send a cowboy up here from the country and the first thing he does is try to tell us press people and library people and everybody what we can read and what we can't read, and he doesn't know half the implications." He just really took me apart. But I didn't think much about it because I wasn't particularly concerned about my constituency. They weren't going to worry about it.

Later on, I had to go to some function, so I went out the south door of the capitol and headed east. I looked up and here was Will walking about 20 or 30 paces ahead of me. He was a little nervous and glanced around and started speeding up. So I speeded up, too, and came alongside him and slapped him on the shoulder and said, "How are you doing?"

"Okay, Bruce," he said.

"Well, that's good," I said.

We walked along in silence for awhile. He must have been wondering what I thought about the column, but finally he said, "How do you like the session?"

"Real fine," I said. "I'm beginning to enjoy this."

We walked along a bit more and he looked up and said, "Don't you read my column?"

"Sure, I read your column."

"Well," he said, "didn't that irritate you? Didn't it upset you?"

"No, Will," I said. "It didn't make any difference to me. You write 'em and I'll read 'em, and that's all right with me."

From that day on he never got near as much fun writing anything negative about me, so he began to write much nicer things. At the end of the my first session he even voted me the legislator most likely to succeed. He would always list four or five of the key legislators and he gave me the prominent spot. Later on when I started my second term, he began to say that he'd like to see me run for higher office. Then when I ran for governor, he actively supported me and helped my campaign through his column.

⋙

Throughout my first legislative term, many of my supporters who had been around the political scene for years continued urging me to consider running for a higher office. It must have been obvious that I had my sights set on bigger things. For instance, Louie Trujillo would come and take his seat right down in front of mine and when it came to voting on certain bills that were before the House, he'd give me advice.

"*Mira!*" he would say in Spanish. "Look, Bruce, be careful how you vote.

We want you to run for land commissioner." He and others watched closely to see I didn't get too far afield in voting for legislation that might alienate me from the people of the north. I had that following already and they wanted me to establish a good voting record. But I was never interested in just making a good voting record. When I ran for major office in later years, I did have a good record because I had a highly diversified constituency and I tried to do what was fair to everybody. I was careful about legislation and that in itself gave me a voting record I could stand on.

One time, though, I took one vote casually and caught an earful from my old mentor Dennis Chávez about the responsibilities of voting on legislation. The bill in question seemed harmless enough. Ike Smalley had introduced legislation in the Senate to develop a new Pancho Villa State Park at the town of Columbus in Luna County, on the Mexico border. In 1916, the Mexican revolutionary Pancho Villa raided Columbus with about 500 of his followers. During that skirmish, the Mexicans killed ten American civilians and eight soldiers and lost about a hundred of their own. Not too many of the legislators seemed bothered by the association of Pancho Villa's name with the park, and the bill sailed through the Senate without any dissenting votes. When it came over to the House, I noticed it, but although I had some reservations about naming the park for Pancho Villa, I didn't say anything. The bill went right on through committee and out onto the floor. It passed unanimously in the House—I voted for it just like everybody else.

That bill hadn't much more than gotten passed when someone handed me a note that said, "Senator Dennis Chávez wants to talk to you on the phone." So I went to one of the phones we had for House members in the back halls, and I found a furious Dennis Chávez on the other end of the line.

"Bruce, what the hell is going on?" he asked. "We got the information back here that they passed a bill to name a park for that outlaw Pancho Villa, who murdered our people there in Columbus. They're going to memorialize him by naming a park for him, a Pancho Villa state park."

I tried to humor him. "Aww, senator," I said, "I don't think you're getting the right meaning. They're just building a park, and they thought this would attract interest in it."

"That's the stupidest damn thing I ever heard of," he said. "Did you vote for it?"

Well, there wasn't anyone who voted against it. "Yes, senator, I voted for it," I admitted. "But everyone else had already voted for it in the Senate, and everyone in the House, and all of them that have been here for a long time. I did have some reservations about it. You know, if there had been some 'no's,' I would have voted 'no,' too."

"Bruce, how in the world are we ever going to get you elected governor if you go around voting for stupid stuff like that? Don't you know it always comes back to haunt you? You knew better, you saw it comin'. I don't care if there's not another member in the House who votes 'yes' or 'no,' whatever the case may be. If that's your convictions, you vote that way anyhow! When the people go to looking at the type of individual you are and what your philosophy is, it won't help you having voted 'yes' for such a piece of legislation as this. It all goes on your voting record. That is just really derogatory to the state of New Mexico."

I took his words to heart, because I knew he wouldn't have gone to all that trouble to call me if he hadn't felt strongly about it. The next day, the headline in the paper said, "DENNIS CHÁVEZ BLASTS PANCHO VILLA PARK LEGISLATION." And he said everything in the paper that he said to me, plus more. It was a good lesson and I took the senator's advice seriously. I came to realize that when the speaker of the House calls your name, you vote "yes" or "no," you don't vote "maybe." From that day on, if something came up that I didn't think was right, as they were tallying the vote I would ask to be recognized by holding up my hand and I'd say, "Please show me voting 'no.'" This went on for a while, and on some of those bills, I would be the only one opposed. By the end of that session, however, other members would come up and say, "Why did you vote against that bill?" A few of them would even hold up their hands and say, "I want to vote 'no,' too."

When I would cast a 'no' vote, often enough other members agreed so that we could say, "Maybe we'd better bring this back and look at it." Sometimes we would kill legislation just on the strength of my opposition. It got to where many of the legislators would come by to visit with me about their legislation, asking if I had any objection to their bills. I'd tell them, "We'll have to wait until we get it on the calendar," because that's where I always liked to look at legislation—as it was coming up. I wouldn't commit to something before it was explained on the floor. I came to feel that the House needed a member who was willing to take an unpopular stand once in a while, someone who didn't have any preconceived ideas, had not been involved in strategy on the issue, didn't mind if it was hurting someone's feelings, and wasn't paying back favors.

≋

Those years in the House of Representatives were some of the best times of my life. That's when the House was fun. We worked hard, putting in long hours nearly every day, but we also had our own social events. Some of them were evening functions, and from time to time others were in the House chambers. Among the most memorable were the spur-of-the-moment musical performances put on by several representatives who had musical talent. Whenever we got the chance to let down, we encouraged the House Cats, as they were known, to show off their talent. Hy Overton liked to play the banjo and sing. Representative Harry Allen played the tub, of all instruments, and played it well. Jim Palermo of Santa Fe played the accordion. Representative Al J. Parker played the fiddle left-handed, and staff member Hal Thornburg, who had a deep bass voice, sang and played guitar. Together they would perform pop songs and country music, and sometimes even some of the press would join in the singing.

Many times when we had night sessions, we might work until 9 or 10 o'clock completing our work, then someone would say, "Let's have a little entertainment from the House Cats!" That's all you had to say. They immediately got down front and began to pick the strings and put on a show. It was never too late for them. These days, that would never happen. The press would probably call it a waste of ta1xpayers' money. That's a bygone era.

≋

The legislature met every other year until 1964, when we added the 30-day session in the off years for bills related to finances. So during my first term of office in the House, my only official service was the 60-day session of 1959. I won re-election and when I came back to the session in 1961, we once again had a great deal of turnover among the members. Democratic Governor Burroughs had lost the 1960 election to former Governor Edwin

Mechem, a Republican. As we got ready for the 1961 session, all the changes sparked a close race for speaker of the House between judiciary committee chairman Jack Campbell and his main opponent, Mack Easley, who unlike Campbell had been a strong supporter of Governor Burroughs. With Burroughs out, Easley's position was weakened. Also vying for House speaker was my friend and fellow cattleman, W. O. Culbertson. I let all three would-be speakers know that I wanted to chair the agriculture committee. I had thought it would take me years to reach that position. But in the 1960 election, Hy Overton had run for state Senate, relinquishing his House seat and the agriculture chair with it, then losing the Senate race. The former vice chairman of the committee, Albert Matlock, made the same strategic error, running for Senate, giving up his House seat, and then losing the Senate race, so there was no one in line to lead agriculture.

I talked to all three speaker candidates about my interest in chairing agriculture. Culbertson and Campbell both expressed their support. Easley was less enthusiastic, wanting to put me on the legislative finance committee. Although I was officially supporting W. O. for speaker, it was obviously going to develop into a race between Campbell and Easley. I tried to talk W. O. out of running, but he declined to release me and, in fact, asked me to nominate him, which I did. None of the three candidates had a majority on the first vote, so W. O. dropped out because he had the fewest votes. On the next ballot, I cast my vote for Jack Campbell and he won—by one vote.

The next day, Speaker Campbell announced the committee assignments, naming me chairman of agriculture. That was a big day for me. This appointment was my greatest accomplishment so far in the legislature. By chairing the agriculture committee, I could do what I set out to do when I ran for office. The committee members were Alva J. Parker of Roosevelt County, Bob Martin of Grant County, Frank Foster of Curry County, Charles Sedillo, a Republican from Sierra County, Toby Lovato, a Republican from Union County, Isidro Romero of Guadalupe County, Dr. Charles Harris of Bernalillo County, and Fred Foster of Grant County. An excellent committee, they were loyal to me and looked to me for leadership.

I broadened the scope of the agriculture committee a great deal. Until then, all game and fish legislation had gone to the natural resources committee. I persuaded Speaker Campbell that game, particularly deer, elk, and antelope, were forage animals and had a great bearing on agriculture, so bills related to them were referred to my committee. In the 1961 session, we considered a lot of legislation that pertained to revamping the state Game and Fish Commission, including changes to the hunting season, rate changes for licenses, regulations about the storage of meat, and other ways to strengthen the laws. We worked closely with commission director Fred Thompson to completely review and update the legislation. That drew a great deal of attention to the agriculture committee and broadened my knowledge of hunters and fisherman and their interests in New Mexico. A rift had grown between these sportsmen and the farmers and ranchers over the issue of hunters and fishermen abusing private property. I worked to resolve these differences by holding meetings with them, persuading the sportsmen to respect property rights, and persuading the landowners that we would have a great deal less vandalism if we had sportsmen supporting agricultural interests.

I also spent a lot of time in the 1961 session on the debate over the fee charged for grazing on state-owned lands. Buddy Wamel, chairman of the Senate conservation committee, wanted to maintain a low fee, as did many of the rural organizations. I felt we should slightly increase the rate, which had been about 7 cents an acre. Those seeking an increase wanted to hike it up to around 50 cents an acre. I thought a better rate would be 17 or 18 cents, so I convinced other legislators to go with me and we had a bill drawn up. Soon thereafter, the Cattle Growers Association led the other farm organizations in a unanimous vote to oppose any increase at all. Despite my ties to these groups, I went on over to the Legislative Council Service, which was drawing up the legislation, and told council director Clay Buchanan to go ahead and give me the bill. He told me some of the sponsors of the bill had already come in to cancel their request for the bill—they were backing out. "Just put me down as sole sponsor and give me the bill," I told him.

We had an introduction session that day, so there wasn't any committee activity or discussion on the floor. After I introduced my grazing-fee bill, the session adjourned. I went home to Stanley and worked around the ranch. When I came inside, Alice said, "What did you do up there today? That phone's been ringing off the hook!" And that evening, the president of the Cattle Growers, John Stark, called. "Doggone, Bruce," he said. "What are we gonna have to do? Gonna have to fight you, too?"

I said, "Look, you guys, I'm trying to be your friend. I'm not at all sure we can even hold the figures I've got in my bill, when it comes right down to it. The increase may be even more. I think I can get it passed in the House, but the bill they have over in the Senate will increase the fee to 50 cents an acre. Let's see what happens to it. I'll hold mine in my committee until we get the one coming out of the Senate."

That Senate bill came over in a day or two. Buddy Wamel had opposed it and his conservation committee gave it a "do not pass" recommendation, but the Senate had revived it on the floor and passed it by a good margin. We discussed the bill for a while in the House agriculture committee but I knew we weren't going to be able to kill it, so I just amended the fee to 17 cents. However, the bill had also been referred to the House taxation and revenue committee, which preferred 50 cents.

On my trips back and forth to Stanley, I began to wonder how I could argue for 17 cents and show it was fair to rural communities without hurting the rest of the state. At that time the King Brothers Ranch had a total of one section of state land—640 acres—which was small compared to all our holdings, so the state grazing fee didn't affect us much. Still, I knew the difficult circumstances of the livestock industry in those days. To make my case, I needed facts and figures on what the earnings would be if the fee were raised and on how the different fees would impact ranchers. I did some research and came up with a good argument for setting the fee at 17 cents, based on the expenses of raising a calf—the costs of grazing, of having a pickup for transportation, of maintaining windmills to provide water, and so on.

Finally, the bill came up on the floor one day about noon. All the press from all around came to watch the proceedings. I remember Jeff Good of DeBaca County leaned over to me and said, "They're just sitting there waiting to pick our bones like a bunch of buzzards."

I moved to substitute my bill for the 50-cent bill. We discussed it most of the afternoon. After my presentation Tony Hillerman, who had plenty of experience around farms himself, teased me by saying, "After you explained how difficult it is to make a farm pay, and how high the expenses are, and the details of feeding cattle and caring for windmills and so on, I almost felt like sending you a note, saying, 'I don't think we'd better increase the grazing fee at all!'"

When we voted, the 17-cent fee prevailed. I was feeling pretty good, but that night at a social function the chairman of the House taxation and revenue committee, Representative Larry Goodell, found me and said, "Bruce, I have to tell you that I've got a couple of people to change their votes and we're going to reconsider it tomorrow in the original form, with the increase to 50 cents." He said those in favor of the larger increase included majority whip Austin Roberts, who had voted with me that day, and most of the other members of the House leadership.

In those days we had an awfully hard time keeping any bill killed or passed, because we'd vote on it one day and the next day they'd move for reconsideration to bring it back. You could only reconsider once, so immediately after a bill was passed on a close vote, often someone would move to reconsider the vote, hoping to get the same result and rule out further reconsideration. With bills I was especially interested in, I learned to immediately befriend some of the opposition after a close vote and persuade them to vote with me on the reconsideration. It wasn't too difficult to enlist their support if I got there before someone else began to maneuver for those commitments. Sometimes it was a better strategy to delay the move to reconsider, if I needed more time to change votes. In later years when I was speaker of the House, I discouraged reconsideration on close votes.

The next day after I got the bad news from Representative Goodell, the grazing bill was going to be the first order of business. I went back to the capitol early in the morning and began to visit with legislators, particularly my friends who had voted for the Senate bill the day before. I told them, "This is not a situation that I have a large interest in personally. But I just feel the 50-cent rate is too high, and we did have a fair vote yesterday, and we prevailed, and I would hope that some of you would vote with me against reconsidering."

Representative Matt Chacon of Rio Arriba County had been one of the strong proponents of the 50-cent fee the day before. He said, "Bruce, I agree. I was committed to stick with the figures as they came over from the Senate, but my commitment is fulfilled, and I will vote with you today." He was just one of many who decided to vote my way.

As the session came to order, Matt was at my desk visiting, along with several others from the northern areas who had opposed me the day before. Speaker Campbell called me up to the podium and asked, "What are you working on?"

"I'm trying to get enough votes so you can't overturn the vote where we killed that Senate bill yesterday," I told him.

"Aw, you don't have to worry about that," he said. "The guys are just teasing you. Shoot, we're not going to reconsider it today. Let's get on with the other business of the House."

It all seemed lighthearted, but I knew that if I hadn't gotten to work, they would have voted to reconsider. Once again, working on a piece of legislation I learned lessons and made friends that would help me later in my political career.

≈

Jack Campbell did several things that later proved helpful in positioning me for my own run at House speaker. Of course, being chairman of agriculture, I was already in a prominent leadership position. In the 1961 session, Campbell was planning to run for governor in 1962 and I was supporting him. So when Governor Mechem, a Republican, would send down messages about legislation that Campbell didn't agree with, he took that opportunity to broaden his name recognition among the public. He would call me up to take the speaker's chair so he could take the floor and blast the governor's position. That gave me a chance to increase my exposure in front of the House.

Another break came when Speaker Campbell appointed me to the state Board of Finance. The board was an accommodation to the biannual schedule of the legislature—it could make monies available to meet interim needs that were unforeseen when the legislature made appropriations during the regular session every other year. The board had one voting member from the Senate and one from the House. This arrangement was later ruled unconstitutional because legislators cannot serve as voting members of an executive branch body, although the board continues to operate with the state land commissioner, the state treasurer, and four appointees by the governor. Much of the board's work had to do with property transactions, since board approval is required for disposing any state property, whether it be land or vehicles or office equipment or anything else. The board is responsible for selling all the bonds of the state and its subdivisions for capital outlays or other purposes. It also oversees transfers from one political subdivision to another, such as a city to another city or to a county. While I served, the position gave me a broad view of the working needs of state government. During the board's monthly meetings, I gained great respect for Governor Mechem and his department of finance and administration. I also became acquainted with the people who did the nuts-and-bolts work of state government. Those ties with state employees served me well when I was speaker and, later, governor.

Working with Governor Jack Campbell (second from right) gave me a glimpse of the influence and the responsibilities that attend the state's highest elective office. Pictured with Campbell are Joe Montoya (left), who would become U.S. Senator, and General John Jolly (right) of the New Mexico National Guard. (Photograph courtesy Museum of New Mexico, #30374)

When it became apparent that Jack Campbell would run for governor in 1962, several House members announced as candidates for speaker, including Albert Lebeck of McKinley County, who was majority leader, Jerry Brasher of Bernalillo County, who was chairman of the appropriations committee, and Dick Dixon of Quay County, the Democratic caucus chairman. At first, I wasn't involved, but some of my friends in the House offered to support me. Then one day Wayne Scott, the capitol columnist for the *Albuquerque Journal*, came by to talk about a story he was writing on the probable candidates for speaker in the 1963 session. He said he would mention my name. "Okay," I said, "let's see what kind of reaction we get."

In his column Scott went through the long list of names. At the bottom, he put a review of my background and interests, adding that I always wore cowboy boots and I was interested in the speaker's job. That column encouraged many of my fellow House members to offer their support. When I finally did nudge over and become a candidate, I got my first real taste of the competitiveness—and some of the hardball tactics—of the big-time political scene.

During the 1962 primary campaign, I served as co-chairman of Jack Campbell's campaign and ran for re-election to my House seat. In the general election, I was the Democratic statewide campaign coordinator and Calvin Horn was the state party chairman. We worked closely together. Campbell won the governor's race, I was re-elected, and many of my Democratic friends were elected to the House. During my travels around the state for Campbell, I made a point to drink coffee with the legislators and mention I was a candidate for speaker of the House and would appreciate their support. I tried to get as many commitments as I could, and finally I felt I had enough to win. But I knew better than to stop working.

In early December after the election, I was still waiting to go around just before the party caucus to visit with the legislators and again ask for their votes. Up until then, we had always held the party caucuses and elected officers the night before the legislature convened in mid-January. However, some of the other candidates for speaker began to say they wanted to organize early. There was a lot of horse-trading and finally they decided to meet in December. Dick Dixon earlier had called a meeting at the Western Skies Hotel in Albuquerque. With Matt Chacon and others, he had finally persuaded a majority of Democratic members of the House to support me. But that didn't end the speaker's race. It just reduced the number of candidates to three: Jerry Brasher, Al Lebeck, and myself.

So in December we came to Santa Fe for the organizational caucus, although some members still wanted to wait until January. Governor-elect Campbell had set up an office at La Posada Hotel, and we convened in the capitol in the afternoon. Calvin Horn presided. When we were nominating candidates for speaker, word came to us that Campbell wanted to talk with one person from each candidate's group, preferably an attorney, before we voted. I assigned Matt Chacon to represent me. Al Lebeck assigned Terry Boucher, who had been chairman of the judiciary committee, and Jerry Brasher assigned Fred Boone from Roosevelt County. They met for an hour or so, then came back and said we would have to postpone the speaker's election for a day or two.

"We're not supposed to say why," Matt said, but when he saw I intended to go ahead with the vote, he explained the situation: "There have been accusations that you and your brothers have registered some land with the Soil Bank and taken payments for it, but also planted crops on it." This would have constituted fraud, because the federal Soil Bank was supposed to pay farmers to conserve land and limit production.

"That's ridiculous," I said. "We'll adjourn until tomorrow morning and I'll see if we can get this cleared up."

I went to see Campbell. When I got there, he had just heard back from U.S. Senator Clinton P. Anderson, who had made a quick check with the Agriculture Department and confirmed that the rumor was not true.

When the caucus reconvened the next day, some members were still demanding we vote on whether to hold the speaker's election then or wait for the night before the session began. Their play was to use the extra time to find a compromise candidate. By then I thought for sure I had two-thirds of the votes, so I said, "If I don't have two-thirds of your votes today, we can wait until January to organize." Matt Chacon, being the scrapper he was, jumped up and said, "I don't care if Bruce disagrees with me. As his lawyer and a member of this body, I say a majority vote is all we have to have." He moved that we vote. When they called the roll I lacked one vote of having two-thirds. Jerry Brasher withdrew, and Al Lebeck and I ran again. That time, I got a two-thirds vote where I only needed a majority.

I greatly appreciated Matt Chacon having the foresight to push through that vote. "You never know," he said later. "You think you have commitments, but sometimes. . . ."

And indeed, some of those I thought were committed would have agreed to wait till January.

After all this was settled that afternoon, I went home to Stanley and told Alice, "If politics is going to be this tough, and they're going to make that

Soil Bank type of accusation when you start up the ladder, I'm going to get out of this business as quick as I can."

"No, that's not right," she said. "They'd like nothing better than to see you get out. You've worked hard to get up this far, and you should go ahead."

Senator Anderson had similar words for me. He was in Albuquerque, so I called the next morning to make an appointment to see him. I knew Senator Anderson, a leading Democrat in New Mexico politics, but we'd never been close friends. He told me to come in any time, so I showed up around 10 o'clock. The senator congratulated me on being elected speaker and I thanked him for clearing up the Soil Bank matter.

"Well, Bruce," he said. "I've known you boys all my life and I figured you can make money easier than that. I know you wouldn't do anything wrong, and I told them so."

"I have thought about politics," I said, "and I just feel that if that's the type of accusations and rumors that go around, and people put that much faith in them, then I'd better get out.

He laughed and said, "Bruce, that's just what they would like for you to do. Those of us who intend to serve the people, we just have to put up with that." He convinced me to stay in politics and from then on we were good friends.

3

Speaker of the House

The afternoon in December 1962 when I was elected speaker of the New Mexico House of Representatives, I came home and was sitting on the divan when I saw a limousine pulling up to my house. It was one of the lobbyists around the legislature. As he came up to the door, I thought, "This is a pretty key position, for these people to seek me out clear down here to the ranch, just to get my views."

The gentleman came up and knocked on the door. My sons Bill and Gary, who were about 11 and 7 then, ran to answer it. I heard the gentleman say, "I'd like to talk to the speaker of the House."

With that, Bill and Gary went running back to the kitchen, hollering, "Mama, Mama, there's a man out here who wants to talk to you!"

In my years as an elected official, I had often reflected on the needs of the state. As speaker of the House, I felt I had attained a position where I could influence the direction of New Mexico. Having grown up and been educated in the Estancia Valley—which is a three-cornered area of Bernalillo, Santa Fe, and Torrance counties—and then later having attended the University of New Mexico in Albuquerque, I knew the needs of those areas. They represented the basic make-up of New Mexico. In Bernalillo County you had the largest city, Albuquerque. In Santa Fe County you had the capital city of Santa Fe and the old, traditional northern areas, and then Torrance County pretty much resembled the high plains, with its agricultural areas. So I felt I brought a broad, statewide perspective to my new leadership role in the House.

From my four years of experience in the House, I realized the tremendous responsibility of the speaker, who appointed all the committees and their chairmen, and referred all legislation to those committees. One decision I made as I took this new position was that it would be in the best interests of the state for me to work with all 66 members of the House. Because each one of them represented a particular area—they were elected countywide at that time—obviously they would know the needs in their home districts. So I structured the legislature to where I could assemble all their thoughts and utilize them. I cautioned all the members that if anything should affect their districts positively or negatively, they should speak up. On the other hand, I urged them to resist injecting things into the session that would not necessarily be advantageous to them but would slow the process down, just because the day before, someone had introduced a bill they thought was an attack against them.

The 1963 legislative session would start January 17, some six weeks later. It was a blessing in disguise for me that we had gone ahead and organized the House early. Otherwise I would not have had time to review the duties of the speaker, who often has to make decisions on the spur of the moment. To prepare for the job I virtually memorized the New Mexico constitution and *Robert's Rules of Order* in my spare time, which served me well in later years. I also studied the names of all the legislators and worked on pronouncing them correctly. I tried to think of every situation that could develop when we convened the House. I knew that many knowledgeable legal minds and other highly educated, sophisticated members would try to show that selecting me as speaker, with my agricultural background, wasn't the smartest move the legislators could have made.

Finally the day came. Secretary of State Betty Fiorina called the House to order and everyone signed the roster. Then we held the official election for speaker and I was elected by acclamation. I rapped the gavel and began to read off the names of those selected for staff positions: chief clerk, sergeant-at arms, and so on. I was doing fine until I came to one name I had not had the opportunity to review, the Republican minority leader from Lincoln County. Even though I knew him and he later became a good friend . . . well, it was a long name: Bill Shrecengost. I said, "We have selected Representative *Shrinkinghost* to be minority leader of the House."

Everyone laughed. I was embarrassed, but didn't let on. I read through the rest of the names, then we sent representatives to both the Senate and the Governor's Office, as prescribed in the constitution, to tell them we were organized and ready to do business. In a joint session in the House chamber, we would all hear Governor Campbell's opening message. While we were milling around waiting for the senators I ran into Albert Amador, a senator from Rio Arriba County. He said, "Bruce, don't let them kid you about pronouncing those names. You may have botched some of them, but on the Spanish names, you got every one of them exactly right."

Immediately after I was elected speaker in the 1963 session, members began to come up and tell me that when they had supported me, they thought they were going to be chairman of this or that committee. When it came time to name the chairmen and members of committees, I wanted to be fair to all areas of New Mexico and to each representative, appointing everyone to the committee of his choice, if I could. I hadn't made any commitments in exchange for support.

Matt Chacon and I looked over the committee assignments, with help from some of my other key supporters. We named one of the strongest groups of committee chairmen that we ever had in the House. I appointed Matt chair of the ways and means committee, Ernest Miera chair of public affairs, and John Mershon chair of appropriations and finance, which raised a few eyebrows, because Jerry Brasher had been chair. But Jerry still worked closely with us. I appointed Bobby Mayfield chairman of the taxation and revenue committee. I reappointed Terry Boucher as chairman of the judiciary committee, even though he had been one of Albert Lebeck's main supporters in the election for speaker. Terry told me he hadn't expected to be reappointed. "I didn't support you, and you knew that."

"That doesn't make any difference," I told him. "You have the ability and you've been a good friend."

We elected Austin Roberts of Farmington to be majority leader, and he proved outstanding in that position. He and I became very good friends. On Austin's suggestion, we rented a room at La Posada Hotel and spent many hours looking over legislation and planning strategy. And since Governor Campbell's wife, Ruthann, had remained in Roswell to finish the school year with their children, we often went over to the governor's mansion to discuss legislation with Governor Campbell and the leaders of the House and Senate. I began to see the attractions of becoming governor of New Mexico. The executive mansion was beautiful, with a view overlooking the city of Santa Fe, and I couldn't help but be impressed with the considerable influence a governor has on the well-being of the state. But for the present, I was also impressed with the influence of the speaker of the House.

The question of how to increase state revenues generated some pretty hot and heavy discussion at the mansion. The 1962 campaign had centered on the legislature's need to raise about $75 million in additional funds. Then-Governor Mechem had said the only recourse was to increase the gross receipts tax. But now Governor Campbell said there were other ways to raise money—perhaps by increasing the income tax or the ad valorem, or property, tax. I fought against a high property tax because it would be hard on homeowners and people in agriculture. They would pay more than their share. I argued that we didn't have good property appraisals and that some counties assessed at much higher percentages of actual property value than others did. The property tax just wasn't a good vehicle for increasing state revenues.

After two or three discussions at the mansion, Governor Campbell began to lose patience with my insistence. He finally said, "Oh, Bruce, we're not gonna hurt your farmers and ranchers. Let's just go ahead and work this around to where we can get the money."

Then Gordon Melody, who was still chairman of the Senate finance committee, jumped in, saying, "Look, Governor, Bruce knows exactly where that money is going to come from if you go to the ad valorem tax. I haven't been thinking much differently, but I've been letting him carry the load. I think we had better look at other taxes."

So we considered other options, but they all were quite difficult and divisive. We finally agreed to increase the gross receipts tax by 1 percent, with myself, Austin Roberts, and Bobby Mayfield introducing the legislation without the consent of the governor. But he finally conceded and signed it.

≋

In those nightly sessions in our hotel room, Austin Roberts and I would prepare ourselves for the upcoming day and develop strategies for dealing with the various bills. We were able to find ways to eliminate many divisive issues, including right-to-work, which would have let non-union workers work on union jobs.

We used "paired votes" as one strategy to deal with hotly contested issues. Pairing worked when a representative knew he was going to miss a vote. If he was in favor of the legislation, he would tell the speaker to go ahead and pair him with someone who was against it and planned to be present. It was easy to pair if some other representative had expressed his stand against before it came to a vote. If not, you just had to use your judgment. Once in a while, someone would resent being paired and might want to change his vote if he came after the absent member in the roll call and realized that his own vote was being neutralized. The pairing would state that it applied to all votes pertaining to that particular subject—whether they were about procedure, amendments, or whatever. Sometimes the pairing might get the absent member into voting in a way he hadn't exactly intended. Done properly, it enabled members to vote on major legislation when they couldn't be present. I would keep six or seven pairings in my desk, and they told me to vote them however I wanted to. I could influence legislation that way. For instance, on right-to-work, when the labor committee chairman, J. B. McCoy, had to leave the House early, he would give me his pairing. Since he was a supporter of Governor Campbell and me, I was able to protect his vote against right-to-work in his absence. But I always tried to use pairs to express the views of the representatives who asked me to pair them on a given vote. This strategy was later ruled unconstitutional.

In the 1963 session and 1964 special session, we worked on quite a bit of legislation related to education. We sought to fund public schools more adequately, although it would be several more years before we completely overhauled the system for funding them. We also concentrated on a couple of large projects for the University of New Mexico and New Mexico State University and on funding and siting the Albuquerque Technical Vocational Institute. My agricultural background gave me working knowledge of the interests of New Mexico State, and we appropriated money to construct an agricultural building at its Las Cruces campus. We also worked hard to expand the University of New Mexico medical school against strong opposition to funding it, since many legislators felt it would be too expensive to keep it going.

At that time, Tony Hillerman had left the *New Mexican* and gone down to UNM to teach in the journalism department. They also made him assistant to UNM President Tom Popejoy, particularly with respect to legislation. Perhaps one reason for this latter assignment was his close association with me in prior years, and of course my door was always open to Tony. When Tom Popejoy came to Santa Fe, he and Tony always wound up in my office. I became a good friend of Popejoy and a strong supporter of the University of New Mexico. I was an alumnus and Austin Roberts was a graduate of the UNM law school, so he and I devoted a fair amount of time to the needs of the university.

⁓

In the 1964 special legislative session we were under court order to reapportion the House districts based on the 1960 census. This would be my first experience with reapportionment, an issue that would pester the legislature after every ten-year U.S. census throughout my political career. From 1950 to 1970 and beyond, the general trend in New Mexico was a rapid population shift from the rural areas to the cities, where people went looking for jobs. Agriculture didn't pay well—it still doesn't—and the dry years pushed people out. In addition, the vastly improved machinery—threshing machines, irrigation systems, tractors, and other kinds of automation—has allowed the consolidation of larger farms while reducing the need for hands. People like us at King Brothers Ranch would buy the land as neighbors left. But the result was fewer people living in the older agricultural areas, particularly on the east side of the state.

I felt that the House could do a much better job of reapportioning the districts than anybody else, including the courts, and I convinced Governor Campbell to call us together in a special session. We looked at two or three model plans that were going around—every state was in some phase of reapportionment—and we worked out a system that became known as the King Plan.

I appointed Terry Boucher to chair the reapportionment committee. We put a third of the House members on this committee and accomplished the job in about ten days. In my plan, we redesigned the House districts so each county would still have at least one representative, but we gave the small counties a fractional vote. For instance, Harding County in the northeast part of the state had only about three-tenths of the population needed to have one representative. Under fractional voting, we gave Harding County one representative, but he would have only three-tenths of a vote. Torrance County had about six-tenths of the population it needed, so it got six-tenths of a vote, and so on for the smaller counties.

We never used this system. Representative David Cargo, a Republican from Bernalillo County, filed a lawsuit challenging the fractional voting method. This was just the first of many scraps I had with Cargo, who became a longtime adversary and friend of mine. The lawsuit was assigned to Judge Caswell Neal's court in the fifth judicial district, the Carlsbad-Roswell area. The constitutional lawyers opposing us argued that the King Plan gave disproportionate influence to counties with small populations by allowing them one representative, even though that person only had a fractional vote in the House. I guess the idea was that the person could have greater influence through their presence on committees and in discussion of legislation than their fractional vote might suggest.

After long hearings and deliberation, Judge Neal ruled that each member of the House must have one full vote. He also held that the next session would be the last time we could convene with each county having one representative regardless of population. Then we would have to reapportion, and we would have to do it in the less populated areas by creating districts made up of more than one small county. So for the 1965 regular session we had a 70-member House, which was up from 66, and the Senate still had 32 members. In the 1967 session, we put these numbers in the constitution by amendment and apportioned the Senate to 42 members. Bernalillo County gained considerable power, all at the expense of rural counties. The loss of rural strength changed the flavor of the legislature, as it began to more noticeably reflect the interests of the urban members.

≋

My friendship with Will Harrison shows how a politician and a journalist covering the legislature could be friends even through those times when their respective jobs set them crosswise of each other. In the 1963 session, the House was considering a bill to create a pre-primary nominating convention, so the parties could weed out some of the weaker candidates from the primary election races. Will asked me what I thought of it.

"I don't like it much," I told him.

"All right," he said, "if you're against it, we won't have it. You can block any bill. But Clinton Anderson and Joe Montoya, they're going to call you jointly and they're going to say, 'Bruce, we want you to implement that pre-primary nominating convention,' and then what are you going to say about it?"

I said I'd tell our two senators that we could do without it.

"Fine," he said, and he wrote in his article that the pre-primary convention would not pass during that session because the speaker was against it.

Well, Clint and Joe did get on the phone with me and Austin Roberts. They really leaned on us. So in a weak moment I finally agreed we could go ahead with the convention. But I knew better than to cross old Will by announcing that his story had been wrong, so I told him, "Will, those guys did like you said they would. They really expounded on the virtues of the pre-primary nominating convention for Democrats and they convinced me it would be the best thing." He knew it a couple of weeks before anyone else.

"Damn you," he said. "You're going to eat crow over that one. I'm going to blast you!"

Of course, he blasted me a lot easier than if I hadn't told him. Then, sure enough, the bill did pass and Governor Campbell signed it.

All in all, I felt I was a success as speaker of the House. When I was completing my second term in that position in 1966, many people began to ask me to run for governor. I rather liked this idea, because I saw so many things I could do for New Mexico. I was interested in improving our public school system, expanding vocational education, streamlining government, and clarifying the role of the executive branch.

When I began to run for governor in earnest, Will Harrison told me,

"Bruce, you've done a good job. You and your family are great people and I'd just like to see you as governor. I think you'd be great for this state. But I'm not going to write in favor of you all the time. They'd think I was your promoter. I'm going to do like I've always done. I'll write the facts and you had better do a good job."

Will and I went over to La Fonda Hotel on the plaza in Santa Fe to eat. I told him that Alice and the boys really wanted to go to the World's Fair. "They all understand it's a crucial time in the campaign, and maybe I shouldn't go."

"No, that's fine, Bruce, you go ahead and let me watch it while you're away," he said. "How long are you planning to be gone?"

I said a couple weeks.

"Well," he said, "I'll guarantee we won't lose any ground during that time if you'll call me a couple of times a week and we can discuss things that are going on."

"I'll call you religiously," I told him.

"You'll go by Washington on the way back and visit Clint?"

"Yes, fine," I said, I would see the senator.

So we went to New York for the fair and son of a gun, I made more progress on the campaign back home in those two weeks than in any other two weeks I ever ran. I made a regular report twice a week to Will and he would write about what I was doing, then the other media would pick it up, and he did a beautiful job. Will was read all over the state, too. He went through how I was visiting the World's Fair and what was going on there. Of course, we had a New Mexico pavilion, so Will wrote one column about my report and he made it sound like it was the "in" thing to do. Then when we got to D.C., he really wrote that up big.

For Alice and me, that 1966 race was our first taste of statewide politics. We campaigned all over New Mexico for delegates who would back me in the Democratic pre-primary nominating convention that year. I worked hard to get on the ballot—you needed 20 percent of the delegates or you could get on by petition. I didn't really have anyone actively working on my behalf. On the other hand, former Governor John Burroughs was running to regain the position with the backing of many of the old-line Democratic politicians, including the Joe Montoya faction. Another strong candidate was Gene Lusk, who had been Senate majority leader for a number of years. His mother, Georgia Lusk, had been a New Mexico representative in Congress. They had a good organization and were popular on the east side of the state. Governor Campbell supported the Lusk campaign and as the sitting governor he had a great deal of clout in the nominating convention.

Senator Anderson at first had tried to lend me some support, but then he worked back in with Governor Campbell and the Lusk faction, and finally he decided to just stay out. Many of his key followers had advised him that I wasn't going to get on the ballot, but I had a strong following particularly in the Albuquerque area among the independent Democratic bloc and the newer voters, and in Santa Fe County.

When we got to the convention, all of us candidates worked throughout the day attempting to swing as many delegate votes as we could. I visited with Filo Sedillo, the dean of the Democratic county chairmen. He was from Valencia County, where he had a loyal contingent. I also had friends who had worked for me in Valencia County and I thought I might get some votes there. Filo told me he was supporting Burroughs, but he said, "Bruce, if you need just a few votes, Valencia County will vote last, alphabetically, and I'll give you enough votes to get on the ballot."

The voting went late into the evening. Valencia County had 44 votes. When it came out that I lacked a few, Filo moved for a recess while they polled the Valencia County delegation. Everyone kind of caucused in place, and we had the general milling around that you sometimes get when you take a break in the convention system of politics. Everyone was wondering what was going to happen. After about 30 minutes, Filo announced the vote for Valencia County. He gave me 13 votes, which put me over the 20 percent I needed to get on the ballot. Burroughs received the largest vote, about 44 percent. Gene Lusk was second with 29 percent. Roy Walker dropped out of the race, with only 10 percent of the delegate votes.

Now my big problem was that everyone thought Filo and I were working out some type of deal in the recess. Even though I probably had 13 votes in Valencia County before then, it wasn't clear to many Democrats how deeply involved I was in party politics or how indebted I would be to Filo Sedillo. Meanwhile, I had been trying to distance myself from the Democratic political machine. I knew I hadn't made a deal with Filo, but I also knew lots of people assumed I had. That wasn't the kind of image I wanted among the people. I also thought if I did lose the governor's race—and I hadn't been too successful up to that point—then I would be out of the picture altogether. Finally, I was a bit discouraged, having thought I would get a larger vote. So I waited a month after the convention and when the filing day came I filed instead for re-election to the House of Representatives and campaigned to get back my position as speaker. I won both positions without opposition.

Part of my decision to stay in the House and run again for speaker was the new capitol building, which was completed in 1966, so 1967 would be the first legislative session in the Roundhouse. Built in 1900, the old capitol had been starting to show its age, so that the House and Senate chambers were getting a little dangerous. Sometimes the heels of women's shoes would break through the floor. One time we had about 75 children visit. Since we didn't have a gallery where citizens could observe the session, these school kids had to sit up front on the floor, and it starting cracking like it was about to crash down on the Senate below us. We also needed office space for the legislators.

Governor Campbell had thought we needed a new building, and I did, too. Together we appointed a commission to pursue the project. Willard Kruger was architect and John Gaw Meem, who is famous for his Pueblo revival style buildings around New Mexico, worked with him on the design. They came up with a round, four-story territorial-style building with four short wings, one in each direction of the compass. The shape is based on the Zia sun symbol, which is the emblem on our state flag. The new capitol was built just a block or so east of the old one, which the state converted to offices and renamed the Bataan Memorial Building to honor all the New Mexicans who died in the Bataan Death March of World War II.

I still have a warm spot in my heart for the old House chambers in the Bataan Building, where I started out as presiding officer, but in the new building, I was greatly intrigued by the speaker's rostrum. I thought it would be a shame for me to have worked so hard with Governor Campbell and the Senate leadership to make money available for the new capitol building and then not get to use that rostrum.

After I dropped out of the governor's race in 1966, Senator Anderson moved into the Lusk camp. He and others leaned on me quite heavily to co-chair the Lusk campaign with Roy Walker of Clovis. I reluctantly agreed to serve.

As it turned out, I enjoyed working with Roy, who was a great fellow, and we had a lot of latitude in running the primary campaign. We got along exceptionally well, and Lusk won the primary by a large margin. However, we had a difficult time helping Lusk make the transition from primary winner to Democratic nominee. Although we did get most of the Burroughs faction to support Lusk, we still lacked the real push that it takes to elect a Democratic candidate as governor.

I chaired the state Democratic party and managed the Gene Lusk campaign for governor in 1966. The campaign was tough, but we still enjoyed the lighter moments. Shown with me are former Governor Jack Campbell, my longtime friend and ally Fabian Chavez, Senator Joe Montoya, myself, Democratic gubernatorial candidate Gene Lusk, and Senator Clinton Anderson.

I also wound up as Democratic chairman that year, mainly because Senator Anderson was running for re-election and wanted me to head the party. I learned that being the state Democratic chairman wasn't all a bowl of gravy.

Senator Anderson had his own philosophy on how to campaign and he set the agenda. Then, too, the gubernatorial candidate always has a great deal to say about orienting and operating the campaign. On top of all that, the Republican opponent, Dave Cargo, was a smart campaigner. He got on issues that attracted the press and he tried several strategies that were quite new and intriguing to politicians in New Mexico.

One thing Cargo did quite successfully, I thought, was to focus on the Indian reservations and on small Hispanic communities in Mora and San Miguel counties, too. They didn't have many votes, but he put some of those communities on the map, like Villanueva and others on the Pecos River. At that time, many news reporters were newcomers to New Mexico. Few were familiar with Mora and San Miguel counties, so they were captivated by the communities and the old-time Hispanic customs that made up those voting precincts. It didn't hurt that Cargo's wife, Ida Jo, was of Hispanic descent from the town of Belen, either. His basic tactic, which he did so well, was to generate a great deal of free publicity by developing his campaign around those quaint, northern communities. He drew on the appeal of local folklore in that scenic region, and he captured the narrative that goes along with campaigning in the Hispanic communities of northern New Mexico.

Dave also worked in the Indian communities. He would go out on the reservation, to little places like Torreon that few people even in New Mexico had heard of, and he would find some Indian friends and get them to put up a big "Cargo for Governor" sign in their window. Then he would persuade the press to go out there and he would say, "Well, look, here's an Indian friend way out here on the Navajo reservation who's supporting Dave Cargo."

Cargo didn't just run against the Democratic candidates, as other Republicans had. He ran more against the political machine of the Democratic party, and he avoided alienating the average Democrat. He also kept some distance from the Republican party itself, instead relating more closely to individual voters. At one point, someone asked him, "If you get elected, are you going to listen to the Republican party?" He said, "I'll listen if I think they are going in the right direction, and if I think they aren't, I'll just go my own way." That spirit earned him the nickname "Lonesome Dave." Many independent voters said, "That's my type of guy. He thinks like I do."

I watched Cargo closely. His approach impressed me and I used some of his strategies in my own successful campaigns in later years.

On the Democratic side of the general election campaign, I could see we were tripping over our own mistakes, including the way the party handled the furnishings for the new capitol building. Senator James Patton of Las Cruces had supported the Campbell administration in appropriating money for furnishings—desks, file cabinets, chairs, and so on. He also happened to own a store in Las Cruces called the Inkwell, which stocked school supplies and furniture. Campbell had commissioned Patton as chair of the committee to specify the furniture we would need, then Patton got the contract to supply it, so he sold furniture and curtains and other items to the state. I'm sure he won the contract on a competitive low bid, but it looked like a sweet deal. Even though Patton's merchandise proved satisfactory, it left the Democrats and the administration open to attacks for being too cozy an operation in purchasing the capitol furnishings.

Sure enough, it came back to sting us. One day Gene Lusk had stayed overnight in Albuquerque, and he and I and some other candidates planned to fly to Silver City together. I drove over from the ranch to the airport and I hadn't had a chance to read the paper. When we got on the airplane, Gene handed me the *Albuquerque Journal*, still wrapped up. As we sat back in our seats, I unrolled the paper and began to read. The first thing that caught my eye was the front page headline that said, "PATTON RECEIVES CONTRACT FOR OFFICE FURNITURE." I was worried.

"Gene, when the plane lands in Silver City, we'll have a lot of press. Besides the local press, the Associated Press will be there, and UPI," I said. "I think you ought to say that you don't condone it when a senator who has worked closely with the Campbell administration and has helped specify the furnishings of the capitol receives the bid and provides the furnishings."

Lusk thought about it. He said, "I can't do that. They're two of my best supporters." He and Senator Patton had served together in the legislature, and Governor Campbell was supporting Lusk.

"Well, Gene," I said, "that's be as it may. They are good friends of mine, too. But I still think that's the strategy we should use. I imagine if we don't refute it today, Dave Cargo will take his swing at it, and we'll probably be making that statement in a couple of weeks, anyway." Having served with Dave as I did for four years in the legislature, I knew he would make a case out of this. Sure enough, in a couple of weeks we ended up making a statement that Lusk didn't condone the deal, but it was too late.

On election night, the race seemed close at first, with Lusk edging out Cargo. We were at the old Hilton in Albuquerque, and Lusk was thinking about going down to give his victory speech. I rode down the elevator with Bob Beier, the political writer for the *Albuquerque Journal*. Bob nudged me and said, "Where are you going, Bruce?" Since I was Democratic chairman, I said I was going down to declare victory. "It's all right, isn't it?" I asked him.

"Well, I don't know," he said, "I guess if you can lose the Northeast Heights of Albuquerque by 18,000 votes and still win. . . ."

"Gosh, no," I said, surprised by that information. I knew he had the latest numbers from the *Journal* news desk.

"Well, I don't want to see you get embarrassed," he said. "You better be careful."

I didn't even have a chance to say anything to Lusk or Senator Joe Montoya, who was also there. I got up and opened the meeting, saying, "We *think* we've won, but we do need just a little bit more time to be certain before we actually declare victory." Then they both made very short speeches, the same way. They knew if I wasn't doing it, I must have a reason. We went into the elevator and by the time we got to the ninth floor, we knew darn well we'd lost.

The race ended up with Cargo beating Lusk mostly on the strength of his Albuquerque showing. In fact, the El Paso newspaper printed an early edition saying, "LUSK WINS," but the Albuquerque returns came in late and all at once, shifting the tide for Cargo.

≋

The 1967 session brought many changes to state government. We had a Republican governor, more Republican members in the House, and some turnover of House leadership. My friend and former majority leader Austin Roberts had lost his election in San Juan County. He had voted against right-to-work, and a strong young Republican businessman in the oil field industry, Greg Marion, had opposed Austin on that issue. That was the first casualty of the right-to-work vote that I had experience with. I felt badly about Austin losing, because he was a close friend and ally of mine. I was also disappointed that he would not get to move over to the new capitol building that he, too, had a great part in creating.

Another change, of course, came in the form of Republican Governor Dave Cargo. Bill Feather of the Associated Press had called me early the morning after the November election and asked, "Bruce, what's the election of a Republican going to do to your chances for speaker of the House?"

"I don't think it will have any effect," I told him. "I wasn't running for higher office." In fact, I was unopposed in both the primary and general elections.

But Bill said he had heard some rumbles that I might not be able to maintain the speaker position. Even though I had had a long night and hadn't gone to bed until about 2 A.M., I got on the phone about 6:30 A.M. and began to call legislators at random, not necessarily the ones I knew were with me. I got Eddie Yunker in Gallup, who was in the wholesale oil business and a Bataan veteran. I said, "Mr. Yunker, I understand you won the election in McKinley County?"

"Yes."

"Well, I am again a candidate for speaker of the House, and I would appreciate your supporting my candidacy."

Eddie said, "Yes, I was figuring on it. But I would like to be a member of the appropriations committee."

"Well, we'll get around to working out the committee membership, but right now I'm just checking to get a count on the representatives who would support me again for speaker."

He said, "I think I'm going to support you, but I would just like to have a commitment that you would put me on the appropriations committee, and then I will commit my support."

I remembered Mack Easley and I had gone through a similar situation, when he said he thought he "probably" would make me chairman of the agriculture committee, and then he lost the speakership by one vote.

I reflected that we would have about 20 members on the appropriations committee anyway, and we'd need someone from the McKinley County area. Knowing that he was a businessman, I said, "All right, Eddie, I'll go ahead and put you on the appropriations committee, but I want your vote for speaker."

"Well, you just mark it down," he said.

So I put it down, and then after two or three more calls I realized that there wasn't going to be any opponent, anyway.

Since I was state Democratic chairman that year, I called the caucus to elect the speaker. Even with no opposition, I felt a bit awkward about that, so I turned the meeting over to one of the senior representatives. I was elected by acclamation, as we had expected. Then I took over as chairman and thanked all our members for their confidence in me. I reminded them we would be moving into the new capitol, which would mark a new era in New Mexico politics.

We elected Dave Norvell to be majority leader. A talented young attorney and a friend of mine, Dave had served in the legislature since my first days as speaker. As majority leader he proved compatible with my thinking, but like some energetic, young lawyers, he sometimes made mistakes that caused us problems. Nonetheless, he was hardworking and developed into a good majority leader—so good, in fact, that when I left in the next term he became speaker of the House.

The 1967 House was a mixture of old and new. I had to work with several blocs and factions, both within and outside the Democratic party. The Republicans had gained many seats under reapportionment. The 1967 House had 43 Democrats and 27 Republicans, which kept my party on its toes. The minority leadership of the House provided a strong nucleus for the Republican party and began to develop some muscle. I had a lot of support from that side of the aisle as well as on the Democratic side, and I enjoyed strong support among the Hispanic legislators from northern New Mexico, who made up about 20 percent of the legislature. They held an Hispanic caucus and insisted that I caucus with them, which I felt was an honor. The 16 legislators from the Albuquerque area formed a bloc in the House, while the east-side legislators also still formed a bloc. Though I had to reckon with these various groups, I was successful in working with all of them, and I often got unanimous decisions on controversial legislation. We managed to avoid taking up some divisive legislation, like right-to-work, and we accomplished a great deal in 1967.

One highly divisive issue was fair trade in liquor. This law allowed the liquor industry to set minimum prices, forbidding discounts. But the courts had thrown out the fair-trade law, and there was a move to reinstate it. I felt that once it was out, we should not be reinstating fair trade, since it had given us an awful lot of trouble. We would kill the legislation and it would keep cropping up. I fought that as hard as I fought Indian gaming in the

1990s, and we stayed in session an extra day or two to kill the fair trade law. That was a real turning point in preventing liquor lobby control of the legislature, which had considerable influence until then.

We also had problems stemming from the liquor licensing law, which limited the number of licenses in a county or city based on population, making them a hot property. It cost $50 to get the license from the state, but the licensee could resell it for $350,000 because there was so much demand and the license would generate so much business. The whole situation was an opportunity for organized crime to get involved. We also had a different problem with the licenses, since they were granted for a specific area, either in a county or within the city limits of a municipality. So if you had a county liquor license, you couldn't use it inside the city, where it was more valuable, because more people lived there and you'd have a bigger market. We had eight politicians from the South Valley area of Bernalillo County, outside of Albuquerque, who had eight licenses. In little shacks they operated bars just beyond the city limits for the required period of a few months. Then they worked to get the city limits expanded to annex the bars. Once inside the city, they could resell the licenses for a big profit. It goes to show that if there's enough money involved, people will figure out a way to twist the law around to work for them. We weren't able to clean up this situation until my second term, when Jim Baca and State Senator Les Houston helped me reform the liquor laws in the late 1970s.

In my last two years in the legislature, 1967-68, the schools were running short of money for the teachers. They finally went on strike in Albuquerque, which caused a great deal of concern among the citizens. We realized we were going to have to do something different. I visited with Governor Cargo and we decided to hold a special session and let local school districts raise their gross receipts tax to increase the teachers' salaries, but only temporarily. After lengthy discussion, we convinced the teachers to go back to work. During my first term as governor, teachers again were demanding higher pay at a time when state revenues couldn't support a large raise.

Another ongoing subject of debate through much of my time in the legislature was revising our antiquated state constitution. Many of us felt we needed to streamline state government and create a cabinet in the executive branch.

Other areas under review were the method of selecting judges and the structure of interactions between state and local government. I supported legislation that passed in the Campbell administration establishing a constitutional revision commission. Governor Campbell appointed Harry Patton of Curry County as chairman, and I appointed Roy Davidson and Dave Norvell as the two members from the House. The commission worked throughout 1967 to develop recommendations for a revised constitution and to see if we had enough enthusiasm to call a constitutional convention, which we finally did in 1969. I was honored to play a key role in that important aspect of New Mexico politics.

≈

In our home, Alice and I have a painting that we bought from Tommy Macaione, a well-known Santa Fe artist who worked around the capitol a great deal. It's a very pretty scene of the Santa Fe River just down the street from the capitol. We enjoy it very much. Tommy was a colorful figure, a very talented artist who also ran for mayor of Santa Fe several times. He usually got just a handful of votes.

In the 1960s, Governor Cargo commissioned Tommy to paint his portrait. So Tommy set up his easel in the governor's office. When we went in to confer with the governor, I thought he would excuse Tommy while we were discussing legislation. But no, Dave didn't do that. Anyhow, I went ahead with the meeting, knowing Tommy wouldn't create a problem. We got to discussing some in-depth situations, and Tommy ran around from behind the picture and said, "No, no, no, boys, that's not right. It's this way." And he went on to tell us how we ought to be handling the issue. Finally Governor Cargo said, "Now look, Tommy, you're painting the portrait. You stay out of our business."

Tommy had a piece of sculpture that he kept wanting to present to the House of Representatives. I thought a presentation like that would be frivolous, so I kept dodging him. Tommy would try to set up an appointment with me through Eloisa Block, my personal secretary. She would say, "Tommy, the speaker is busy today. You'll have to come back in a day or two." Well, the new coffee shop and House lounge was just a few steps away from my office. I made several trips a day over there. So Tommy would wait to catch me in between the lounge and the office. He would say, "Now, Mr. Speaker, I've got this fine sculpture that I want to present to the House of Representatives." I would say, "Yeah, Tommy," and just keep walking by him.

This went on for two or three days until finally he ran around in front of me and said, "Now look, Mr. Speaker, you cannot just brush me off this way. I'll have you know I've been a candidate for mayor of this city of Santa Fe four times."

That struck me as humorous, so I stopped and put my hand on his shoulder, and I said, "Yeah, but Tommy, how many votes did you get?"

"It doesn't make any difference how many votes I got," he said. "The point is I've been a candidate for mayor and you're gonna have to listen to me."

I thought anybody who was that intent, I better listen to him. I took him in my office. He made a nice little presentation, and I thought, "Oh, we'll get into a lot of trouble with something like this," so I said, "Tommy, I'll tell you what I'll do. I'll appoint a committee of three to look at your presentation and if they think it's worthwhile for the House of Representatives, I'll let you set it up and show it to us."

"All right, that's fine," he said.

So I appointed a conservative Republican, Merrill Taylor from San Juan County, as chairman of that group. I thought, "This will be the last I'll hear of that."

Lo and behold, in about ten days Representative Taylor gets up on the floor and says, "I'm carrying out your orders and we have reviewed Mr. Macaione's presentation of his sculpture. I think it warrants viewing by the members of the House."

I was absolutely flabbergasted. And I was stuck. We spent about 30 minutes looking at the piece, which resembled a large ice sculpture, and by the end of that time I was somewhat impressed by it myself. We never took any action on it and nothing more came out of this incident, except I guess Tommy gained some prestige. Even after that, he continued to be a supporter of mine. He was very smart, and I always liked and respected him. One time when I was running for governor, I came to a big meeting of environmentalists in the North Valley of Albuquerque. Tommy was up front presiding, and when he saw me he said, "Here comes that Bruce King. I guess he's going to be asking for our vote." I thought, oh, boy, here it comes.

But he said, "You know what, I'm not only going to vote for him, but I'm going to get out and support him. He's a good man."

≋

By the end of the 1968 legislative session I felt I had worked things out quite well with Dave Cargo, but apparently we weren't getting on as well as I had thought.

He came by on the last day of the session when we were within about an hour of completing the work. In those days, we just stopped the clock if we had a number of bills waiting. We had stopped it at noon that day and by about 3 P.M. we still had not finished the business of the legislature. So Dave came up to the rostrum, leaned over my shoulder, and said, "Mr. Speaker, I have to go to Silver City on a speaking engagement and I know you'll be done within the half hour. Most of the basic things have been completed. I just wondered if it would be too disruptive if you would break for about 15 minutes and let me address the House of Representatives, being that I'm not going to be here when you complete the work."

"No, that will be fine," I said. "Just wait a second until we complete the action on the legislation we're on."

Then I visited with Dave and we talked about how the session had progressed. He agreed that we'd had a good session and had accomplished a great deal, particularly in the House of Representatives, because we had good leadership. Then I gave Dave the speaker's rostrum with the loudspeaker. He spoke along the lines of our conversation, and noted that we had done our job diligently, and said we'd been supportive and had given the administration the things they needed. Finally, he said he just wanted to tell us that he appreciated the hard work we had performed in the House of Representatives.

We gave him a standing ovation and he left. Then in Silver City he made a public speech, just blasting the House of Representatives, the leadership, and everybody else. We didn't quite know how to take that. Maybe he got to thinking in the airplane as he went down that I might be his opposition when he ran for re-election.

≈

In 1968 I decided that Dave Cargo had not developed the type of administration that could meet the needs of the state. He hadn't spent the years in New Mexico that many of us had. I felt we should have a Democratic governor and I thought that if I had been the candidate two years before, I could have been elected and we would have maintained Democratic control following Governor Campbell's administration. Many people in the House and elsewhere encouraged me to run for governor, so I became a candidate, which meant win or lose, I was giving up my House seat. I knew I was taking a risk, but I felt like I was the heir apparent. I had done a good job first on the county commission, then as a member of the House, and finally as speaker. The consensus was that Bruce King should be the party nominee for governor. It seemed to me that was pretty well accepted. The press, Senator Anderson, and Senator Montoya had all said as much. It looked like a done deal.

I realized how tough it was going to be one day when I was up at Taos for a county officials' convention. After I had been introduced and had addressed the crowd, with all their cheers, the reporter Wayne Scott said to me with a little smirk, "So, you think you're going to be the next governor?" Now the newspapers all carried stories saying here's this guy who tells corny jokes and thinks he can be elected governor. They just took a direct turn the other way, after they had set me up. Despite that turnabout, I stayed with it, but I didn't have the resources and financial contributions to win the primary. I also wasn't as well known as I thought. One time I went down to Roswell for a meeting at the Roswell Inn with a few people I knew from the legislature, and a few county officials came. When I was speaking, the manager came in and interrupted us, saying, "Is there a Bruce King in here?"

Still, we had a hot primary race that year. After I had gone through the pre-primary nominating convention in 1966, I had decided that the convention wasn't the best way to select candidates, so I had worked with my friends in the legislature to successfully repeal the pre-primary nominating convention. That change of procedure made the 1968 race wide open—too wide, in my later opinion. Mack Easley had been lieutenant governor and speaker, and now he decided to run for governor. Bobby Mayfield got the bug to be a candidate, and my long-time friend Calvin Horn, who was a good friend of Senator Montoya, decided it was time he made a move for the governorship. With the rest of us vying for position, Fabian Chávez decided there was room for him in that crowded field, too, as did Harry Stowers, who was then a young lawyer but later became a state supreme court justice.

Up in the secretary of state's office, we drew ballot positions. Slips of paper with numbers on them—1, 2, 3, and so on—were put in a vase, then one at a time we reached in and pulled out a number determining our ballot position. Fabian Chávez drew the number 1 position and I drew number 6. We each worked at it quite differently, but we were six congenial men and, while it was a hard campaign, no one developed any ill feelings. Unfortunately, there was no way I could get ahead of that particular field of candidates. I predicted Fabian Chávez would win the primary, and he did. I came in second. Like any defeated candidate, I wasn't real enthusiastic about the race after that, but I did get back in the swing of Santa Fe County politics and I got more interested in the general election as the campaign went along. It was a close race for governor, although the final result was another disappointment for the Democrats—Dave Cargo defeated Fabian Chávez by a narrow margin.

I was now out of office for the first time in 14 years, which felt very strange after all that time. I would see the legislature working on bills that I had been deeply involved in, and I'd be homesick for the House. So I took up lobbying for causes that were in the public interest. It wasn't long until I was back in the thick of state politics.

4

Fighting for a New Constitution

In 1969, a unique opportunity to get back into politics came my way when the legislature called the constitutional convention. It couldn't have come at a better time for me. Delegates would be elected from the same districts as the House of Representatives, so I would be running from my old House district in Santa Fe County. I was very interested in changing the constitution, and I also saw the convention as a chance to continue my work as a public official.

The need for the convention had been established by the constitutional revision commission, which I had helped to appoint when I was speaker of the House. Those of us supporting revision felt the original constitution, which was adopted in 1912 when we became a state, was a bit too restrictive. It held us back some, getting in the way of our creating job opportunities and supporting progress in living conditions in New Mexico. In fairness to its authors, they did an excellent job for that day and time, but now we needed an update. We were modernizing our laws through legislation, which was a slow, laborious, and sometimes short-sighted process. By revising the constitution, we felt we could address the big issues all at once in an arena—the constitutional convention—that was less politicized than the legislature. I used to make the point that it was like the choice between buying a new car or buying all the parts and building it one piece at a time. In 1969, you could buy a new car for $5,000, or you could spend $10,000 in parts, and then you'd have to assemble it.

The revision commission's report gave us a good blueprint for change. It pointed out how we could improve the operations of state government and suggested strengthening the executive branch and giving it more responsibility through a cabinet structure. The commission called for reviewing the process of selecting judges and for looking closely at how state government worked with local government units. Other issues included self-rule for local governments, which involved loosening the ties between the state and the cities and counties; equalizing educational funding; and making some statewide offices appointive rather than elective, such as attorney general, secretary of state, and state auditor.

The revision process was straightforward. First the legislature passed the bill calling for the constitutional convention. Then voters would elect delegates in a statewide, nonpartisan special election. They would convene to design the new constitution, which the people of New Mexico would vote to approve or disapprove in a special election.

As soon as the legislature passed the bill creating the convention, a herd of candidates began jockeying for position to run for delegates. Along with many others, I announced my candidacy, then I declared my intention to run for president of the constitutional convention. The news media, particularly in Albuquerque, said, "That's just like Bruce King—run for governor, get beat, . . ." I was still smarting from my defeat in the primary, so that kind of talk kept alive my interest in running for governor again. For the moment, though, I concentrated on becoming a delegate to help devise a new constitution for the people of New Mexico.

I found plenty of encouragement. Albuquerque lawyer Dick Modrall told me the convention would be an ideal setup for me. Likewise urging me to run was my longtime friend Albert Mitchell. A Republican and a real "gentleman's gentleman," he had been president of both the New Mexico Cattle Growers Association and the National Cattle Growers Association. Albert told me, "Look, Bruce, governors come and go, other elected officials come and go, but the constitution is lasting. Those of us with rural interests and agricultural interests need strong representation. There is no position where you could better serve the citizens of New Mexico than being the president of the constitutional convention."

I had already begun to work back into political life with my friends in the House. By then Dave Norvell was speaker, George Fettinger was majority leader, John Mershon was chairman of the appropriations committee, and Seferino Martinez was still majority whip. All were close friends of mine.

The state had advertised for the most talented people to run for those delegate seats, hoping to tap the widest possible cross section of the New Mexico population, whether they were Democrats, Republicans, or Independents, men or women. Clearly, being a member of this body was highly desirable, so competition was intense. In my old House district in Santa Fe County, the candidates included a fine, outstanding young woman, Charmaine Crown, who could call in many IOUs for her hard work in the Democratic party and in Santa Fe county and city politics. A number of Democrats and others on the city council actively supported her. Another candidate was Reuben Rodriguez, a young attorney supported by the Republican element. My old district leaned heavily Republican. In fact, they had held that House seat for the term before I was first elected to the legislature. Now they were sore from losing the last election and they hadn't learned a great deal about campaigning since then.

I gathered a few close friends to work on my campaign. One was Richard C De Baca, a shrewd politician who had been county road foreman back in my days on the Santa Fe County Commission. He and I put together a campaign strategy and worked hard at it for about 60 days, going door to door and talking with the people in the district.

We held our 1969 state Democratic convention about that time, in the spring. Some of my friends said, "Oh, that's too bad, Bruce. You ran for governor and got beat, and now they say you're not even going to be able to get elected to the constitutional convention."

"Don't worry about me, you guys," I said. "I'm looking at it pretty closely, and I think I'll be in there." When they came up to me that way, though, I got to thinking, "Boy, if there's that kind of feeling, I better get out and do this up right." Their comments show the value of your friends being candid with you. If they'd all run up and said, "We know you're gonna win, Bruce— just go ahead and do your thing on the ranch and don't worry about it," then I would have lacked the incentive to get out and campaign so hard. All that work paid off. On election day, to my surprise I received more votes than just about any other candidate for the constitutional convention, statewide. That was partly because there happened to be more voters in my district, but I won it by a large margin over Reuben Rodriguez and the others.

After the election, we had to call the convention within 60 days. The legislature and revision commission had suggested that we complete the work in another 60 days, but there was no legal time limit. Once convened, a constitutional body has a great deal of latitude. We used the House chambers in the new capitol, and we could have kept them even if the legislature had assembled while we were still sitting, adjourned until after they met, or arranged our time however else we wanted to. We chose to stay within the 60-day time frame, convening during most of August and September.

Right after I was elected delegate, I began to visit with my friends in the Santa Fe area to promote my candidacy for president of the convention. I was not alone. Other candidates included Judge David Carmody, another friend of Senator Dennis Chávez who had been a lifelong friend and supporter of my father and me. He had resigned as chief justice of the state supreme court to run for convention delegate from Santa Fe County. The judge was keenly interested in developing a better plan for selecting judges. Many of my friends, particularly those in the legal profession, began to seek me out and say things like, "Well, look, Bruce, you would like to run again for governor, and it would be much better if you would let Judge Carmody be president—just shift your support to him. He thinks he has sufficient support anyway." I made it clear I had already announced for the presidency and had no intention of withdrawing. I added that there would be no hard feelings—we would all work hard and see what happened.

Of course, we weren't the only candidates. Filo Sedillo, my friend from Valencia County who had complicated my first attempted run for governor in 1966, also joined the race for president of the convention. His father had been a member of the original constitutional convention back in 1910. Another candidate was Dorothy Cline, a professor of political science at the University of New Mexico and a student of constitutional issues. She was also a practical politician, having been a Bernalillo County commissioner. Representing the conservative interests was Lewis Cox, a member of the legal profession from Roswell. The other serious contender was Herb Hughes, who had dabbled in politics for years in Albuquerque, worked in the state Department of Finance and Administration, and helped in many other government positions. A delegate from Farmington and member of the revision commission named Bud Tansey also felt he should be president, though he lacked significant support.

Between the election and the official start of the convention, we all maneuvered for position. The process was new to many of the delegates, the ones who had been elected without previous political experience, but it was all very familiar to me, especially since the convention was using the House chambers, where I felt very much at home. From my years in the House, I knew exactly how to organize the delegates in my campaign to be president. I took the same approach that had made me successful running for speaker. I called each delegate on the phone, then I met with each of them, trying to convince them I wanted to design a constitution that would benefit all of New Mexico. I told them I thought I had the expertise required to organize the convention body. Frank Papen, who later became a state senator from Doña Ana County, coordinated Judge Carmody's campaign for presidency. I developed a great deal of respect for him and the judge as we ran against each other.

When we finally gathered in the House chambers to organize, about a month ahead of the official opening of the convention, I felt I had enough support to win the presidency that day. Starting at noon, we were going to select the officers and assign committees so we could do the detailed preparation for the next 30 days before we convened. About ten that morning, a reporter from the *Albuquerque Tribune* named Jim Boyer came around looking for a story for that afternoon's paper. Since I was feeling pretty confident, I thought, "What's the harm? The papers won't be out till 3 o'clock and we convene at noon." So I said, "I think I'll be elected president, because I have sufficient commitments to win." He was a friend and I thought I'd give him a scoop.

That was one of the biggest mistakes I made in politics. Harold sent that story down to the *Tribune* immediately and they must have brought the papers back by air freight, they arrived so quick. To this day, I don't know how they got the papers out that fast. We had gone through quite a few procedural steps by 12:30 P.M. and were just getting ready to elect the president, when Bud Tansey came rushing into the chambers with two or three copies of the *Tribune*. He didn't even stop for the proper protocol. Right at the door, he said, "Look, this guy thinks he's already elected! It says so here in the paper." They spread those papers around the chambers and I could see what a mess I'd made. Right there, I learned a good lesson—don't talk too quick. So I had to backtrack pretty fast. I made a motion to suspend the vote until we convened in 30 days, even though I knew I had the strength. Under the current circumstances, my supporters felt they'd be hard-put to back me now, although they promised to stick with me until the election.

We decided to name a temporary group to help us organize. I nominated John Irick, a Republican from Albuquerque, to chair the organizing committee. I had talked with him several times and knew he was an able businessman. My friends who supported me for president voted for John, and he was elected. I visited with him and he didn't express any particular interests or concerns, but after we adjourned he drove all the way out to my house in Stanley. I was surprised he knew where I lived. He said, "Okay, coach, what are we going to do? It looks to me like you'll probably be the president, so I would like to get your thoughts on how we should organize." We had given him authority to hire the staff, print up stationery, buy supplies, and things of that nature. I gave him my views and we stayed in touch the next few weeks. Filo Sedillo was also quite involved and had gotten the authority to work with John in hiring the employees. Despite his own aspirations to lead the convention, Filo evidently also thought I would be the president, because they filled all the positions but secretary to the president. They left that slot open but hired Eloisa Block without assigning her any particular job. She had been my secretary when I was House speaker.

The night before the official first day of the convention, I met with Filo Sedillo; Raymond Sanchez from Albuquerque, who was just out of law school and would become speaker of the House in 1983; and others. We discussed who might be committee chairmen and the makeup of the various committees, if I did become president. It was much like organizing the House during the party caucus on the eve of a legislative session, but I had become much more cautious after my brash announcement to the newspaper backfired in my face. I wasn't nearly as far along in naming delegates to key positions in the convention as I had been earlier.

Finally on August 5 we convened. I was still confident I would be elected president. Even though Filo Sedillo and I were friends, I had been unable to convince him and his Democratic group to withdraw and help me. On the other hand, I had the backing of the agricultural contingent and many others. By then I also had convinced Judge Carmody that he didn't have the numbers to win, so I picked up most of his votes, including delegates from Doña Ana County and the Santa Fe area. Dorothy Cline still had her bloc, and Herb Hughes still had his, while Lewis Cox had garnered quite a bit of support from the southeast.

Early that morning, a delegate from Valencia County named Boleslo Romero came by and said, "I think you and Filo had better get together. Things don't look good. I'm a good friend of both of you and we're going to get into trouble." I guess he was worried that we'd split the vote and both lose out to one of the others.

"Well, tell Filo to come over," I said. Since no one had an office yet, we got together out in the hall and talked. Finally Filo said, "Well, okay, I'll withdraw and I'll give you my support."

We reconvened after the keynote address and the swearing-in formalities. The floor was open for nominations for president. Raymond Sanchez stood up and nominated Filo for president. Filo said, "I'm going to withdraw and I'm going to nominate Bruce King." I thought by then that maybe the rest of the field might do the same. I had been nice to all of them and I avoided making any enemies during the campaign—I had learned better than that, through the years. Still, the other candidates had gone so far that they went ahead with the nominations and we held the election. As the voting moved along, I had the vast majority of delegates. About halfway through the roll-call the other candidates began to withdraw, so I was elected president of the convention.

I enjoyed that job immensely, but it took every ounce of strength and intelligence I could muster. In many ways, the duties were similar to those of speaker of the House, so I was in my element. On the other hand, the convention involved a lot more work on the floor as a committee of the whole than the House did. I had to give everyone their say so we could fuse all the ideas together. My first official act was to name the four defeated candidates for president—Filo Sedillo, Dorothy Cline, Lewis Cox, and Herb Hughes—to be vice chairmen of the convention. In making appointments of that type, it's not unusual to recognize the talents of the opposition, but in this case those appointments proved extremely beneficial. By appointing them, I also made it clear I wanted a close-knit operation. Although John Irick's team had made committee assignments in the past few weeks, I knew they were not going to work out properly because his team had to leave the task of assigning the committee chairmen up to the president. So I asked for a one-hour recess to work it out. I met with the four vice chairmen to go over the names I was thinking about for chairmen. They all agreed I had done a good job picking those people, which I had not selected from among my personal supporters. I tried instead to name delegates who had shown talent and interest in particular areas. We needed to balance out the committee assignments by region. We also wanted to structure the committees not so they would be agreeable, but to make sure every side would have a spokesperson, which saves work for the committee of the whole. Otherwise, you just end up hashing out disagreements on the floor, which is more time consuming than resolving the big issues in committee.

I named Judge Carmody to head the committee on the judicial article of the constitution, John Irick to head the elections committee, Raymond Sanchez to head the local government committee, and S. P. Sahd to chair the natural resources committee. I named Claude Leyendecker, a longtime friend from Deming, to chair the legislative committee and Mel Aragon, a former (and future) city councilor of Albuquerque, to chair the bill of rights committee. John Bigbee had been a minority member in the legislature when I was speaker, so I'd never been able to assign him as a committee chairman. Now he was a delegate, and in the nonpartisan convention I named him chairman of the revenue committee, where he did an excellent job. Everyone agreed these appointments would provide good leadership. I also asked Jim Martin to be my personal coordinator and assistant. An attorney from Doña Ana County, Jim had worked with me in the legislature since 1959 and had served on the state school board for a number of years. Other key employees of the convention were Betty Fiorina, the chief clerk, and Eloisa Block, my special assistant. Shirley Hooper worked closely with us and later went on to be elected secretary of state. She and Linda Kehoe, who became my assistant when I was governor, kept a running diary of proceedings during the session and helped me review the day-to-day workload. Jeff Bingaman, who became attorney general and today is a United States senator from New Mexico, was legal counsel to the convention.

After naming the committee chairs, I reviewed the committee assignments made by the organizing committee and took the choices of the various chairmen. Then we had to decide the hours when the different committees would meet so that each member could serve on two committees without a scheduling conflict. I got all this done and succeeded in maintaining good feelings among the delegates.

By the next morning, the second day of the convention, we were ready to do business. In my remarks, I made it clear that every delegate should represent his or her district, and in voting should back the positions that would enhance their districts. Even so, I urged them not to form pressure groups on behalf of the big city of Albuquerque or the interest groups to the north or east, and so on, but to vote for the well being of the entire state so we could design a good constitution. As our work proceeded, the delegates did conduct themselves that way. In fact, in all the years I have been involved in different political positions and in various aspects of government, I never worked with as dedicated and harmonious a group as we had in the constitutional convention. I enjoyed being the presiding officer, where I could exercise my flair for harmony. I worked at creating good working relationships, using everyone's talents, and letting them all realize they were needed.

Every delegate wanted to design a constitution that would guarantee individual rights for all without intruding on the rights of others. They did look out for the needs of their districts, and they did stay true to their personal philosophies. Some members, such as Bill Warren, Dorothy Cline, and Mary Walters, could be considered liberals. Mary Walters went on to be a justice of the state supreme court, while Bill Warren served in the legislature for many years. Leaders among the conservatives included Noel Rankin of Grant County, who was a long-time rancher and former president of the Cattle Growers, Lewis Cox, and H. C. Pannell, an educator from the junior college in Lea County. And of course we had many in-between viewpoints. Among the delegates, I also developed great respect for Bob Poole, who was then a young Albuquerque lawyer and who accepted much of the responsibility for putting together some basic viewpoints in the constitution. David Townsend, an educator from Otero County, worked hard to develop a good educational system. Former Alamogordo Mayor Dwight Ohlinger devoted much time to the work, as did Dennis Salazar, who represented the younger element of northern New Mexico and later served as president of the board of regents of Northern New Mexico Community College when I was governor. With such a diverse group, I felt I was able to use humor and reasoning to head off major conflicts that could have derailed the convention. We didn't have any head-on collisions, either.

The constitutional convention was a unicameral body, a structure that influenced how we went about our job. I never had been quite able to figure out how you got a unicameral legislature to work because party politics would always come into play. Also, a great deal of legislation is based on friendship and horse trading, and having two houses helps weed that out. For instance, House members might count on the Senate to kill a bill that got through the House more on the basis of internal politics than on its merits. On the positive side, as a House member I would often find out what my bills needed by taking them over to the Senate.

In the convention, on the other hand, all the delegates knew their work would go straight to the voters without another review. You didn't see delegates voting frivolously for proposals the way members did in the legislature. There was no other house, no chief executive, and it was nonpartisan. This setup encouraged the convention delegates to work with maturity and genuine consideration. We had to be right the first time. Under that pressure, we saw the familiar spectacle of both the liberals and conservatives moving toward the center, until most of the delegates were in the middle. As a result, the unicameral system worked wonderfully.

≋

The constitution was made up of more than a dozen articles: the bill of rights, legislative branch, executive branch, judicial branch, local government, elective infrastructure, education, finance, public trusts, miscellaneous, constitutional revision, compact with the United States, and schedule and transition. We assigned committees to specific articles. They went off and prepared drafts, which they brought back to the main body for review. At first, we found a great deal of conflict and overlap among the articles, so we worked long hours, the first night going until one or two in the morning. I began to realize that after about 10 P.M. we were not making progress. Later we had to go back and redo most of the work we did after midnight. Feelings were running high and divisiveness was developing in a way I did not like to see. Something had to give. I announced that if we had to work additional days, we would, but we were not going to stay in session after 10 P.M. I could feel the relief go around the chambers.

We got along much better after that. Every day, we convened about 10 A.M. and worked as a committee of the whole, then we would adjourn for the committees to work on their technical tasks for each article. At that point, I would convene the vice presidents and my coordinator in strategy meetings to anticipate needs that might come up. We then conveyed our decisions to the committee chairmen. In those strategy sessions I developed tremendous respect for Filo Sedillo and Dorothy Cline, who repeatedly demonstrated their understanding of the needs of all areas of New Mexico. Dorothy had arranged for former Governor George Romney of Michigan, her home state, to come and address our body. Romney was a constitutional revision expert. He advised us to show confidence in our public officials and give them the tools to carry out the purposes for which they were elected. He suggested making the divisions of government explicit so that everyone would know their jurisdiction and what their responsibilities were, with the least amount of friction. That was a good statement of our intent in designing the new constitution.

Governor George Romney of Michigan, left, shared with me his wealth of experience in revising a state's constitution.

≋

As the committees began their work, we could sense a great need to address certain areas of government. In addition to strengthening the executive branch, reducing the number of statewide elective offices, and revising the judge-selection process, the committees also focused on education and self-rule for local governments, plus a few special-interest issues that didn't really belong in the constitution.

We discussed the article on the executive branch at great length. Many delegates felt the two-year term was a problem because elected officials wasted a lot of energy running for re-election. It didn't take us long to decide we should have four-year terms for the governor and other executive-level statewide offices, and that we should have at least two four-year terms. The other major bone of contention was how strong the chief executive's office should be. The revision commission members and many others felt we should eliminate most of the statewide elective positions in the executive branch—like attorney general, treasurer, land commissioner, secretary of state, and others—and move them into a cabinet appointed by the governor. We put in long hours in committees and on the floor deciding how many of those offices to keep. After much discussion, debate, and consultation, we settled on a cabinet with about 18 positions and just four elected offices: governor, lieutenant governor, attorney general, and land commissioner. This conclusion would later have significant impact on the fate of the proposed new constitution. We also reached consensus after much discussion about how to design the elective process for the statewide offices and how we could give the governor and the executive branch the powers they needed to carry out their constitutional duties.

I worked with Judge Carmody and his committee on the judicial section. He wanted to streamline the judicial branch and adopt the so-called Missouri plan for selecting judges by appointment. His committee included most of the lawyers among the delegates. Surprisingly, after about two weeks the committee chose not to go with Judge Carmody, and instead concluded it was better to continue electing judges. From that day on, Judge Carmody was a bit depressed about the constitutional convention proceedings. However, he was a lifelong friend of mine and he wanted to see a good outcome for our work, so he continued as one of my chief legal advisors. He wanted to ensure that anything we proposed would pass muster in the courts of New Mexico. With his many years of experience as district court judge and supreme court chief justice, he was immensely helpful in keeping us on the right track regarding the judicial branch.

We devoted a great deal of discussion to the structure of the education article of the constitution, which would have made the state board of education appointive, given more authority to local school districts, and equalized funding across the state. Generating even more enthusiasm and support among the delegates was the self-rule provision for local governments. Many delegates wanted to give city and county governments additional authority to meet the needs of their constituencies. Under the existing constitution, their hands were tied in many instances. So we wrote a strong self-rule article, which earned us great support for the proposed constitution from the municipal and county government people.

My friend Elliott Barker, the well-known outdoorsman, had been the champion supporter of the New Mexico Game and Fish Department for several decades. He wanted the department to become a constitutional body, with a place in the cabinet. I disagreed, and I tried at great length to persuade Elliott to see it my way. Most of the delegates agreed with me, but Elliott kept saying, "Bruce, if you don't put it in the constitution, we're going to oppose it." Well, we didn't put it in and that opposition turned out to be costly, although Elliott and I remained good friends. He helped me when I ran for governor, then in 1971 as governor I declared Elliott Barker Day in New Mexico. He was Mr. Game and Fish of the Year many times and did much to conserve the state's natural beauty and wildlife. He continued working with the Natural Resources Department into the 1980s.

Another special interest I fought off was brought by delegate Tillman Bannister, who came to the convention with the express purpose of getting a water works for his small community of Otis in southern Eddy County. I tried to convince him there wasn't a place for a water works in the constitution, but it took long hours.

"Now look, Bruce, I understand," Bannister said. "But I'm interested in us having a waterworks, and this is the way we're going to get it. On other things I'll vote with you, but you're going to have to work with me for our waterworks."

"We'll try to get you a waterworks through the legislature," I said, "but we can't put it in the constitution." Otis did later get a water works through a legislative appropriation and federal funding.

≋

Come October, our 60 days were up. We had designed a constitution with most of the provisions we wanted, but now we had to structure the document, styling it so each article was in the right place and had the least conflict with the other articles. I appointed Don McCormick, a lawyer from Carlsbad, to oversee this task. He devoted a great deal of time to that work, along with the Legislative Council Service, where Clay Buchanan was still director. Clay had initially hesitated, unsure whether to get involved. Mercedes Romero, a staff worker who kept the convention calendar, talked to Clay and told me, "Bruce, if you'll go visit with Clay, I think you can convince him that the legislative council staff could style the constitution." So I visited with Clay and he agreed to have the council work with Don McCormick, the other committee chairmen, and the delegates who had been assigned to draft the different articles. This was a 16- to 18-hour-a-day task with no extra pay or consideration, but they did an excellent job. When the styling committee finished its work, we put in another 30 days making sure we had a document we could take to the public.

The new constitution went on the ballot for a special statewide election December 9, 1969. Most of the delegates worked hard for it. We tried to pair up in teams making presentations to the public around the state, explaining what we tried to accomplish and urging adoption of the new constitution. Unfortunately, we didn't take near enough time to present it to the public. The timing was bad. We were running into the holidays, and we decided we should go ahead with the election before Christmas. About the only open day was the second Tuesday in December, so I set that date. Pat Baca, Dorothy Cline, Raymond Sanchez, Mary Walters, and others took advantage of the considerable exposure offered by the media and TV to promote the passage of the constitution. While most of the delegates were in favor of the proposed constitution, there were a few exceptions, including Agnes Head, publisher of the *Hobbs Flare*, a small newspaper in Lea County. She turned out not to be a great admirer or supporter of mine, and she remained that way for years.

We worked hard and did well in Bernalillo County and elsewhere, but we ran into problems in parts of the state where we didn't have sufficient workers. That was true in Lea County and other areas in the deep southeast and in some of the northern counties. The new constitution also ran into opposition from many of my friends. Emilio Naranjo, the leading political figure in Rio Arriba County, didn't think it would be good. Neither did Tom Montoya of Sandoval County. Along with a few others, they spread the feeling that the proposed constitution was anti-Hispanic. I was very concerned about that. Their main complaint was that Hispanics had not been as well represented at this convention as they were at the original convention in 1910. Furthermore, they opposed eliminating elective political offices, and they didn't like having two four-year terms because that took away their political base. Their thinking was that if you put politicians in office too long, they would be less responsive because they wouldn't feel as accountable to the voters. Holding more elections gives the average voter more influence, they argued.

Along in November, so many rumors and false statements were flying around that the constitution looked doomed. Talking with some of the people working in the office, I had expressed my grave concern that we were running into too many problems, too many innuendoes, and too much undercurrent, and the new constitution was about to get scuttled. "Aw, heck," I finally thought to myself, "I better get on back to work," so I headed for Mosquero, New Mexico, to buy stock to put in the feedlots. We were out in the pens weighing cattle when someone came to get me, saying I had a call from the convention office in Santa Fe. I got to a phone and called back. Filo Sedillo had come into the office and heard about my concerns. "Bruce," he said, "they say you're a little despondent and you're having great concern about whether it has a chance of getting adopted."

"It's sure taking a bad turn," I admitted.

"We don't have any money to run advertisements or attempt to sell our proposal," Filo said, "but I could turn around the rumor that it's not in the best interests of all the citizens, and particularly the Hispanic population of New Mexico, if I just had four or five hundred dollars. We could have a little evening function somewhere and I think I could turn that viewpoint around."

I said immediately, "I know a guy who could get us four or five hundred dollars to have a function."

"Who?"

"Me," I said.

"Okay," Filo said, "let me invite some of the leaders in the Hispanic community and we'll see what we can do." He realized that it was rapidly getting out of control and we needed to respond quickly. That was about Tuesday and by Friday night he'd set up a nice function at the Sundowner in Albuquerque, which was run by a friend of ours. Filo had invited about 40 people, community leaders like Roberto Mondragon, my future lieutenant governor, and others who were influential and the people trusted as friends that would look out for their best interests. We had legislators and even had some convention delegates we wanted to firm up.

I never saw anyone perform like Filo Sedillo did that night. He said, "Let's not let them tell us the new constitution is anti-Hispanic, not with myself working on it, Bruce working on it, and Raymond Sanchez, Joe Baca, Pat Baca, Ray Baca, Mel Aragon. . ." and he went on to name the many others who had worked hard on the new document. "You know this is a good constitution," he continued. "I have been involved in politics and I know those who question it are concerned over some short-term political reasoning, not the best interests of the people of New Mexico." He turned those viewpoints completely around. He said, "Everyone here who feels they can help us, we'd like you to stand up. If you can't help us, we understand." Everyone stood up. From that day on, we had a much better push with the Hispanic voters.

As I had worked on the constitution that previous summer, some of my friends who had helped put earlier constitutional proposals before the public in other states gave me a warning I wish I had followed. They suggested breaking the constitution down into about four articles for the ballot. Then some voters might vote "no" for one article, but approve the others, rather than rejecting the whole thing out of hand. Since the opposition would be split up, the whole constitution might pass. For instance, the pro-elective office faction might have voted against the article that made those positions appointive, but approved everything else. Meanwhile, other people might have approved that article about appointive positions and rejected another article. Taken all together, maybe no single article would have been voted down.

≋

Despite our last-minute efforts to persuade voters, the proposal to adopt the new constitution lost by some 2,000 votes in the December election. We got beat badly in deep southeastern New Mexico, but carried Bernalillo County strongly, where our people had campaigned hard. I was disappointed because I felt we had created a document that would improve government for the people of New Mexico.

The constitution failed for many reasons. Looking back on it, I can see how the "short ballot" provision eliminating many of the statewide elective offices hurt its chances of passing, because several then-current state office-holders became formidable opponents—in particular, my old friend and fellow Santa Fe County Commissioner Jess Kornegay, who was state treasurer at the time. Also, many professional politicians were opposed to elections at the longer four-year intervals, because they felt that running for election every two years was a big part of their strength. In hindsight, I think if we had named the Game and Fish Department in the constitution, we probably would have gotten it passed, because then Elliott Barker and his supporters would have backed it. Our cause also would have benefited from putting the constitution on the ballot as four separate articles. A few of these little slips cost us dearly.

The night after the election, I attended the annual reception sponsored by Schwartzmann's meat packing plant in Albuquerque. Dick Modrall happened to be there. He came up to me and said, "I know you're very disappointed—I can tell when I see you on TV—but I'm going to be very honest with you. I went down and voted for it, but I sincerely think the best thing that ever happened to you was that the thing got beat. If it had passed, you'd be out there every day trying to defend it. This way you can say we had a good fight and it got beat. It's all right. You can go back and adopt portions of it now." And that's what we did.

In that light, I could never see the loss at the ballot as a failure of the revision process. For one thing, out of that defeat came some impressive subsequent victories for the concepts it contained. Since then, maybe 80 percent of the important changes in the proposed constitution have been adopted through individual constitutional amendments, approved at various elections by the voters. Of those subsequent amendments, I was most enthusiastic about the four-year term for the governor and other statewide elected officials. I was the first governor to serve four years in one term under those provisions. In addition to the four-year term, we now have self-rule for local government entities, the cabinet system, and other proposals that we made in the convention. In fact, changing the constitution by amendment may have worked out better than passing the revised constitution. If the revision had passed, we would have faced the daunting task of revising all our statute laws at once.

This process of constitutional change by amendment was helped by several of the convention delegates—such as Raymond Sanchez and Ray Leger of San Miguel County—who went on to serve in the legislature where they were instrumental in bringing forth the amendments derived from the proposed constitution of 1969. Many other delegates were later elected to public office. Doris Miller of the San Antonito area, for example, remained active in politics and government. David Townsend of Otero County and Bill Warren of Bernalillo County, both Democrats, won seats in the legislature. Mary Walters became a justice of the state court of appeals and Herb Walsh became a long-time member of the state board of education. Pat Baca became chairman of the Albuquerque city council and Joe Baca went on to be a district judge in Bernalillo County and later chief justice of the state supreme court.

With all these positive effects coming out of the constitution revision attempt, I think the whole process can be seen as beneficial to the state of New Mexico. Everyone learned more about the constitution, whether they were for or against the revision. I had been warned when we started that everyone would say we wasted the $500,000 appropriation for the convention, but no one ever said that afterwards—not a one, even the opposition. In all my years of campaigning, it never came up.

The constitution revision effort certainly gave my career a shot in the arm, too. The many friends I made in the convention among delegates and employees later helped me in my next run for governor. By the time the convention was over, those people knew of my ability and my concern for efficient government, my legislative experience, my service on the county commission, and my leadership in the constitutional convention itself. Once again, I had furthered my own political education and gained deeper insight into building consensus among groups with diverse needs. The convention also prepared me to run and serve as governor by giving me a chance to develop my abilities and add to my knowledge of the functions carried out by the chief executive of the state of New Mexico. Dorothy Cline spent much time writing about our work on the constitution.

5

Corny Jokes and Baloney Sandwiches

As the governor's race began to shape up in 1970 before the primary election, I wasn't even sure I was in the race. The roots of that contest could be traced back to the 1968 election, when I had lost the primary to Fabian Chávez and then David Cargo had beaten him in the general election. That had been a crowded Democratic primary, with perhaps too many strong candidates for our own good. Having worked real hard, I naturally had been very disappointed when I didn't win the nomination. After that, I felt burned out on politics for a while. Alice and I and our families had done a lot of the work in the 1968 primary campaign, so we needed to regroup. Maybe it was a blessing in disguise for me, though, since I was able to go on to become president of the constitutional convention in 1969, which meant a great deal to me. I devoted most of my time during that year to the constitution. Many people thought I did that so I could position myself to run for governor, but that really wasn't true. It just worked out that way. At the time, I was thinking I might just end my political career after being the president of the constitutional convention.

In the meantime, the east side of New Mexico decided it was their turn to have a governor. Jack Daniels of Lea County started running for governor almost before the 1968 campaign was over. A distinguished businessman and legislator, Jack pulled together considerable support. Under a three-year contract, he hired a politically astute former *Albuquerque Journal* editor to manage his campaign. Then the New Mexico Amigos, a group of business and community leaders who served as goodwill ambassadors for the state, decided they wanted to influence the Democratic nomination by backing him. With considerable financial support from Lea County, as well, the Daniels candidacy was off to a great running start.

I was toying with running for governor when the primary season began to shape up, but I hadn't committed myself. Another potential candidate was David Norvell, who had succeeded me as speaker of the House when I left that position to run for governor in 1968. Fabian Chávez considered running but finally decided against it, which was good for me. Meanwhile, state Senator Jerry Apodaca of Las Cruces was Democratic Party chairman in 1970. He was deep in the Daniels camp, which was trying to manipulate the party into selecting the primary nominee without the division that crippled our campaign in 1968. So one day, the Democrats under the direction of Apodaca called a meeting of all the proposed candidates. They managed to talk Norvell out of running for governor. Instead, he would run for attorney general. Realizing I was their main contender, they proposed I run for lieutenant governor. Being forever the political conciliator, I said I would think about it.

Well, somehow the press reported I was running for lieutenant governor before I even got back to the ranch. Word could get around just that fast, in those days. Alice and my brothers, Sam and Don, had already gotten together and talked it over. When I got in at about 5 o'clock, they said, "Look, we'll do everything we can and devote 100 percent of our time for you to run for governor, but if you go for lieutenant governor, you're going to lose us." We also realized that the more liberal elements of the Democratic party who had been backing Norvell were unhappy he had pulled out, and they wouldn't back a more conservative east side candidate like Jack Daniels. So they helped talk me back into running.

With brothers Sam and Don in 1972, I checked the corn crop on King Brothers Ranch in Stanley. Besides running the ranch together, we shared an interest in politics. (Photograph by John Littlewood)

The fairly liberal grassrooters in the Democratic party were very strong in Albuquerque. Their membership included Irene Mathias, Bert Lindsey, Bob Harris, Grace Williams, Bill Byatt, and Stanley Brasher. They all met in Jo Salyer's house. A number of the former constitutional delegates were urging me to run, too, including the Doña Ana County group, which was very keen on my candidacy and had a good organization down south. I also had strength in the Albuquerque and Santa Fe business communities. My old nucleus got behind me, too—the New Mexico Cattle Growers Association, the Farm Bureau, the Soil Conservation folks, county officials, rural people, labor, and the teachers. That was a coalition you probably couldn't assemble under one tent anymore, since it brought liberal and conservative elements together.

So I was in the race. In those days, we didn't have any paid political consultants in our campaign, and no one from out of state. I had Larry Hamm, who was a radio man, and Keith Dotson working Santa Fe County.

My campaign treasurer was Marshall Rowley, who had retired from the oil and gas business over in Artesia. He raised the most money with absolutely no strings attached of anyone I ever worked with. If they told him what they needed in exchange for a campaign contribution, he'd just say, "Thanks, I don't have anything to do with that," and he'd walk off. Lew Thompson had an advertising agency in Santa Fe, as did Ed Delgado, and those two made our television commercials. Businessmen Hickum Galles and Bob Weil helped, along with all the candidates I'd run against in the 1968 primary, especially Calvin Horn and Fabian Chávez. That showed good rapport within the party.

I probably didn't spend more than $75,000 on that primary campaign, while I'm sure Jack Daniels spent considerably more. We could really feel it when he dropped in another $100,000 for advertising. He ran a more high-tech campaign and kept close watch on the polls, whereas we just did it on hard work and having friends all over the state. We built our grassroots support, literally going person-to-person in every little town. I was also happy to have the support this time of Senator Clinton Anderson and his son, Sherburne—I had done my time in the trenches and I guess they figured I deserved the nomination.

The field in the primary sorted out to just three Democrats: Al Sceresse, who was the Bernalillo County district attorney, Jack Daniels, and myself. I won with a good margin and Roberto Mondragon won the lieutenant governor nomination. On the Republican side, Albuquerque City Commission Chairman Pete Domenici beat Steve Helbing, the House minority leader from Chávez County, and Junio López of San Miguel County, and Joe Skeen would be their lientenant governor candidate. After the primary election, I immediately called Al Sceresse and Jack Daniels to say I needed them. Al had already conceded, and the press had asked if he would help me. All he said was, "I'm going to vote for him." They pushed him a little harder, asking, "Are you going to *help* him?" He wouldn't comment any further. When I thanked him for conceding, he said, "You saw what I said in the paper, that I would vote for you." And I told him, "I really appreciate that. In the last campaign, we didn't even have that kind of support." I'll never forget his response: "I feel badly about losing, but a week from today, let's get together and have lunch and talk about it." I told him I knew exactly how he felt. He turned out to be one of our best supporters. That's when we got Pete Pence, a former *Albuquerque Tribune* editor who had been press secretary for Al, to go to work for me.

≋

After I won the primary, Alice and I took a week's vacation up into Canada to let things settle down a bit. When we came back, we started focusing on the general election campaign against Pete Domenici, which turned into a close, hot race. The two big issues were how to handle the University of New Mexico, which was in a period of great unrest, and who had the best plan for creating jobs, improving the economic conditions of New Mexico, and increasing the tax base. I contended we could boost the economy by focusing on education, bringing in light manufacturing companies, and taking care of employers that we already had. I made a big point about the need for vocational education to prepare our workers for better jobs and to provide a better-trained workforce as an inducement to industries considering relocation in New Mexico.

UNM was suffering from poor relations with the general population in those days. As a subject of discussion and concern, it extended beyond its home territory of Bernalillo County. A few events had brought the university to the forefront. Student riots had broken out in the late spring of 1970, which had prompted Governor Cargo to call out the National Guard to restore order. The publication of the controversial—and some felt obscene—"Love Lust" poem and a sit-in at UNM President Ferrel Heady's office had also raised serious questions about the university. Many New Mexicans felt the situation at UNM was out of control and wanted to see strong measures to bring it back in line. The legislature was increasing its scrutiny of UNM, chiefly through the University Study Committee. Domenici committed his support to the committee, but I didn't want my hands tied that way. Many people in Bernalillo County were opposed to this legislative intervention, so it was not a clear-cut issue. I felt that if I were governor, I wanted more options, including working with the board of regents. Therefore, I didn't commit myself to the legislative committee, and I took some heat for that decision but it also helped me in Bernalillo County.

Another big issue was no different than today—what to do about crime and prisons. Crime was on the increase, and Albuquerque had been ranked second-worst in the nation, so law and order was on everyone's mind. In the corrections system, the Cargo administration had management problems, with a troublesome turnover of wardens and Corrections secretaries, and a Santa Fe grand jury was investigating the state penitentiary. This was something they did as a standard procedure whenever a grand jury convened in the county. Governor Cargo had just recently brought in a professional, Howard Leach, to fill the slot of Corrections secretary after he fired John Salazar, who had caused a lot of problems for Cargo. Felix Rodriguez was warden. The grand jury later reported that Leach and Rodriguez were both doing a good job, and they stayed on after Cargo's administration.

In Albuquerque, garbage collection also became a campaign issue. Domenici and the commission had decided city residents should start stacking garbage out front in the street instead of in the back alleys, and people in the Northeast Heights of the city had a hard time getting used to that. So I made a big to-do out of that. In an editorial page cartoon, Mac McGinnis of the *Albuquerque Journal* showed a mangy dog and the garbage stacked up in front of the houses. Domenici was trying to shoo that dog away, but it wouldn't leave. The point we tried to make was that if he couldn't run the city properly, how could he run the state?

I also campaigned on meeting the needs for education, which included equalizing the funding for all our schools, so the rural districts weren't at such a disadvantage. It didn't seem fair that students in poorer communities should be denied access to the basic educational opportunities enjoyed by urban kids. The federal courts were getting ready to rule about equalizing funding, so that was a big issue.

On the other side, the Domenici campaign was trying to make an issue out of my work as speaker of the House and my voting record. He also made fun of my rural background. I remember one time he was ridiculing my corny jokes and my style of leadership. In response, my friend, state Revenue Director Victor Salazar, wrote a letter to the editor saying he would rather have a governor who tells corny jokes than a guy who tries to feed us baloney sandwiches. To our surprise, it got into both Albuquerque papers.

We also debated on television that year. Newsman Dick Knipfing was the moderator and Jim Baca, a friend of mine who later worked in my administration and went on to elective office, was the questioner. Domenici was unhappy with the station because Jim kept referring to him as "Mr.

Domenici," while calling me "Bruce." Thinking I wouldn't do very well, the Republicans rented Johnson Gymnasium on UNM campus to watch the debates on closed circuit TV. They wanted to see the smooth Albuquerque commission chairman maul the country politician, but it didn't come out too well for them. Our scouts sent people over there and they reported back that things got pretty solemn. I had good issues and having been speaker of the House, I had some abilities that you don't learn out gathering cattle on horseback.

≋

My rural supporters helped me a great deal in that campaign. Domenici had much more money than we did, and he had access to good airplanes for traveling around the state. Albert Black—rancher, owner of the Seven-Bar Airport, and a great friend of mine—loaned us a plane, too, but we didn't do that much flying. We drove everywhere. One time I had been way down in the far southeast at Lovington and was driving back to Portales. I stopped at Pep, the way I did at all those little towns. Pep was a small, dryland farming community with a store, a post office, and a gas station all in one building. I went inside and found an elderly gentleman who had run the store and the post office for 40 years. I tried to strike up a conversation.

"You know, I'm from the little community of Stanley that's very similar to Pep," I said. "I'm just running for governor and I thought I'd stop in and see if I could get y'alls' help, because I understand your situation in the rural areas. I'm a farmer and a rancher myself."

He didn't warm up much. I was used to that kind of reaction at Stanley. I bought a bottle of soda pop and a bar of candy and that made him feel a little better. As I drank the soda pop, he decided that maybe I was in earnest.

"Now where exactly are you from?" he asked me. So after we visited about 10 or 15 minutes, I asked him if I could leave a little campaign literature around the store—stickers, buttons, matchbooks, and so on. I went out to the car and got three or four stickers and four or five pieces of literature and took them back in to him.

"That all you got?" he asked.

"Well, no," I said.

"We've got about a hundred voters over here, and I need at least one of those campaign cards for every voter. I don't need any of those stickers, but give me plenty of those cards and some buttons."

I gave him some more, and then I drove on. On election night I particularly watched the returns for that area to see how we did, and we got every vote. Out of 99 votes, we got 99. I thought he was a pretty cheap campaign worker. In later years, Pete Domenici told me, "I learned one thing: not to just fly over those guys."

Torrance County also gave me great support. Of course, those were home folks to me, since Stanley is just a few miles from the Torrance County line. Alice grew up there, too, in Moriarty. I had been chairman of the Torrance County Farm and Livestock Bureau as well as being on the fair board and participating in so many of their activities. Like Stanley, it was my home community. In those little towns like McIntosh, I got just about every vote there. I really appreciated how the people in Torrance County were excited about having one of their own run for governor who could relate to them and be their friend. They all had many friends and relatives in Albuquerque and on the east side of New Mexico, so we suggested they could help us out if every one of them would just write three letters telling how well they knew us and asking for support. People in those days were earnest enough to do it, and that strategy proved very effective.

〰

With all this support—Senator Joe Montoya even campaigned door-to-door, which helped me a lot—I finished strong. On election night, once again the Northeast Heights of Albuquerque came in late, and they came in Republican for Pete, but that wasn't enough to overturn the big numbers I was getting on the east side, in the north, and in the valley areas of Albuquerque. The King/Mondragon ticket managed to beat the Domenici/Skeen duo by 25,000 votes. Despite the natural animosities that develop during a campaign, Pete and I respected each other, so after the hard campaign, it all blew over. Since then, we've gotten along wonderfully and after he became a U.S. senator we were able to work together on dozens of projects that benefited New Mexico.

All the Democrats had been unified this time. We were good friends and we wanted to see each other get elected. Just about everyone did well that year—my friend Jess Kornegay was re-elected as state treasurer, Dave

Norvell was elected attorney general, Alex Armijo was elected land commissioner, and Betty Fiorina was elected secretary of state. Although Republican Manuel Lujan was reelected to one of the Congressional seats, Harold Runnels unseated the Republican incumbent Ed Foreman for Congress.

Voters also approved the constitutional amendment giving four-year terms to the statewide elective offices, including governor, which was one of the provisions we had hoped to enact through the constitutional revision. Though I was actually running for a two-year term (1971–1972) in that election, the constitutional amendment on the ballot was effective immediately, so it applied to the incoming officers. I think Alice was more excited about that amendment passing than she was about me getting elected, because it meant I wouldn't be campaigning in two years, or even four years hence, since you couldn't succeed yourself in office then. Alice always worked hard when I campaigned, so she was relieved to have it over with for a while. For my part, I was looking ahead to my duties as governor. Sixteen years after I entered politics by running for county commission, I had been elected to the highest office in the state, the realization of a dream I had held onto most of my life.

During the interim between the election and inauguration, I headed off to North Carolina to attend an orientation meeting of the National Governors' Association, a group that would turn out to be a great source of professional and political support for me throughout my career. We governors developed great camaraderie, even across party lines, based on the common challenges we faced. During that December orientation, I met many people who would become lifelong friends, including Dale Bumpers of Arkansas, Ruben Askew of Florida, David Hall of Oklahoma, Cecil Andrus of Idaho, and Jimmy Carter of Georgia. We were all first-time governors that year, and we swapped war stories about our campaigns.

Jimmy Carter and I had agriculture in common, so we talked about farming and about our kids. Amy Carter was about four years old at the time, and he told a funny story about his little girl warning her neighborhood friends not to cross her or she'd call security. I guess the advantages of being a governor roll all the way down the family line, although during my first term, our son Gary took an opposite stance. He flat refused to have security drive him the 40 miles from the governor's mansion in Santa Fe to Moriarty High School. Teenagers are like that.

Jimmy Carter and I became good friends when we met at the National Governors' Association conference in 1970. Jimmy always kidded me because Alice came out in support of his presidential candidacy before I did.

A few years later, I was at a luncheon with Jimmy in Georgia. It was 1973 or so, and both our terms were coming to an end. Jimmy asked me, "What are you going to run for now, Bruce?"

"Aw, I don't think I'll run for anything," I said. "I'll just go back to the ranch."

"Well, I think I'll start off trying to run for president, and see where I get," he said.

I didn't think he'd have much chance at that, so I suggested he try for vice president, instead. Of course, things started to go pretty well for Jimmy. As the 1976 primary developed, I was following the lead of Senator Clinton Anderson in supporting Scoop Jackson, and I thought we had a lead-pipe cinch. About then, Rosalyn Carter called Alice and asked her if she would help raise the $5,000 needed to qualify for the election in New Mexico. Alice asked me what I thought, and I said, "Well, that's fine. Maybe he'll be picked as a vice president. He'll never make it to president."

Jimmy loves to tease me about that. "Alice is smarter than you are," he says. "You were behind Scoop Jackson."

It was amazing how Jimmy Carter caught on, running very well without a lot of money. It was the right time for him. He was one of the brightest people that I ever worked with, and one of the most honest, hardest working, and sincere. The way the press and his detractors branded him as a weak leader responsible for the "malaise" was unfair. He is just a wonderful man.

6

Taking the Reins of State Government

I was sworn in as governor at midnight on January 1, 1971, in the governor's mansion in Santa Fe. We had just gotten the key to the mansion from Dave Cargo that afternoon. An old friend of Alice's and mine officiated, New Mexico Supreme Court Chief Justice James Compton. Just a few people were there: our children, my brothers and their families, a few friends, and a photographer. Alice had baked up some biscochito cookies and put on a pot of coffee. The whole ceremony didn't last an hour.

Because the term of the outgoing chief executive expires at the stroke of midnight on New Year's Eve, each new governor is sworn in at the first moment of January 1st in case an emergency develops before the public ceremony at midday. Otherwise, the state could be caught without a governor for a half day. So the inauguration and public swearing-in ceremonies were held 12 hours later, at high noon inside the state capitol rotunda. As a native of Santa Fe County, I had seen too many inaugurals held outdoors in nasty weather, and I didn't want to take that risk. As it turned out, my hunch was right but my timing was off by just a few hours.

Alice headed the inaugural committee, which had done an outstanding job pulling the festivities together. A large crowd gathered inside the capitol in the rotunda, where they could look on from upstairs. The National Guard band played for an hour, Homer Tanksley of Clovis Baptist Church sang, "How Great Thou Art," and the Archbishop conducted the invocation. Even Lieutenant Governor Roberto Mondragon, an excellent folksinger, performed the state song. When it came time to start the ceremony, first we swore-in Roberto. Then Judge Compton again swore me in, and I was the chief executive of the state of New Mexico for the next four years. I couldn't help reflecting on the responsibilities that go with taking the reins of government and the problems that might develop. Here I was, heading off on a totally new endeavor. It was like starting my life over again. I felt very humble, and I also felt greatly blessed. My mother was always a deeply religious person, and she felt your life was God's will and you needed God's guidance to move on.

I knew it was going to be a heavy job, but I felt up to it. Of course, I realized I was taking on responsibility for the needs of all the citizens, as well as trying to see they got the opportunity to enjoy the quality of life and protection they were entitled to. Later, after four years as governor, I came to realize that everyone is responsible for himself or herself. Right then, however, I didn't see it that way. I wondered what problems might develop in the upcoming session of the legislature or any other aspect of state government. I didn't have to wonder long. The first crisis I faced came on so fast that there was no way to prepare, and it had nothing to do with politics. It was the weather.

New Mexico Supreme Court Chief Justice J. C. Compton performed the swearing-in when I became the state's 31st governor in 1971. We held the ceremony inside the rotunda of the Roundhouse, our state capitol.

Right after the inauguration, I was busy visiting with friends and welcoming those who came from out of town. The capitol was crowded and noisy with the sounds of people talking and milling around. Alice's parents, Kenneth and Audra Martin, and their family were there, along with my mother, Molly, my brothers, Sam and Don, my sister, Leota, and our sons, Bill and Gary. We stole away for a brief time-out as a family to eat sandwiches and enjoy the moment without a large crowd. I slipped up to the fourth floor to take a quick look around at the governor's office. Then we headed over to the public reception at the Palace of the Governors on the Plaza, where hundreds of people came by to welcome us as the new Chief Executive and First Lady of New Mexico. The weather had been quite nice at noon. I was thinking we would have been better off if we'd had the swearing-in ceremonies outdoors, but by three or four o'clock that afternoon, a bitter north wind blew in. Many of the people standing in line at the Palace were out in the cold. And it kept getting colder.

We had announced we would be in the receiving line from 2:00 to 5:00 P.M., but at five o'clock long lines still stretched down the sidewalk. My brothers, Sam and Don, were going up and down the line visiting with people, and many of those waiting began to think of leaving early when they saw they weren't even going to reach the door by five. But Sam and Don came in and we took a short break, and they asked, "You will stay and greet the folks who are still in line, won't you?" They knew I would, of course, and I agreed. So the line went on until six-thirty, and we were proud and pleased, and also humbled that so many people would come to wish us well and participate in the inauguration of the first family. We took a 30-minute break and that, along with keeping the reception line open an extra hour and a half, delayed us to where we had little time to get to the inaugural ball. In the past, it was held at the historic La Fonda Hotel, kitty-cornered from the Plaza. Because of the large crowds, though, we moved the ball out to the College of Santa Fe. We joined together two of the large field houses, and even those facilities were completely overtaxed.

After a long night, we got back to the Inn of the Governors around 1 A.M.

The next morning was Sunday—still not an official work day. I made some calls to key people in state government, then we had a luncheon at the mansion for the visiting kinfolks—both Alice's and mine. Many had come from other states. Alice had the lunch catered and we started promptly at noon.

Snow began to fall. The weather quickly turned bad the way a northern New Mexico winter sometimes does. Alice and I stayed at the mansion until about four that afternoon, then went back to the Inn of the Governors to retire for the evening, since we hadn't completely moved into the mansion yet. Many of our visiting relatives were struggling through the snow to get home to southeast New Mexico and Texas. The driving conditions were so treacherous they ended up spending the night in little towns like Clines Corners and Vaughn, though some made it on to the larger city of Roswell. Even our families from as close as Stanley and Moriarty—40 miles from Santa Fe—barely reached home. This was just the start of a record cold spell that nearly paralyzed New Mexico during my first few days in office. Before long, we found ourselves in a full-blown winter crisis that called for prompt action from a still-green governor.

The second morning I was up early. Along with the snow, a deep chill had settled onto our part of the world, but I wasn't going to let that stop me. Since it was my first official work day, I was eager to get started. I had told the security men, Lieutenant Red Pack and Sergeant Dudley O'Dell, to pick me up around seven-thirty, which was when I had always gone to work, a habit I would continue as long as I was governor. The constant presence of security people was new to me, and it's a difficult adjustment for any new governor. Unfortunately, the many threats from radical movements that had sprung up in New Mexico made them necessary. In time, I saw for myself how concerned and diligent the security men were about protecting my life and my family.

Ironically, that first Monday morning when the time came to go to work, I didn't have any security. I waited and waited. Finally about five minutes before eight o'clock, Lieutenant Pack called and said the weather was so cold they couldn't start the car. I had a key to the capitol, so I walked over from the Inn through about eight inches of snow to meet them at the Round-house. Santa Fe was uncharacteristically quiet under its blanket of snow, since few people had ventured out into the weather. The scent of piñon smoke hung heavy in the air. We went upstairs to the fourth floor, unlocked my office, and went in. I looked around to see where I was going to begin work. The rooms were bare, dead quiet, and it seemed like there wasn't any heat on. It was a lonely feeling to be in that vacant office. Governor Cargo had cleaned out every desk drawer, and there wasn't even a paper clip or a rubber band. I soon found that Cargo had cleaned out more than paper clips—in fact, his legacy gave me more than a few headaches.

Unfortunately, I had bigger problems on my hands. Right off, I had to deal with a series of weather-related crises. The snow kept piling up and the temperature just plummeted, getting colder and colder. We had record low temperatures throughout New Mexico—40 below around Gallup, and 20 and 25 below in Santa Fe and northern New Mexico. By my third day in office, another emergency threatened when natural gas supplies started running short. Nearly everyone heated with gas, so private residences got first priority and the gas company shut off all the heat in the capitol. I didn't worry much about that, having worked outdoors all my life. I just put on heavy underwear, extra clothes, and an overcoat, then headed for the office every day, anyway. I let one or two staff people who felt they could brave the cold come in and work with me, so we kept the office open.

That was fine for me, but a severe cold-weather emergency was threatening northern New Mexico. People were suffering. Transportation had ground to a halt and folks in outlying areas were stranded without food and medicine. Since ranchers couldn't haul feed out to their livestock, cattle were dying on the range. It was devastating. I began to see that the governor had even more responsibility than I had imagined for the welfare of the citizens in a crisis. It became vividly clear to me that I could not simply rely on an overall plan for operating state government, though I certainly needed one. Over a number of years I had developed a detailed plan for what I wanted to do as governor, but it didn't cover record-cold weather and gas shortages. I couldn't worry about the far-reaching issues of state government when we had to solve this immediate crisis. I soon realized the emergency was dragging on and as chief executive I had to act quickly. I felt like my horse had stumbled on a rattlesnake, threw me off, run away, and left me lying on my back. That often happened to me.

To review our options, I called a meeting with Martin Vigil, chief of the State Police, General John Jolly, head of the National Guard, and Stretch Boles, Secretary of the state Highway Department. We decided we would have to secure livestock feed, open the roads, and use the National Guard to bring in food and supplies. We put on quite a coordinated effort, which helped us get through those tough days. That's when you realize you really need experienced people, and I was so impressed with how Martin Vigil handled the situation that I kept him on from Cargo's administration, and we became very good friends.

Finally, as the sun came out, the snow melted, the gas supply came up, and everyone began to see the humorous side of it, too. I was speaking to the Santa Fe Chamber of Commerce and I kidded them that I didn't know if I was welcome there or not, since they shut off the gas. They all laughed at that. Despite the fun, we realized we needed to be better prepared in the future.

In the midst of this wicked cold snap, the Navajo Nation inaugurated their newly elected chairman, Peter McDonald, who had replaced Raymond Nakai. Like me, McDonald was a new leader with new ideas. I wanted to show respect for the Navajo people and their new chairman, so Alice and I planned to visit Window Rock, Arizona, for the inauguration on January 5.

Along about this time, someone decided that the mansion—for some unknown reason—was part of the capitol complex and they shut off our gas. The line out there didn't have any pressure, anyway, and that whole area of town didn't have gas. People were moving into the hotels and motels, but we didn't have reservations and the road was clear to Stanley now, so we decided to go back home and stay in our house, which was only about a forty-minute drive from the capitol. We left Santa Fe after the day's work, about six-thirty or seven that evening, and drove down. When we stopped at the Stanley post office about eight to get the mail, I hadn't thought it was much colder than usual, and I hadn't been overly concerned, but one of our neighbors who kept the official weather data for the area drove up and said it was 20 degrees below zero right then. We drove on the two and a half miles to our ranch house, where we had a butane/propane tank for heat, like most country people around there, so we were cozy at home.

The next morning was the inauguration of Peter McDonald. I wanted to leave early so we could fly out of Santa Fe by 8:00 A.M. and reach Window Rock in time for the ceremony. I got up in the dark and went out to start our car, a 1970 Buick Special. I left the car running to warm it up and came back in the house to have a cup of coffee, then finish getting ready to catch the government plane. I went back out 15 or 20 minutes later and the car had overheated. It had blown all the water and antifreeze out of the radiator and was burning the paint off the engine. I knew the engine was too hot to add new antifreeze without completely ruining that car.

About that time, my brothers stopped by to see how we were getting along. I told them about the car, and they said they would take us to Santa Fe. I managed to call Lieutenant Pack and told him to meet us halfway. So Sam and Don drove us to Galisteo, where we met Lieutenant Pack, who took us on to the Santa Fe airport. Then we flew out to Window Rock. If anything, it was even colder there, but the Navajo people came in great numbers to the tribal grounds—actually, the rodeo arena—and sat in the grandstands. That day the thermometer crept up to 11 below zero. The Navajos gave us blankets, which we wrapped around ourselves to keep warm. Alice said she had never been so cold in all her life. Afterwards we had a brief lunch with chairman Peter McDonald, who appreciated that we had come despite the weather. The tribe served their traditional mutton stew, which was cooking outside in big pots, and along toward evening we finally headed home. My presence had demonstrated to the Navajo people the kind of recognition they would receive from me and it helped me to gain their confidence. I was impressed with Peter McDonald and we worked very closely after that.

I met a couple of my neighboring state governors there at Window Rock. Jack Williams, a Republican, had been governor of Arizona for four years, and he turned out to be an excellent friend and ally. Cal Rampton, a Democrat, had been governor of Utah for four years, and we became good friends and developed a strong working relationship. All three of us were governors of states that included the Navajo Nation. I also visited with Wilson Skeet, the vice chairman of the Navajo tribe, who had been a good friend and supporter of mine when I had run for governor. Wilson also belonged to the New Mexico Cattle Growers Association—he lived in New Mexico, while Peter McDonald lived in Arizona.

~
~~

I was barely open for business that first Monday of my term when the young Associated Press reporter Larry Calloway came by, and I let him in. We were acquainted from my years as speaker of the House and president of the constitutional convention. Larry looked around the bare office, and he said, "Governor, what happened to the moon rocks that used to sit on the desk?"

"I don't know," I said. "There weren't any moon rocks here when I came in this morning."

Larry looked around some more, and he said, "There were two flags in stands, a New Mexico flag and a United States flag. They were one to either side of the state symbol on the wall behind the governor's desk. Where are those?"

"I don't know. There wasn't anything of that nature here when I came in."

Larry looked over at the bookshelf. It was empty. "This shelf was full of law books Friday evening. What happened to them?" he asked.

With that, I looked around and saw a driftwood carving of a roadrunner, the New Mexico state bird. Former Governor Campbell had made the roadrunner a gift to the people of New Mexico before Cargo came into office. The carving had a red spot on it, and to me it looked more like some other bird, not a roadrunner.

"Well, Larry," I said, "there wasn't a dang thing here but that woodpecker when I came in."

That remark got national publicity. The first cartoon about my administration by my friend Mac McGinnis, the *Albuquerque Journal* cartoonist, suggested I didn't know our state bird, and didn't even know what a roadrunner was. Mac showed the roadrunner and our state insignia, the Zia symbol, which is a circle with four lines radiating out from the top, bottom, and each side. I was pointing at the Zia symbol, saying, "What's this little thing with all the straight marks?"

My son Bill looked in the paper that evening and asked me, "Daddy, you do know what it is, don't you?"

"Yeah," I told him. I was born in the country, and I sure enough knew what a roadrunner was, and a woodpecker, too.

We looked around to see what happened to the moon rocks, which the astronauts collected at the lunar landing site. The United States government had given samples to the people of each state. When he left office, Cargo had taken the rocks and the flag stands. He had also moved out an old piano with him from the governor's mansion. All this soon caused a great deal of controversy. The gentleman who had contributed that piano to the state of New Mexico was concerned about its whereabouts, and he called me wanting to know about it. I told him there wasn't any piano in the house when we came in, not like the piano he was looking for. So he tracked it down and found it had been taken up to Cargo's home in Pojoaque. The gentleman wanted to know if he could bring it back to the mansion. "You and Alice will have to work that out," I told him. He chose to take it home to Sapello.

When Cargo was asked where this or that item was, he would say, "I was going to hold a ceremony and present them to the people of New Mexico." He gave the moon rocks to the Museum of New Mexico. Those three things—the flags, the moon rocks, and the piano—inspired a lot of cartoons and a lot of interest in state government right at the start of my term as governor, but all this confusion didn't make for the smoothest transition between administrations.

≈≈

I knew that if I was going to operate state government successfully, I needed a first-rate staff. I looked over the agency heads in charge of the various departments. Even though I was taking over from a Republican governor, I felt that at least half of his top administrators were competent people and that it would be best to leave them in office, where we could benefit from their knowledge and abilities. Among those I kept were Bob Kirkpatrick, director of the Department of Finance and Administration; Franklin Jones, commissioner of the Bureau of Revenue; Stretch Boles, the state Highway Engineer; Martin Vigil, chief of the State Police; John Jolly the adjutant general; Ladd Gordon, director of the Game and Fish Department; and Steve Reynolds, the State Engineer, who oversees all water rights.

I brought in several new staff members, too. I named Dick Heim to run the Human Services Department. Dick had been an assistant to Senator Clinton Anderson in Washington and before that, Bernalillo County manager. With his background, he knew the needs of the Human Services Department. I brought in Bill Giron, who had been deputy land commissioner, as secretary of the Department of Hospitals and Institutions, where he did excellent work. I appointed Roy Davidson as the bank commissioner. Roy had been in the legislature with me and had been chairman of the House banking committee. As state tourism director, I named Fabian Chávez, who of course had extensive experience in state government and as a lobbyist. That group gave me a nucleus of administrative skills to work with in state government.

For my administrative assistant, I picked Toney Anaya, who became governor of New Mexico in 1983. I also named Keith Dotson and Larry Hamm to my staff. Keith was a longtime friend from the Santa Fe Chamber of Commerce, while Larry had worked with the electronic news media in Santa Fe. He became one of my assistants in Boards and Commissions and I later named him director of the state Film Commission, which he handled well.

My appointments didn't escape criticism, but I was surprised to find myself under attack in the newspapers from my own lieutenant governor, Roberto Mondragon. In early 1971, he told reporters that of the 60 or 70 appointments I had made since taking office, none were people he had recommended. He told people not to come to him for a recommendation, because it didn't work out that way, adding that my rejection of his choices had become a pattern. In reply, I answered, "If they want to be governor, they should run for governor." Fortunately, that situation blew over and we worked very well together for four years.

♒

The legislature was to convene just two and a half weeks after I was inaugurated. I organized a group to help me draft the annual state of the state message that would open the session. My aim was to be quite inclusive in my proposals. I wanted a professional state government that would respond to the needs of all the citizens of New Mexico and improve the quality of life for everyone. An immediate problem that I had to note in my message was deficit spending: state revenues were falling short of projections. Inadequate funding for education was an issue—as it would be for years to come—particularly with regard to public school teachers' salaries.

I tried to mention as many of the problem areas I saw in state government as I could. We needed to modernize the state Motor Vehicles Department, which had faltered quite badly, and I wanted to update the equipment of the state Motor Transport Division. I knew we would have to bring professional attitudes and methods to these offices, and I said so in the message. I asked for additional help for minority groups that had been neglected. I wanted women's rights, and we went on to accomplish a great deal in that area, starting with my executive order creating the Commission on the Status of Women. It worked to ensure that women were treated equally in all aspects, such as pay and property rights for women after divorces or the death of their husband. Then in 1973, New Mexico passed its own Equal Rights Amendment.

In my speech, I noted that we needed huge capital outlays to improve the state highway system. I asked for a stronger state personnel system and I wanted to improve our prisons and correctional system. Finally, I pointed out that I had served a number of years in the legislature and that I wanted the support of all legislators, Democrats and Republicans alike, to participate in these steps to strengthen state government. Unfortunately, I never did develop the collaborative working relationship with the legislature that I had hoped for.

During that session, we worked on bills creating a state correctional board, tightening controls on drunk driving, and providing $1.1 million to fund the new cancer research center at the University of New Mexico. I vetoed a bill that would have raised interest rates for small loans, since I felt that anyone who had to rely on the small loan companies shouldn't be gouged by a high interest rate.

With all those significant issues at stake, we came into a great deal of unexpected criticism concerning my request for $50,000 over four years to fix up the governor's mansion. This lovely territorial-adobe style residence sits on a hill a couple miles north of downtown and the capitol. After looking it over, I felt the mansion was in poor repair. Though heavily used for public entertaining, no substantial maintenance had been done for six or seven years. The carpet was getting worn, the drapes were in poor condition, the plumbing needed repair, and much of the furniture had to be reupholstered.

By this time, Cargo had gone to work as a political commentator with an Albuquerque TV news program, and he quickly became highly critical of me. As a television reporter, he didn't try to discuss issues. Instead, he used the position to editorialize against me. For instance, when I noted the steps we needed to take before we could open the Anapra port of entry with Mexico, Dave said everything had already been done under his administration. Actually, all his people had done was to go put up a sign saying, "Future Site of Anapra Port of Entry." Then he wasn't happy I said the governor's office was bare. When Alice and I expressed concern about the condition of the mansion and some of its furnishings, Cargo claimed it was a "perfectly good million-dollar mansion" when he left it.

Cargo laid into me: "Well, the hay kicker goes to Santa Fe and takes over the governor's mansion, and the first thing he does is to say it has to be re-done." He implied we were couple of country people who immediately wanted to live in New York style. None of his charges were true, but the place was in bad shape. We just wanted a respectable mansion that New Mexicans could be proud of, because it belongs to the people. We knew that thousands of visitors from the general public would pass through the mansion in the next few years. In fact, after Cargo stirred up the controversy over our request, we kept track and found we had 10,000 people a year—that's over 800 a month. Visiting the mansion was the "in" thing to do for awhile and everyone wanted to come by. Alice was there for any event. I would look in as much as I could, just to make an appearance, which didn't take long. I would take a coffee break once in a while, anyway, and run out to the mansion to greet people.

In those first years, we hosted the Mexican ambassador to the United States two or three times, plus visitors from Japan and Korea, governors from other states, Governor Oscar Flores from Chihuahua, Mexico, and a group of cattlemen from Mexico. We also had supreme court justices, legislators, church organizations, civic clubs, and so on. We kept the mansion readily open for such affairs, and any state organization could schedule an appointment. We gave lots of tours for schoolchildren and 4-H clubs. The mansion was even on the Gray Line sightseeing tours of Santa Fe in my first administration. Every bus would circle the mansion, letting tourists view the grounds and the rock garden. Sometimes people would come by unannounced. Usually they were friends, but one lady came and claimed that since the mansion belonged to the state, she was going to live there. She threw her bed out on the lawn. I guess she stayed about a half day.

Well, Cargo and I got into big arguments about the condition of the mansion during the first month or so of my administration, and the papers put our pictures on the front page, with Cargo stating his accusation and me saying, "these are the facts." I soon decided we had better get away from this kind of controversy, and I quit debating those issues publicly. I said I wouldn't have any further answers to Cargo's comments, but that I would take a strong approach to improving state government.

Others in the press were derogatory about our needs for the mansion, too. Eventually, my brothers became as fed up as we were with the whole subject. One day they came by and said, "If everyone is going to fuss about it so much, let's go ahead and do the remodeling and the King Brothers Ranch will pay for it."

To clear things up, Alice and I went in to visit C. Thompson Lang, the publisher of the *Albuquerque Journal*.

"Alice," he said, "don't listen to that criticism any longer. We're going to come strongly to your defense, because we want the mansion to look nice, and we know that's all you're trying to do." On the other hand, syndicated capitol columnist Fred Buckles made a great fuss about the money we spent on the mansion. He used up a lot of paper space working over the expenditures he thought were extravagant.

Eventually, most of the press moved on to other topics. We showed many legislators through the mansion to see the needs firsthand. When the bill for refurbishing the mansion finally passed, the legislators played games and held up the emergency clause, which would allow us to use the funds immediately. The House appropriations committee under my friend John Mershon wanted to send the bill back for the emergency clause, but I was afraid the floor would kill it altogether, so I signed it without that clause. Then I told Alice to go ahead and have the work done—we would personally sign a note at the bank and pay it off when the state money came in. That's what we did.

⁂

Education had been one of the major themes of my 1970 campaign. I felt we needed to improve education at all levels in New Mexico for the betterment of our citizens. It was also sound economic development policy. Giving people a solid education meant they could get good jobs, and as a state we could attract new industry. On the negative side, we also were going through a period of unrest at two of our state universities, the school teachers were unhappy about their low pay, and schools in rural or poor communities were at a distinct funding disadvantage compared to the big urban districts. I spent a good deal of time in my first administration resolving these issues, but all-in-all, we succeeded in improving education in New Mexico.

I always saw the tie between economic growth and education. Along with several other leading figures in state government, I was interested in measures to increase individual earning capacity and develop job opportunities in New Mexico. We approached this from a couple different angles by working to bring more jobs into New Mexico and developing better job training.

A basic problem in New Mexico was the lack of good employment for young people when they completed their education. To meet the demand for jobs, we passed legislation creating the state economic development board. Then we needed an economic development director. So I enlisted some of my close friends in the business community to help me locate the best we could find. After searching a couple of months, this committee recommended Bill Simms, a former commissioner of banking in New Mexico who was well informed on the needs for economic development. I appointed him director of the state Economic Development Division. Then I convened meetings of the board at different communities around New Mexico, and we set the stage to encourage different industries to move into New Mexico, bringing new jobs.

In the area of training, John Mershon shared my feeling that we needed a school of economic development. With Bill Simms, we decided to focus on doing a better job of training our people for the service-oriented and hospitality industries, which were—and still are—a large part of the New Mexico economy. Numerous job openings were turning up in that area and we weren't adequately preparing people to fill them or training them in how to meet the needs of the public. Having well-trained people in the hospitality sector—cooks, hotel managers, front desk people—is a good way to promote New Mexico. So we set about developing the first program in the country to provide education at all levels for careers in the service sector. The legislature met my request by appropriating $1 million to develop service industry training in the statewide vocational program. We then provided the training on-site all around the state, at places like La Fonda Hotel in Santa Fe or the Lodge down in Cloudcroft. Anyone in the area could send their employees to the training free of charge. Working with the University of New Mexico's school of business, we brought in experts to develop management training and a program to match training with open positions. This effort was successful in placing graduates in well-paying jobs.

I appointed an advisory board to look at the needs for training and to watch over the expenditures. I named Harry Wugalter, the director of finance for public education, and Joe Menapace, who was then director of the New Mexico School Board Association. He later became the lobbyist for the Santa Fe railroad in New Mexico. Others included Alex Mercure, then president of Northern New Mexico Community College. Alex later went to the University of New Mexico and moved on to Washington in the Carter administration as one of the three top deputies in the Department of Agriculture. He returned to New Mexico as director of Commerce and Industry in the Anaya administration. Another member of the advisory board was Louis Saavedra, who became the first president of the Albuquerque Technical Vocational Institute and later mayor of Albuquerque. I also named L. C. Cousins, superintendent of schools at Portales, to represent the public schools, and David McNeill, deputy director of the state Department of Construction Industries, who did a lot of work in developing the capital expenditures plan.

The legislature was soon appropriating $15 million annually for capital outlay projects for the schools. We set up a board to dispense the money, which was intended particularly for the poorer school districts that otherwise could not have afforded the facilities they needed. Some of it also went to the branch colleges of the major universities and the junior colleges who were strapped for funds.

Despite these efforts to improve education, some teachers felt that neither the legislature nor I moved quickly enough to raise their salaries. New Mexico's teacher pay ranked very low nationally. I proposed to the 1971 legislature a 7 percent pay increase for school teachers, and the legislature cut that back to 6 percent, which did not meet the expectations of the teachers. They had been good supporters of mine, and I had talked a great deal about a pay increase and what we would be able to do to support the public schools.

Many teachers were disappointed in the outcome of the 1971 legislature. Just days after the session ended, members of the New Mexico chapter of the National Education Association urged me to immediately call a special session to seek increased funding for the schools. However, when I reviewed the appropriations and the state's tax structure, I concluded that we could not justify a larger appropriation for the public schools. I dealt openly, as always, with the school people on this issue. I explained that the 6 percent raise was the best we could do without a tax increase, but I said I would try over the next four years to provide the raises they wanted, bringing salaries up several percentage points in national standing.

The issue didn't die there. In reference to the 6 percent raise, an *Albuquerque Journal* cartoon showed teachers saying, "Ye gods! Half a loaf again!" Dissidents in the NEA called a statewide meeting in Albuquerque, which I agreed to attend. They aired all kinds of complaints. For example, they were concerned about the number of students in the classrooms. At the meeting, they kept pushing me to call a special session, and I repeated that I failed to see adequate justification, but I would continue to review the need. The dissidents held several other meetings around the state in which they were quite critical of me and of the legislature. The threat of a teacher strike hung in the air. Remembering how devastating the strike had been in 1966 during Cargo's administration when I was speaker of the House, I did not want one on my hands now.

At this point, my ability to influence the NEA leadership became important. I had befriended the president of NEA-New Mexico, and persuaded him that we had done all we could do. I also visited with others on their executive committee, particularly those who had been close advisors and consultants to me during my campaign for governor. Of course, my supporters in the NEA also wanted better pay for teachers, but they realized that the legislature's 6 percent was the best we could do that year. I reminded them that we had three more years to look at appropriations, and told them that perhaps we could do better later on. Finally the school funding issue came to a head at the NEA meeting in Las Cruces on May 2. To my great relief, the executive committee voted 160 to 64 against calling a teachers' strike. I was grateful to my friends on the committee for taking a stand against striking.

In the early 1970s, the state wasn't doing a good job of sharing the wealth among all the school districts. With funding based largely on county property taxes, obviously the poorer counties would have less money to work with. They couldn't give their kids the same opportunities that the larger city schools provided. During the next couple years I worked with the state superintendent of public instruction, Leonard DeLayo, to determine the proper direction and funding for our schools. The end result was our proposed 1974 school equalization bill, which included a school funding distribution formula that used state revenues rather than county revenues to pay for school operational costs on a per-student basis, thereby spreading the money equally across all the districts. Each district's funding level was based on average daily attendance, with special weighting factors for the smallest, most isolated rural schools.

We got help from Larry Huxell, who was assistant to Harry Wugalter in the Public School Finance Division of the Department of Finance and Administration. Larry was a numbers man. He showed the needs of the poorer districts and demonstrated how those needs could be met by redistributing state-level funds so that each student would get about the same support, no matter where they lived. People tended to think the poorer districts were in northern New Mexico, with its largely Hispanic, low-income areas, and western New Mexico, where we have large Indian populations. But when we looked hard at the numbers, we found that the Albuquerque district would also pick up substantial additional funding, to the tune of about $8 million. That gave us a good voting bloc from the Albuquerque area to support equalization and the bill passed the legislature to become law in 1974.

The funding formula was a milestone and it was one of the greatest and most lasting achievements of my first administration. We were one of the first states to provide equal funding for all students. With our considerable mineral wealth concentrated in a few areas, we had greater discrepancy of resources among our school districts than most other states. Through equalization, we vastly improved our public school system, and I campaigned hard on that accomplishment when I ran for governor the second time, in 1978.

∿

We were also having trouble in 1971 with two of our institutions of higher education, the University of New Mexico and New Mexico Highlands University. Several high-profile incidents at UNM in 1970—including Cargo's calling out of the National Guard—were damaging its reputation around the state. Bringing order to UNM was a big campaign issue around Albuquerque and the legislature was extremely concerned about the university. Senate President Pro Tempore Ike Smalley wanted the 1971 legislature to continue its close scrutiny of UNM with the University Study Committee, which provided a vehicle for the legislature to review operations at UNM. Plenty of people opposed this committee because they felt it wasn't a proper role for the legislature, but with Smalley and others feeling so strongly about, I signed the bill to continue the committee and came in for a great deal of criticism.

By this time, much of the controversy at UNM actually had already blown over. I knew, however, that a good part of improving the situation lay with the regents and I was due to make two appointments to the board. After I was elected, my old friend and advisor Calvin Horn told me he strongly wished to become a regent of UNM. His financial position allowed him to devote virtually full time to university affairs. He had put together much of the research and many position papers for my campaign, and I was happy to name him regent. I also named my old friend Austin Roberts, who had been House majority leader when I was speaker. He was a graduate of UNM law school and his daughter attended UNM.

That left three regents who remained from Governor Cargo's administration. I saw that it might take a while before my interests were fully represented on the five-member board, but I at least wanted Calvin to be chairman. I visited with one of the holdover regents, Cyrene Mapel, who was a friend and neighbor of his. She agreed that Calvin would be a good choice. With those three votes—his own, Austin's, and Cyrene's—Calvin was elected chairman. He also became the liaison between the regents, the university, and myself.

I had other friends at UNM. Many people there had worked in my campaign, including Marion Cottrell, a professor of engineering and later an Albuquerque city councilor and Bernalillo County commissioner. Marion was an excellent liaison with the university faculty. He organized monthly meetings alternately on the UNM campus and in my office in Santa Fe, with about 25 to 30 members of the faculty senate attending each time. I insisted that Calvin also come to those meetings. My approach was something new. The faculty had not met with a governor before. I enjoyed meeting with them, and soon found they provided as wide a viewpoint as you wanted on any topic.

I tried something else new. In September 1971 I called the first-ever meeting of the members of all the state boards of regents and all the presidents of the state's six four-year institutions of higher learning. I wanted to deepen their mutual understanding to help eliminate duplication in academic programs. I felt that the better rapport these leaders developed, the better off we would all be. That meeting established a precedent, and now all the regents meet together regularly.

It may seem unusual for a governor to take so much interest in a state university, but UNM was of such concern throughout the state that I felt if we made the university go well, many other things would improve in New Mexico. And if we didn't get our leading institution of higher learning accepted as the fine university it was, then it would be difficult to meet the other needs of our citizens.

By the 1972 legislative session, a year later, things were running smoothly at UNM. Calvin Horn and the other regents had been able to resolve many of the university's problems to the satisfaction of the public, as I had planned, and we soon got away from the controversy. By my second term, UNM was much less visible and no longer such a great cause of contention. I feel I made the right decision in signing the bill creating the University Study Committee, because it helped us avoid a showdown over having the committee as oversight to the university. If that controversy had erupted, we might have lost the gains in public confidence we were establishing for the university.

Meanwhile, major problems were developing at New Mexico Highlands University in Las Vegas in 1971, where people were bitterly divided over the university. Those divisions worked their way into the political system, too. Deep splits were developing between ethnic groups in the community and the region. Tensions ran high, worsened by poor communication and lack of understanding between two disputing groups of citizens in San Miguel County, and among the students. The pressure built till it just flat boiled over.

Highlands had become known as a racially oriented, highly volatile place. Enrollment was plummeting. About that time, a magazine came out calling Las Vegas the drug capital of the USA. Obviously, responsible parents didn't want their children attending that type of school. Meanwhile, the radical Hispanic political group La Raza Unida was making demands on how the university should be run. Besides holding parades and demonstrating, they even built fires all around the president's house. The atmosphere got so tense that my security people didn't like me to go there, but State Police Chief Martin Vigil said, "If you're going, I'm going, too." I would meet with La Raza leaders, sitting right down on the sidewalk with them and talking about whatever they wanted to discuss. As this went on, they started to get a little bit friendly with me.

I knew we had to correct the problems at Highlands. No one was sure exactly how to move. A few years earlier, at Governor Cargo's request the board of regents had named Dr. Ralph Carlisle Smith as interim president of Highlands. Then several members of the board had resigned about the time I took office, so I needed to appoint their replacements. That seemed like a good place for me to start, but I had a difficult time persuading some of the people I wanted to serve on the Highlands board of regents. I did convince Tom Wiley, who had been state superintendent of education. He was known in San Miguel County and was acceptable to both groups as a professional who understood the needs at the university. I also was able to convince Highlands graduate Ben Roybal to serve as chairman of the regents. Ben had been the administrative assistant to Congressman Tom Morris, and was later a municipal judge in Bernalillo County. He was more than willing to go in and try to straighten out the situation, with my backing.

As we were taking these steps to resolve the problems, Stuart Beck, editor of the *Daily Optic* in Las Vegas, resigned from the board of regents over the hostile treatment that interim president Smith had received at a mass meeting on the campus. According to Beck, Dr. Smith didn't have the community support and backing he needed. I saw that the key to turning this situation around was setting up a board of regents that had the confidence of the community and could relate to the needs of the people. In Beck's place I appointed Ernestine Evans, who was the immediate-past secretary of state, had been Governor Campbell's assistant, and was familiar with educational needs. That left Dean Robb as the only hold-over regent who remained on the board. A pioneer in electronic music and professor of music at the University of New Mexico, Robb had been a Republican congressional candidate some years earlier and I imagine that was one reason Governor Cargo had appointed him to the board. Fortunately, he proved most helpful in working with us to try to resolve the tensions at Highlands.

We named Frank Angel as interim president after the dissidents all but ran President Smith out of town. Angel happened to be the brother of District Judge Joe Angel of San Miguel County, and that relationship was an asset in trying to bring order to the situation. State Representative Sam Vigil was also of great help as vice president to Dr. Angel. Throughout this difficult time, many wonderful people of Las Vegas stood up to be counted— the supporters of the university far outnumbered the dissidents. It was still a long haul before we got Highlands University back up to par, but in my four years we made a great deal of progress. Turning that university around was a significant achievement of my first administration.

☲

Being governor isn't all work. Sometimes it brought me recreational opportunities that might otherwise never come my way. I always enjoyed traveling to Mexico on official business, making friends there, and seeing how their political system worked. I also took great pleasure in traveling with the New Mexico Amigos, the group of 100 business people and others who spread the word around the country about the opportunities for economic development and tourism in our state. They pay their own way and invite the governor as their paid guest. The Amigos got their start in 1962 with a focus on bringing enterprises and job opportunities into New Mexico. Unfortunately, about the time I came in, the people we visited were starting to resent anyone trying to pirate their industry. So I made it into more of an ambassador's visit to maintain the goodwill of the governor of whatever state we were visiting and to emphasize that we are a unique, tourist-oriented state.

At first I was hesitant to travel with the Amigos as governor. I wondered if it wouldn't be seen as a waste of time and taxpayers' money, but after I went the first time and saw the tremendous amount of publicity and friendship the tour generated for New Mexico, I became an ardent supporter of the Amigos. As the years went by, the group's emphasis shifted from strictly business-related economic development to tourism. I continued my involvement since tourism remains one of our most important industries.

I first toured with the Amigos in May 1971. That trip was a nice mix of serious business and more lighthearted activities. We started in Oklahoma City, where my friend Albert Mitchell had arranged for my induction into the Cowboy Hall of Fame. I also met with Governor David Hall of Oklahoma. From there we dropped into Texas, where I met with Governor Preston Smith. This was still a drought year throughout the Southwest, and we three governors decided the federal government was not doing right by us in providing drought relief. Governor Smith and Governor Hall let me be spokesman, and I stated that the Nixon administration had been less than responsive to the emergency needs caused by the drought in our three states. Rapping the Nixon administration brought us a lot of press coverage, and after that we also received a great deal more emergency drought relief in our states, the kind of help that only the feds could bring. A good example was the situation in the remote village of Pie Town in west-central New Mexico.

The well had gone dry and we were having to haul water in. With federal funding, the village drilled a new well and set up storage tanks.

During my first Amigos tour, I was piped aboard the USS *General Wainright* at Charlotte, North Carolina with full military honors for me as governor of New Mexico. Since I had served as a corporal in the army, I was impressed by the ceremony. But the trip had disappointments, too. In Texas, we were supposed to visit the LBJ ranch for a barbecue to meet former President Johnson. We made it to the ranch, but we couldn't find LBJ. Then we spent a couple days in the Bahamas, which was the first chance I'd had to relax as governor, and by the end of the week I could tell how much I'd needed it. That was usually the case, as I continued traveling with the Amigos on their annual tours during my later administrations. I remember in 1981 we visited the West Coast and Hawaii. During the trip, my staff called to tell me that a prisoner had escaped from the penitentiary by hiding in a van. This was after the prison riot of 1980 and all the subsequent work we had done to straighten out our corrections system, so that was depressing news. My old friend, *Albuquerque Journal* cartoonist Mac McGinnis, showed me sitting by the seashore in Hawaii, and he portrayed all the problems I had had throughout the year—the penitentiary, the demands for special sessions, the Highway Department problems, and other issues. In the cartoon I was saying, "You just tell them I might stay an extra week before I go home."

During my first tour with the Amigos, a goodwill group of business people who represented New Mexico in other states, I was piped aboard the USS *General Wainright* at Charlotte, North Carolina with full military honors.

One evening in May 1972, my friend Governor Holcomb of Indiana called our home and my 17-year-old son Gary answered the phone. When the governor asked for me, Gary told him I was in Silver City, but he expected me home shortly.

"Can you take a message?" Governor Holcomb asked.

"Sure, I'm his son," Gary said, explaining that he was a senior in high school.

Governor Holcomb realized he had a friend there and he said, "I just wanted to invite you and your dad to come to the Indianapolis 500 race."

Gary was a sports enthusiast and he fired back, "We accept! We'll be there."

When I came in the door that night he said, "Daddy, Governor Holcomb called from Indiana and invited you and me back to the Indianapolis 500 the day after tomorrow, and I accepted."

"Well," I started, "I don't know about our schedule."

"It won't make any difference, Daddy, whatever the schedule," he told me. "We've *got to* go to the Indianapolis 500."

"All right, Gary," I said. Gary never injects himself into situations, and he never fussed about his last two years of high school when we didn't have the time to spend with him that we'd like to have had. This automobile race seemed so important to him that Alice and I made a special effort to revamp our schedule so Gary and I could go to Indy. We were greeted with great distinction by Governor Holcomb and by the Tillman family, which operates the Indianapolis 500. We enjoyed the race, and had a chance to visit with Bobby and Al Unser of Albuquerque, two of the leading Indy car drivers and part of a long dynasty of great Unser race car drivers. They were always ready to participate in public events when we asked them to. Bobby was picked to win the 1972 race. He led until he broke a rotor in his car about the sixth or seventh lap, forcing him to drop out. But Al stayed in the race and ran well.

That year Gary graduated from Moriarty High School as valedictorian of his class. Even though we lived in the mansion at Santa Fe, he had finished his school years at Moriarty. Alice and I attended the graduation and watched him deliver the valedictory address. Gary had become interested in politics, in the positions we were taking on the needs of young people in New Mexico. In 1986, he was elected to the House of Representatives, where he continues to serve with distinction, supporting many of the same issues that I championed in my years as a public official.

≈

Under the Cargo administration, a film commission began bringing more movie business to New Mexico. Our state has wonderfully scenic locations and skilled workers to support movie making, and down through the years the film commission did a fine job bringing in more and more production companies. In 1971, motion picture filming projects had brought in $24 million. I felt we needed to continue this state support of the film industry, and I had said I would go to Hollywood to help further that cause. Late in the year, the Albuquerque Chamber of Commerce set up a trip, so I went with them to invite the Hollywood people to produce films in New Mexico.

Alice and I went with the group in November. We met many leading actors and producers, including Mike Landon of the television series "Bonanza." I told him we always watched his show. He spent considerable time with us and took us all through the "Bonanza" set. We also watched filming of the show "Alias Smith and Jones" and we met Anthony Quinn, who had starred in the biggest film made at the time in New Mexico. It was first called "The Drunken Indian," but that controversial name was changed to "The Navajo."

In 1974, Alice and I again went to Los Angeles to sing the praises of New Mexico in Hollywood. My old friend Dr. George Fischbeck, a Los Angeles TV weatherman who had done the forecasts on Albuquerque TV for years, invited me to appear on his show. Afterwards he took me to meet Cissy King, a former University of New Mexico cheerleader who was now a dancer on the Lawrence Welk Show. When we got to the studio and met Lawrence Welk, he invited us to appear on the show they were taping that day. I tried to say no, but Cissy and Alice insisted. So we taped the show— Alice danced with Lawrence Welk and I danced with Cissy. Afterward, more people commented about our appearance on the TV show than anything else we did. We got wide recognition for the state of New Mexico and for ourselves, just by being in the right place at the right time.

These trips were successful, and our contacts brought new business to New Mexico. Other states observed our success and tried to set up movie commissions patterned after ours, but we were first in that line and kept our lead for a number of years. New Mexico continues to attract the producers of major films, year after year.

≋

At the same time I came into the governor's office in 1971, a group of liberal Democrats gained control of the House. House Speaker Walter Martinez of Valencia County, Gene Cinelli of Bernalillo County, David Salman of Mora and San Miguel Counties, and Raymond Sanchez of Bernalillo County were the main leaders. The group called themselves the Mama Lucy Democrats, taking their name from the restaurant in Las Vegas where they often met to discuss strategy. Most of their support came from north-central New Mexico and the Rio Grande corridor, including parts of Albuquerque and Las Cruces. The Mama Lucy group took in anyone who would join their cause, giving them a majority in the House. To balance what I felt was their excessive liberalism and override the Mama Lucy votes, I helped form a bloc of conservative, east-side Democrats and Republicans, which became known as the Cowboys. Even though it sounds like a gridlock-type situation, we could work together and we all remained friends. Sometimes Hispanic representatives voted with the Cowboys, and Anglos with the Mama Lucies, so there was never a purely racial or ethnic split.

Speaker Walter Martinez tried to be a mediator. He voted with the Mama Lucies, but he would work with me, too. After one or two showdowns on the floor of the House, he took to asking my brother Don, who was a more conservative Democrat in the legislature then, to come up to my office and ask me. Then I'd send someone down to tell Walter to come up and see me. I'd explain our point of view. For instance, one time they wanted to spend $14 million of the severance tax fund, but I wanted to make sure it got set aside so it could earn interest for the state and help meet future needs—that was the purpose of those funds. He'd come around, but then he'd get nervous about what David Salman, Gene Cinelli, and Raymond Sanchez were going to think, and he'd say, "Can I go back and bring all the guys up?" And I'd say, "Sure, go ahead." We'd have a nice, congenial discussion, though nobody pulled any punches. I could always reason with them by stating the facts, after we'd beat them a time or two. First we had to get enough strength together to win a few votes on the floor.

In those days, we had a better system of reconciling differences. It wasn't so polarized between liberals versus conservatives. My strength as speaker of the House had been building harmony among those people who held radically different viewpoints and represented various interests. On different issues, we'd be all over the place. You couldn't mark people—or issues—so easily then as a liberal or conservative, or as being from Albuquerque or the east side. I just wanted to help New Mexico, and do the right thing at the right time, and I think most of us felt that way. These days, maybe it's too much greed and individual interest, rather than having the big picture.

An example is the 1974 school equalization bill, which distributed funding equally to all school districts across the state. These days, you couldn't anymore pass that law than you could fly. But back then, I finally convinced the conservative eastsiders by saying, "Look, we're all in this together. You can either pay it in education, or you can pay it in welfare and assistance." They knew I was right. We had to spread the wealth around to help those living in the poorer areas to help themselves. They finally said, "Look, governor, we're not going to argue with you about what you're going to do, but you don't really expect us to vote for it, do you?"

"No, no!" I said. "I just didn't want you all feeling that I'd done you in. I don't want you to leave here thinking we'd done something that wasn't in the best interest of all New Mexicans." I could understand their problems, and they could understand mine. When they went home, they could say, "Well, I voted against it," and that would end the discussion with their constituents.

Two Democrats who could really tear at each other's throats were the liberal Benny Aragon of Albuquerque's South Valley and Finis Heidel, a conservative from Lea County. They were at opposite ends of the spectrum, but they were both good friends of mine when I was speaker of the House. In the late 1960s, David Norvell of Clovis was majority leader, and he would assemble the Democratic caucus and Finis and Benny would get to arguing over something like right-to-work, and all Norvell could do is call me in to mediate. I would try to stay out of it, but sometimes I couldn't. One time Benny Aragon said, "I'm tired of coming to all these Democratic caucus meetings and we're all agreed that we're against right-to-work, and then Finis Heidel goes and introduces it on the floor."

Then Finis would say, "If you think I'm ever going to quit introducing it, you're crazy."

I'd say, "Now guys, let's settle down a bit. Look, if I lived over there in Lovington where Finis Heidel lives, obviously I'd think right-to-work would be helpful." And I explained why. Then I said, "Now if I lived down in the South Valley where Benny Aragon lives, for sure I better not be for right-to-work, or I wouldn't be coming back. It wouldn't reflect the philosophy of my people. So I think we as Democrats have got to be broad enough and brave enough to realize that we're not ever going to do anything that everybody can agree to. We've just got to call this thing to a vote, and you'll vote however you want. We don't expect you to vote a Democratic line." And that's how it went. The bottom line between those two legislators in particular was that when Finis Heidel started to run for supreme court, his campaign manager in the South Valley was none other than Benny Aragon. I about fell over.

Achieving this kind of harmony is tough. People have to have confidence in you. They have to know you're not playing games with them, which I never did. It helped that in those days everyone truly wanted to get along for the benefit of New Mexico.

〰

As governor, I was able to push forward a few initiatives related to regulating land use and protecting the environment, which were issues I had felt strongly about ever since my early years on the Santa Fe County Commission. The legislature in 1971 created New Mexico's first environmental improvement board and charged it with assuring orderly development that did not unduly pollute the atmosphere. I named a balanced board that could work both with industry and the environmental lobby: Jim Snead of Santa Fe as chairman; Kenneth Brown as secretary; Howard Rothrock, a representative from the mining industry of southwestern New Mexico; Don Alberts, an environmentalist from Cedar Crest; and George Lambert, a land developer from Truth or Consequences who later moved to Albuquerque. This board began serving in 1971 but still had to be confirmed by the Senate in the 1972 session. Dick Heim and Larry Gordon were jointly appointed as paid staff, with Larry as the staff director.

However, one hitch developed with my appointees. Don Alberts had annoyed some of the legislators and ran into difficulty getting confirmed. The problem related to water rights and water policy more than to his job on the environmental improvement board. I told Don I thought it would be better if he withdrew and let me name someone else when confirmation came up in 1972. Don held fast and wanted his name sent down. Senator Mike Alarid, the chairman of the Senate rules committee, told me he didn't think they could get the votes to confirm Don. When I told Don this, he blasted me, and the headlines read, "KING PULLS AWAY FROM HIS APPOINTEE." That was misleading and didn't reflect the facts. I went ahead and sent Don's name down to the Senate, and things developed as I had predicted. When the Senate declined to confirm Don Alberts, I appointed Bill Atkins, who served continuously for the next eight years and became the board's senior member

In 1971, I asked for a moratorium on further development at the Four Corners electric power generating complex until the air pollution threats of those
huge coal-burning plants could be solved. The plants did not use the latest
in air purification technology and the pollution would drift from northwestern New Mexico all the way to Santa Fe and Albuquerque. It was so bad
you could identify the pollution in an infrared satellite image. I wanted assurances that pollution control measures would be installed to prevent the
dispersal of fine particles in the air, which were coming to be recognized as a
serious health hazard.

My request drew wide attention, of course. I felt I was right on those
issues, but that didn't keep some legislators from criticizing me as they addressed citizen groups to explain what had happened during the legislative
session. Often, they didn't represent the positions I'd taken or what actually
happened in the legislature with any accuracy at all. When I was asked about
the Four Corners moratorium, I pointed out that many other legislators,
Democrats and even Republicans, supported my positions, as did U.S. Senator Joseph Montoya. Even some of the conservative legislators from the
southeast corner of New Mexico who sometimes disagreed with me, like
George Blocker and Walker Bryan, were quite supportive on these issues.

In the spring of 1971, the state had the opportunity to buy the privately
held Vermejo Park, a vast, 485,000-acre tract of high mountain peaks, rolling meadows, clear streams, and dense forest in Colfax County along the
Colorado border west of Raton. I thought it would make an ideal state park
and recreational area. I asked Tourism Director Fabian Chávez to personally
make every attempt to buy Vermejo Park and brief the legislators and the
public on how the state would benefit from owning that beautiful parcel.
Fabian did a good job. He developed a slide show for his presentations, and
it got to where he was an even stronger advocate of purchasing Vermejo Park
than I was.

The property's heirs offered it to us for about $25 million. The trouble
was, about 25 years earlier they were going to let the state have it for about
$3 million, so now several legislators hated to pay the higher price. When I
realized we couldn't persuade the legislature to buy the entire area, I proposed we purchase at least 100,000 acres. That would have been a wise decision. It would have cost only about $6 million and the state could have eas-

ily maintained the land, but the legislature said no. In retrospect, I'm amazed that I was unable to get more support to buy such a beautiful piece of property as Vermejo Park. We now see its value has increased many times over that $25 million figure. In later years, Pennzoil Corporation acquired the land and donated a portion to the state. Then in 1996, Ted Turner and Jane Fonda bought the remaining tract and the adjacent Kaiser property, as well.

When I was in the House of Representatives, I had been the prime mover behind the passage of the greenbelt law, which taxed agricultural lands at their production value, rather than their speculative value, as long as they were used for agricultural purposes. Greenbelt laws were catching on as many states passed them. They were not merely agricultural-interest laws, but a means to maintain open space, which is always at a premium in the developing areas around urban centers. Back in the 1950s, I had also been concerned about the absentee landowners in rural areas who would not take care of their fields. They often came in and stripped the sod, breaking the land and farming it for a year or two, then going off and leaving it. You would see big clouds of dust billowing off that bare ground during the spring windy season. I felt that if an owner tilled his land and stripped the grass cover, there had to be some way of enforcing measures to control wind erosion. So I had backed and we had passed legislation allowing the state to do soil erosion-control work on such lands and assess the owner for the cost.

The soil-erosion and greenbelt laws were a step in the right direction, but as I traveled around the state, I was depressed to see certain types of property abuse. Junkyards were perhaps the most depressing. In 1959, I co-sponsored legislation to require approval for unsightly uses that would devalue adjacent lands. We wanted an overall plan, where urban lands would be urban and agricultural lands would remain agricultural. This way, we could provide some protection for those who had invested their money, so they would not find a trash dump right up next to their house, and we could help preserve farming and ranching against urban sprawl. We did get a bill passed that required junkyards owners to fence them off and clean them up a bit.

As governor, to address these issues and others I pushed a proposal in the 1972 legislature to create subdivision controls, which would give planning and zoning authority to counties and put the decisions about land-use planning close to the local people. I had already co-chaired a land use planning symposium in 1971 with former Governor Jack Campbell. The symposium was convened by the state land use planning council to inform the people of New Mexico about the need for enlightened planning. Participants included the state Game and Fish Department, the State Engineer's office, and other concerned agencies.

During a day away from the office, I looked over the pasture at the York Ranch, western New Mexico, 1972. Often I would sneak away from the capitol for a day of gathering cattle and other cowboy chores at the ranch. The York later became the center of a controversial land trade after Congress designated the property as wilderness. (Photograph by John Littlewood)

Many subdividers had come in and taken advantage of the near-absence of subdivision legislation in the state. In earlier years, some promoters couldn't even show clear title to much of the land they subdivided. I wanted legislation to require anyone selling subdivided land, first, to be able to give a clear title. Second, I wanted them to stipulate the availability of water and roads, and have the property marked on the ground so that it could easily be located. We put all this into bills, but though a number of them passed with amendments from one house to the other in 1972, no bill cleared both houses and came to me for signature. Finally, in the 1973 legislature we got subdivision controls through. The *Albuquerque Journal* said it was a far-reaching piece of legislation that gave the people of New Mexico local initiative in determining how land in their area could be developed. The law made counties responsible for land-use planning, which included establishing subdivision controls. Furthermore, it mandated that counties call open meetings to give citizens the opportunity to be heard on questions of land-use standards. I felt that the closer the controls were to the people, the better chance the regulations would have to succeed, and I had sought these powers for local governments ever since I had been a Santa Fe County commissioner.

In 1972, I was concerned about the harm strip mining caused to the environment, so I rallied broad support for a model strip mining act. I felt that if it was not profitable to care for the topsoil, replace it, and return the land to its natural state when mining, then it wasn't feasible to mine in the first place. From that viewpoint, I worked with the legislative leadership in both houses and in both parties to develop legislation that would be fair to the mining industry, the environmentalists, and the citizens of New Mexico. I named a task force on strip mining.

At that time, it was unheard of to include industry representatives on such a body, but I appointed members from the copper and coal industries. Even though they opposed our reforms at first, we got them to work with us and back our efforts. Everyone could see we weren't out to get any particular group, but were trying to do what was right. Giving people input into the decision-making process goes a long way toward creating goodwill. We widened our support by asking experienced people to draft the bill, including Dick Moolick, who at that time was working for Phelps Dodge in Silver

City and later became head of Phelps Dodge in New York. As a result of these collaborations, the environmentalists and the mine operators and owners all felt it was a fair bill. Based on that endorsement, we easily passed the New Mexico model strip mining act without the criticism that often accompanies attempts to tighten mining regulations. The law was later used as a model by other states.

Looking back on it now, I see how the Act has served us well as we have developed coal, copper, and uranium mining, all of which expanded rapidly during the early 1970s. Today we can tour mines around the Four Corners area and see stronger vegetation and better maintenance of the soil than before the land was stripped. The mining people had fussed and cried like a strangled lamb at first, but afterwards we went up there and they were as pleased and proud as I was when they saw the sheep out there grazing on that reclaimed land.

7

Smoothing the Ground

During my first term I had to straighten out a few kinks in government agencies and in the state personnel system, which I had wanted to reform since I was a county commissioner. I was able to get the Highway, Purchasing, and Motor Vehicles departments back on track, but I caught a lot of flak for placing my nephew, David King, in the State Planning Office and for appointing a Sandoval County politico to a job in the executive branch. I also found myself having to defend my old friend Judge James Scarborough in a controversy over his retirement.

When I became governor, I inherited a state Motor Vehicles Department that was in great disarray and had given nothing but trouble for as many years back as I could remember. It was plagued by long lines and inaccurate data. The department functioned so badly that former directors of the DMV used to set up offices across the street and make a good living just expediting the flow of paper for vehicle registrations through the department.

Toward the close of the 1971 legislative session, the Legislative Finance Committee asked for a special meeting with me and my staff, which I granted. They were concerned about the sorry state of affairs in the DMV. I told them we were beginning to reform the program and that I was naming Franklin Jones to oversee the changes we planned. Franklin always wanted plenty of time to carry out his assignments, and he said, "Now, it is going to take us at least a couple of years to get this reform accomplished. So don't get too impatient." Despite his plea, the press became more critical of the mess at DMV as my first year in office was winding down, and the cartoonists had a lot of fun jabbing at me for not improving the agency. I agreed the DMV was one state agency that I had not been able to modernize into a professional operation, and I began to devote a lot of time to it.

The public was well aware of the problems because nearly everyone has dealings with the department when registering a car or getting a driver's license, mostly. I felt that if we could make Motor Vehicles into a professional operation it would send a strong message to the public that we were no longer running state government by politics as usual. I resolved to make the department into a model of efficient operation. George Lovato of the State Planning Office appeared before the LFC and went over the numerous problems of the DMV. His testimony revealed him to be a man of tremendous ability who was well-informed on those particular issues. I realized he might be the one I needed to move over and clean up the department. Further talks with him confirmed my initial impression that he was experienced with that department and interested in trying to improve its operations.

So George went to work at DMV with Dave Urioste, the professional deputy director who I had moved up to director for a while earlier that year. Dave felt it would be better if he dropped back to being a professional manager under George, who would be the administrator working with the public and handling the public relations end of things. George Lovato proved an excellent choice to administer this problem department. With my support and encouragement and the help of many others in state government, we were able to turn the agency completely around. My first decision was to drop consideration of staggered vehicle registrations. Under that system, a vehicle's registrations would be due for renewal on a particular month instead of at the end of the year, as it currently was. George felt that attempting to put in the new system would create too much confusion at that point. I next agreed to name a committee to study the department, and to look at joining it with the Motor Transportation Department into one agency, which was eventually done under the Apodaca administration.

Our improvements to the Motor Vehicles Department began to show. Until then, many times in the final month of registration we had long lines of disgusted citizens waiting to get their papers. By the following year we had shortened those lines dramatically, through the use of mail-in registrations.

I also inherited a state purchasing system that was difficult to administer and had often shown favoritism based on partisan politics. I was determined to eliminate that influence. Caesar Sebastian had been administrative director of the state Purchasing Department in prior administrations and he agreed to serve as purchasing agent in my administration. I named a strong commission to work with Caesar to improve the department. They decided we needed a professional deputy purchasing agent who would bring the expertise the office needed and stay on from one administration to the next. They also wanted a personnel system for the office that could resist the pressures to favor bids unfairly. We all decided on Jim Montoya, the purchasing agent from Sparton Corporation in Albuquerque, and he agreed to come. Jim served four years with me, four years with the Apodaca administration, and then another four years in my second administration. He remained deputy purchasing agent until 1983. So we can say that our plans worked out as we had hoped for the purchasing system.

We also knew we needed to reorganize the Department of Finance and Administration, which included the functions of educational finance and the state Purchasing Department. Bob Kirkpatrick had experts available for this task, including Maxine Gerheart, who had great ability and had worked her way up to deputy secretary. We had large plans for reorganizing this department, and it went on for years.

We also needed to professionalize the Highway Department. Alfred Schwartzmann was a holdover member of the state Highway Commission from the Cargo administration, and I named him chairman of the commission. He ran the big meat packing plant in Albuquerque's South Valley. Other members included Bob Martin, who had served with me all the time I was in the legislature; Ken Tolls from Hobbs; Robert Armijo, a holdover appointee from San Miguel County; and Reginald Espinosa from Santa Fe, a holdover Republican member. Reggie worked constructively with us, despite being a member of the opposition party. When his term expired after two years, I named Jim Chaney in his place. Stretch Boles, the state Highway Engineer, was an outstanding professional who had worked up through the ranks. These individuals became a cooperative group and through them we improved roads all over New Mexico.

Our highways and roads were in bad shape. In addition to developing a stronger road-building program, we needed to widen many bridges, a fact driven home to us vividly by a tragic accident on the plains just east of Fort Sumner one night between Christmas and New Year's 1972. Nineteen members of the Woodland Baptist Church were killed on a narrow bridge when their bus collided with a livestock truck. Both vehicles sheared and all the riders were thrown forward. Admittedly, some error by the driver of the bus was a factor, and the bus was not of a substantial design. Nonetheless, with this tragedy fresh on everyone's minds, I directed the introduction of legislation to appropriate additional funds to widen bridges. The legislature passed the bill and all bridges below a certain width were widened.

We also bought a lot of our own highway equipment and were able to improve outlying roads that otherwise would have remained in poor condition. My view was that for secondary roads, the state can do its own maintenance, directly and less expensively than contractors can. Contracts often involve high costs, such as preparing and advertising for bids, letting the bids, surveying the needs and defining the structure of the road, awarding the bids, supervising the construction to see that the contractor lives up to the contract, and then monitoring the day-to-day operation of the road. The actual work is only a part of the cost of contracting road work, whereas having your own equipment lets you build the road for just those actual costs. In my years as governor, we built many miles of secondary roads, doing the work in a professional manner using state employees to operate our state-owned equipment.

᪲

New Mexico has a large and diverse Indian population. Tribes that call New Mexico home include the Navajos, with a large reservation in New Mexico and Arizona; 19 different pueblos; the Jicarilla Apache, who live in the northwest at Dulce; and the Mescalero Apache, who live in the mountains to the south near Ruidoso. In the late 1960s and early 1970s, the Indian people of New Mexico were becoming more interested in participating in state government. They had stayed away from it up till then, wanting to remain autonomous and to retain their own identify, but that was beginning to change during my first administration.

Benny Atencio, chairman of the All Indian Pueblo Council, felt that state government had not paid enough attention to the needs of the Indian people of New Mexico. Instead of coming to my office and trying to work out these problems, he issued a news release in 1971. I received it when I was in Clayton for the dedication of a recreational project. So I in turn gave my answer back through the news media. People took strong exception to my doing that, saying, "You shouldn't answer those kinds of allegations in the press." I told them, "That's the way I received them, so that's the way I returned them."

After that, though, I did call Benny and we worked out many of the problems that bothered him. We decided it would be wise to bring people together to discuss the plight of the Indian people in New Mexico, so I called the meeting in Santa Fe at the State Land Office auditorium. Those who attended openly discussed their feelings and their views of what state government needed to do for its Indian citizens. They wanted more involvement in decision making, more jobs for their people in government, and a liaison in the governor's office. In return, I pointed out the steps I felt were needed to assure that Indians were represented in state government, including participation in the political life of the state, positions on state boards and commissions, and employment. I noted the things I felt we could and could not do. The meeting resolved many of the problems, misunderstandings, and hard feelings that had developed. From that time on the relationship between Indian citizens and the state government improved markedly, and Benny and I became good friends.

I took these requests to heart and did what I could, naming Indians to state boards and commissions and establishing the Commission on Indian Affairs to give them a stronger voice at the highest levels of state government. Following my own convictions and working closely with the Indian people, I continued urging their leaders and other Indians to get involved in the political system and in state government. By 1972 they were becoming increasingly concerned that we didn't have nearly enough Indian employees in key positions in state government. This question became controversial, and I was trying to resolve it. I wanted the legislature to know that I was making a strong attempt to include the Indian people in state government.

I also worked on Indian range and livestock management with Dean Philip K. Lyendecker of the College of Agriculture at New Mexico State University. We called a conference and invited all the range and livestock people of the Indian tribes and pueblos. The Indian people have been herdsmen for centuries and many Indian leaders came to the Indian Range and Livestock Days program at New Mexico State. Our oldest son, Bill, participated in this program, presenting the facts of feedlot management and explaining what the feedlot operators looked for in cattle raising.

My oldest son, Bill, enjoyed the ranching life as much as I did. In addition to playing a crucial role on the ranch, Bill became one of my most trusted advisors and lobbyists to the legislature when I was governor. (Photograph by John Littlewood)

These were some of the ways I tried to bring the Indian people more into the mainstream of New Mexico life. The basic challenge, of course, was to increase the number of Indian state employees until they roughly reflected their percentage numbers of the state population. I think we succeeded at least in defining the way to involve the Indian people in state government and in supporting their interest in getting involved. I tried to be sensitive to their needs and desires, and to see that we looked at problems in state government from the Indian point of view, as well as from the white man's point of view.

∾

Ever since my first days on the Santa Fe County Commission, when I told the county workers that mere party affiliation wasn't enough to guarantee their continued employment, I struggled against the political machinery to professionalize the personnel system for public employees in New Mexico. In the legislature in the early 1960s, I had helped push through a merit system to replace the old spoils system. The merit system had been started in Governor Mechem's last term and gradually strengthened under succeeding governors. I believed we could attract much more qualified people into state government if they felt their jobs would be protected and they wouldn't be dropped at the whim of a politician on each change of administration. They needed that assurance, and adequate compensation, as well. We also needed to hire the best-qualified applicants, not simply those who had supported a particular candidate for office.

In my first years as governor, I picked two strong professionals to consolidate the gains made by earlier administrations in the area of personnel. I named Chuck Spath as state personnel director and asked Ray Powell to continue as chairman of the state personnel board, a position he had first assumed under Governor Jack Campbell. Chuck and Ray made a good team. Chuck was working in New Mexico for the U.S. Department of Energy, which loaned him to me to help update our personnel system. In my last term as governor, the Energy Department again loaned Chuck to us, this time to help us reform science education.

In the mid-1950s, Ray had come to New Mexico as one of the top personnel people at Sandia National Laboratories, a U.S. Department of Energy facility in Albuquerque. He also became involved with industrial development for the Albuquerque Chamber of Commerce. Ray shared my views on the need for a strong merit system to attract highly qualified people into state government. He also turned out to be a troubleshooter for me in several areas of state government not immediately related to personnel policies, including the correctional system and the state Mortgage Finance Authority, which helped first-time home buyers get loans. The press respected Ray. When he gave his views to the newspapers they were usually accepted. Together, Ray and Chuck were able to improve the personnel system to where we could attract able people to come and work in state government. They made the process of selecting qualified applicants more objective and made it harder to pick an incompetent person just for political reasons.

By the 1972 legislative session, our state personnel system was working well, but some politicians wanted to weaken the system for their own gain. In the 1972 session, hiring practices again aroused considerable debate, as some legislators tried to turn back the clock to the old days of political spoils. Representative Eddie López of Santa Fe County sponsored legislation to water down the strong personnel merit system. His bill would give job opportunities to many people with much lower qualifications than the standards we had set. Eddie and his co-sponsors were looking to place friends from their political organization in state jobs on the basis of political patronage, rather than proven ability.

The way the merit personnel system worked, applicants were screened through a testing procedure. The three top-scoring candidates' names were then sent to the department that had the vacancy. The employer could only pick from that list of three, but the López bill would have opened eligibility to all the candidates who passed the test, regardless of score, rather than just the top echelon. I was sure that approach would automatically turn away the best people from even considering employment in state government.

Ray Powell had developed figures that showed how the merit system had reduced the turnover of state employees from 96 percent when Governor Mechem took office his last term to about 15 percent during the first King administration. That was a normal turnover rate for any business or government employer. In hearings on the López bill, Ray went before the legislative committees and testified on the negative effects the bill would have on the personnel system, if it passed. Ray kept me informed on the progress of the bill and I said quite early that if it passed, I would veto it. My opposition to this bill drew quite a lot of publicity.

Despite our campaign against it, the House and Senate passed the López bill. Rather than sending it straight up to me, they waited until they were considering legislation that I wanted passed and they tried to use that as leverage for horse trading on the López bill. That kind of move might have worked under other governors, but I knew the needs of the state and I knew how the legislative system worked. All those years of studying the law books hadn't gone to waste on me. Still, even some of the experienced observers thought I had a problem. For instance, Wayne Scott, the dean of capitol reporters, wrote that I probably hadn't looked at all the bills that I had down in the legislature and that maybe I wouldn't be in a position to veto the personnel bill when it came up to me. But I felt that each piece of legislation should stand on its own, and if I had recommended a bill, we needed it. I didn't get involved in "you scratch my back and I'll scratch yours" to get something passed. I had many friends in both houses, on both sides of the aisle. I never had a day when I couldn't rally enough votes to pass a bill I felt was crucial. Besides, I was aware of a requirement in the state constitution that the legislators had overlooked: it says the progress of a bill that has passed both houses cannot be delayed. You can't harbor it. The bill must be sent up to the governor. At a social function one night, I pointed this out to Al Romero, chief clerk of the House. The next morning when I got to work the personnel bill was on my desk. I vetoed it and the veto stood. Ironically, many years later during my third administration Eddie López became one of my best supporters.

Nonetheless, political change doesn't come easy to New Mexico. In 1972, Joe Castellano and the Santa Fe County Central Democratic Committee passed a unanimous resolution that I declare all state agency directorships open and appoint more Democrats to those positions. I fired back that I had no intention of returning to the old spoils system. If anything, we were going to put more professional, nonpolitical people into key state jobs. I pointed out that those asking for the spoils did not control a majority of votes in the state, but only a fraction. The proof was that the majority of citizens had elected the Republican Pete Domenici as U.S. senator when he had run on more of a model government program than as a Republican, anyway.

I felt comfortable with my repudiation of that "unanimous" resolution because it had been clear to me that the citizens of New Mexico were demanding professional state government. I had campaigned for years on that principle, and I was gratified that the media backed me.

᪥

My first term was not without controversies over people. I got into quite a scrap with the Legislative Finance Committee and the news media over the State Planning Office and the role of my nephew, David King, in that agency.

The spark that set the issue on fire was one piece of inaccurate information, which often happens, but once those fires get to burning, they take on a life of their own.

I had brought David King into the state planning office in a $10,000-a-year job to help coordinate their programs involving the public, the municipalities, and the county governments. When the deputy state planning officer, Joe Castellano, decided to return to private law practice, I moved David up to fill that position. Keith Dotson, who had worked in my campaign, was the chief planning officer. Along about this same time, Keith got interested in the Four Corners Commission and wanted to work in that area, so it became obvious in 1972 that we were moving David in as chief planning officer.

The Legislative Finance Committee jumped all over this situation. They criticized moving David into the top planning job and threatened to dissolve the Planning Office. LFC staff director Marilyn Budke sent her chief analyst, John LaFaver, over to analyze the Planning Office. About that time, or maybe a little sooner—it depends who related the sequence of events— David and Keith offered John LaFaver a job at a slightly higher salary than he was earning over at the LFC. At that point, all hell broke loose. Somehow, the outstanding *Albuquerque Journal* reporter Wayne Scott heard that Keith Dotson was in line for a $5,000 pay increase, moving him from $16,000 to $21,000. That wasn't so. He was getting the same incremental percentage pay raise as everyone else, moving from $16,000 to $17,000. But Scott ran an editorial page article blasting the Planning Office and harping on this falsely reported $5,000 raise. It started a chain reaction. Every print, television, and radio news department picked up the story, saying we had a state agency filled with politically connected people who were getting huge salary increases, and it was questionable whether the agency even served a legitimate purpose. On top of all that, they criticized me for hiring David to run the agency, even though he was the only family member I ever brought in for a paid position in state government. I kept many cartoons about this issue in my newspaper scrapbooks from this period. In one, drawn by Mac McGinnis of the *Albuquerque Journal*, two cowboys are riding past a beat-up old horse, labeled "State Planning Office," One cowboy says, "I wonder what a poor old animal like that is doing on this high-class ranch?" The other nudges him and says, "Don't say that out loud. That's the governor's favorite horse."

The controversy kept building, which forced the people in the Planning Office to make several presentations to the LFC. This was the one time I appeared before a legislative committee as governor, describing in person the accomplishments we'd made in the Planning Office and also pointing out our efforts to improve the Motor Vehicles Department. I knew we were running an effective planning office and I asked that we finish out the year before making a complete presentation on it. The LFC approved, agreeing we had covered most of the business that we needed to cover during that legislative session. That whole controversy finally just wore itself out as we kept on doing things professionally and for the good of the people.

This episode illustrates the tremendous impact that a legislative committee with strong leadership and the news media can have on the executive branch. It's all part of the system of checks and balances, with the media serving as watchdog.

A good friend of mine suffered under intense scrutiny and criticism by the media in 1971, which caused me a great deal of concern before it was over. My friendship with District Judge James Scarborough of Santa Fe went back to 1954, when he was running for district judge. I was running my first race for county commission, and we campaigned together throughout Santa Fe County.

By my first year as governor, Judge Scarborough had served four full terms, about sixteen and a half years. He had always been re-elected. However, he had been disqualified much more than most other judges, and he got media attention when he expressed his concern about being disqualified so often. He also felt that the court system and the court administrator had been unfair to him by letting other judges take trips and excursions at the taxpayers' expense. He said that some judges had gone to Europe and elsewhere on judicial training programs.

Now Judge Scarborough told me he was thinking of stepping down, which I thought was a good idea. He added that in his more than sixteen years he had taken virtually no vacation, and had gone on none of these judicial training trips that the other judges had taken. As a personal friend, he told me that being a judge in northern New Mexico, he would benefit from a sabbatical to study Spanish at Cuernavaca, Mexico, and also to enlarge his knowledge of court procedure in Mexico at the same time. He didn't want a long sabbatical but he felt that he was entitled to $800 over two months. After that, he said, he would probably resign and stay another couple months on his own and continue to study Spanish. Then he would return to New Mexico and make the knowledge he had gained available to our court system, without any charge.

I agreed that Judge Scarborough had probably been disqualified more than he should have been. It was causing some strain on the court. We had two judges in that district then—Judge Scarborough and Lyle Teutsch, who was the presiding judge. Judge Teutsch needed more help and he felt, along with other judges in New Mexico, that it would be good if Judge Scarborough took his two months sabbatical and then retired, so I could appoint a younger judge to help Judge Teutsch.

The news media picked up on this plan and strongly opposed it, calling it a boondoggle and a waste of taxpayers' money. I went ahead anyhow and worked it out with the courts, and I said I thought it would be all right for him to go to Cuernavaca to study Spanish. So Judge Scarborough went off to Mexico and immediately the press got highly critical about it. At that time, Alice and I attended the National Governors' Association conference in Puerto Rico, where we got daily reports from my office in Santa Fe, saying the print and TV media were full of stories about Judge Scarborough's sabbatical. The media, which couldn't figure out how that trip would benefit the state, demanded that Judge Scarborough and I explain.

Flying back from Puerto Rico, we landed at Dallas, and Judge Scarborough just happened to be there, too. He had been in Cuernavaca about two weeks, where he had been contacted almost daily by the press. Upset about all the controversy, he was sorry that Judge Teutsch and I, among others, had caught so much adverse publicity, so he was coming home on the same flight we were from Dallas to Albuquerque. We visited on the plane.

"Governor," he said, "I never intended to cause anyone any embarrassment or create problems. I still feel I am entitled to this sabbatical, but if this is the feeling, then I'd better drop it. I cut the time short to come home, and I wanted to be there when you got back so we could see what the problem was."

Returning to New Mexico didn't stop the bad press. The Scarborough situation still made headlines almost daily. At one point, he said in exasperation, "If they're going to be that way about it, I *won't* resign."

"No, Judge Scarborough," I countered. "I don't think that would benefit any of us. Why don't you go ahead as you'd planned? And you can go back to Mexico." So he resigned, and I appointed Ed Felter as district judge in his place. I still felt that under the circumstances, Judge Scarborough was entitled to the $515 he'd already spent on his sabbatical, which was quite comparable to the money other judges spent on theirs. We tried to work it around to where he would be paid, but after a great confrontation between secretary of Finance and Administration Bob Kirkpatrick and Judge Scarborough, we all decided it wasn't worth the hassle. He pulled back and never did receive any reimbursement.

That entire episode took thousands of dollars of media time and attention, and nothing significant came of it, except that Judge Scarborough got one month of leave pay that he had more than accrued over the years. On the bright side, Judge Scarborough's son later followed in his footsteps, winning elections to district judge in the first judicial district, then to the supreme court. So things have a way of correcting themselves over time, regardless of the press coverage.

I also took a lot of flak over another person who I defended during my first administration, Reuben Miera. Reuben was a dedicated public official who had also happened to be active in politics as Democratic chairman of Sandoval County for some years. Then it got to the point in New Mexico where the public no longer found it acceptable for a county political chairman to serve in a high-paying state government position. With all the work I'd done to toss out political patronage from our personnel system, I probably had something to do with that change in attitude. Yet at the same time, I also made many friends through Democratic politics, and if they were qualified people I liked to put them in positions where they could contribute to our efforts.

Aware of the change in public perception, Reuben had relinquished the reins of the party and had begun to devote more of his time to being a public official. He had served as deputy secretary of state, but in 1972 he wanted to get out of that job and into the governor's administration, so I began to look around for a position he could fill in state government. Word soon leaked out that he wanted to become manager of the State Fair, which wasn't true. Rumors were also floating around that Finlay MacGillivray was going to retire from that job soon—and that turned out to be untrue. Anyhow, I did think Reuben could be useful at the Fair, so I threw out his name as a trial balloon. It was shot down pretty quick. Many editorials and news stories and considerable TV and radio time were devoted to Reuben Miera and how people didn't think the State Fair was a proper place for someone with his background.

Wherever Reuben went, the press was sure to follow, scrutinizing the state agencies we were considering for him. I finally decided we were taking too much of a beating with Reuben just floating around. I called Roy Davidson, the state banking commissioner and a troubleshooter for me, and Chuck Spath, director of state personnel. I asked them to look over the positions in state government that were exempt from the personnel system.

"Let's find a place where Reuben can fit and do a good job, and we'll go ahead and place him there," I told them.

Roy and Chuck came back with about six vacant exempt positions where we might use Reuben's abilities. I decided that the best place would be as assistant labor commissioner to Ricky Montoya, so I called in Ricky and told him I found an excellent assistant for him and for the commission.

"Oh, I don't know," Ricky said. "Reuben would probably fit better somewhere else." He also said that he didn't particularly need an assistant and that he thought it would be better to forego this proposed appointment.

By now I had gone through too much adverse publicity with Reuben and I felt this wasn't fair to him or me, either one. We had to go ahead and place him somewhere that he could get to work and apply his abilities. So I insisted that Ricky accept Reuben.

"Well, Ricky," I said, "you know I gave Reuben these six choices of positions," although Reuben and I really hadn't discussed it at this point, "and of all the six of those, he looked at you as the labor commissioner and he chose your division, to go in under you."

Ricky Montoya sat there for just a second, then said, "Well, that son of a gun!"

So we sent Reuben over to him, and it worked out well, as I thought it would. He and Ricky became good friends and Reuben did a tremendous job as deputy labor commissioner. When Jerry Apodaca succeeded me as governor he named Reuben director of the Motor Transportation Division, which had been created under the Apodaca reorganization of state government. That was a job Reuben had always wanted, because he had held the port-of-entries job under Governor Campbell and had done well at it. When I became governor again in 1979, I kept Reuben as secretary of the Transportation Department.

It sometimes took the media a while to learn that an appointee may prove to be a top public servant despite having a political background. It was up to me, in making that appointment, to know ahead of time that Reuben would meet that standard, and to defend his appointment. Then it was up to Reuben to do a good job, and his subsequent years of outstanding public service proved he was a worthy choice.

≋

1971 was an eventful year. It began in January with record cold, when the temperature in Santa Fe seldom rose above zero. That cold spell was followed almost immediately by a series of forest fires that flared up because we had seen little moisture in about a year, so we had drought conditions. The fires started burning in the closing days of the legislature, and on April 14 I released badly needed emergency funds for fighting these blazes. Then in June a human catastrophe threatened Albuquerque: riots erupted. Suddenly I faced another emergency that absorbed a great deal of my time and effort. This was during the Vietnam War, which of course was a divisive issue and stirred up all kinds of unrest across the country.

In Albuquerque, a take-over group assembled in Roosevelt Park, part way between the University of New Mexico and downtown, then marched out on a wave of destruction, burning several buildings and trashing businesses. I alerted the National Guard and they moved in on the Albuquerque riots on June 14th and 15th. Soon 283 rioters were arrested and put in jail, and we quickly brought that situation under control. Then on June 17th, riots broke out in Santa Fe as social upheaval boiled over in the capital city. The federal building was bombed and other bombs were planted. Mayor George Gonzales came in to confer with me. "Look, governor," he said, "you go ahead and coordinate whatever we need to do in Santa Fe. Don't take the time to check with me. Just say you did and that we agreed to take immediate action to prevent loss of life and property."

Advocates of all kinds of causes were attracted to the riots, and many who were disaffected or had complaints tried to piggyback on these violent rampages, moving in and demanding this or that be changed in the direction they wanted. We reacted quickly to the situation, but I still spent a lot of time resolving the problems that led to the riots and trying to prevent them in the future. I appointed a blue ribbon riot study committee of 13 citizens representing a cross-section of New Mexico, and I named my old friend Judge David Carmody as chairman. Two of my appointments proved controversial: Chief Don Byrd of the Albuquerque Police Department and Chief Martin Vigil of the State Police. But Martin immediately declined the appointment, which he felt would lead to problems.

The riot probe committee itself became highly controversial during the latter half of June, after the riots. They tried to meet several times, and by enlarging the committee I attempted to involve all the different groups that felt they should be represented. Each time we tried to meet, something would come up. I still marvel at how quickly riots polarize a community when people with different causes jump in to demand immediate attention. The committee was intended to work on resolving the problems of the riots and healing the divisions they caused, but the committee itself kept getting in the way. Working without the committee, we had pretty well addressed many of the complaints that had provoked the unrest. Now we were having more difficulty with the riot committee than we had with the issues that sparked the riots in the first place.

One day Judge Carmody came in and said, "I think we should just drop this committee. I don't think it's doing what you and I hoped it would." With all the history that Judge Carmody and I shared—from his days as a friend of my dad all the way through his work as my legal counsel on the constitutional convention—I knew that he was interested in my success as governor, so I valued his opinion.

"Bruce," he said, "I think the best thing would be for me to announce that I'm resigning as chairman of the riot study committee. Then when they rush in and say, 'Judge Carmody resigned,' you say, 'Okay, I'm going to dissolve the whole riot commission.'" We did it that way, and it worked out well. Although we took a little flak in the media for a day or two, it died down. We went on healing the divisions that had developed in the riots and strengthening our ability to prevent such violent unrest in the future through stronger law enforcement. At least as important as that, however, was giving all citizens the opportunity to air their complaints all the way up to my level and convincing them that they didn't have to act so radical to be heard.

Law and order, and crimes and their punishment seem always to be at the center of political debate. In New Mexico, as in so many states, we have had continual problems with our prison system—we still see it in the headlines constantly—and every governor faces prison-related challenges, including me. In 1980 one of the most horrifying prison riots in the United States fell in my lap, but the correctional system was troubled well before I came to office the first time. I knew we needed stability in the system, along with a better pay scale and a better training program for corrections workers. When I campaigned for governor in 1970, part of my platform was to establish a state correctional board. The crime and delinquents committee had been studying corrections needs in detail. The members included good friends of mine. We all knew we needed to do a better job with our prisons, and we got legislation passed creating the correctional board to oversee the system.

On May 1, 1971, we had a visit from a national corrections consultant who had the job of studying prison systems throughout the country. He had toured our penal facilities in 1969. On this trip in 1971 he found vast improvement, most notably in management. That was gratifying, because I had come to have great confidence in Howard Leach, my secretary of Corrections, and Felix Rodriguez, the warden of the penitentiary. I did have to strongly suggest to the new correctional board that we maintain Leach in that position. They reappointed him by a 4-3 vote, which proved an excellent decision.

On the prison tour with the consultant I found things in good shape, on the surface. But I knew we needed to look at the training program, the rehabilitation program, and many other background needs. The penitentiary was overcrowded and inmate strikes from time to time kept us busy maintaining order. We tried some new things. New Mexico was one of the first states to develop an educational system that provides for teaching college classes in prisons. Despite this and other improvements, in the first week of October 1971 about half of the 573 inmates at the state penitentiary went on strike, refusing to work. Their grievances included demands for a new parole board and improvements in health care, food, pay, and visitor accommodations.

Howard Leach, Felix Rodriguez, and I tried to work with the inmates. I didn't think we could justify changes to the parole board, except as vacancies occurred normally. We did try to improve medical and dental care. Better pay for inmates required legislative action, and the legislators were conservative about paying prisoners. They also skimped on appropriations for food and visitors' accommodations, and I repeatedly had to insist on improvements in these areas. Nonetheless, we made substantial progress during the next few years.

Corrections was an area that Alice got involved in early on. She knew that prisons had a social dimension beyond the realm of law-and-order. The first week of October 1971, Alice and I were going to Raton and decided to leave a couple of hours early so we could stop at the Springer Boys School to see how things were going at that correctional facility. We dropped in and chatted with some of the boys. I could tell they were interested in returning to society as good citizens. Though they were eager to talk about the food and other mundane topics, we found them much more reluctant to start a dialogue about the work load, the supervision, and things of that nature. I didn't try too hard to draw them out. Alice lagged behind to visit and the boys, no doubt remembering their own kind mothers, talked more freely with her about their circumstances.

At Springer and at the girls school in Albuquerque, the administration and the inmates soon learned that Alice was interested in improving conditions and ensuring they had a good program. When they had needs, they discovered she was the first to rally around them. In return, she wanted them to run a professional operation. When we got home from such visits, we'd compare notes and Alice would have secured a much better feel for the needs and opportunities than I did.

On January 6, 1972, I received a report from a Santa Fe grand jury that had looked at our penal institutions as part of its general duties. They found that the penitentiary needed updating, the guards needed more training programs, and we needed to increase the patrols. I was pleased they had found that Corrections Secretary Leach and Warden Rodriguez were capable and were doing a good job.

An April 6 *Albuquerque Journal* editorial commented on the grand jury findings, saying that the Corrections Commission and employees were doing a competent job. They pointed out that despite the change of administration after Governor Cargo, I had not suffered the heavy turnover in staff that had sometimes hit Corrections in the past. On February 17, the *Albuquerque Tribune* similarly praised Leach, Rodriguez, and Maurice Sanchez as the chairman of the Corrections Commission. They noted that former Corrections Secretary John Salazar had worked one 30-day period in that position and immediately afterward, Governor Cargo had ordered the State Police to bar Salazar from entering the state penitentiary. He went around blasting my administration's actions regarding the prisons, but the *Tribune* wrote that Salazar was in no position to make such statements or to influence the correctional system. I felt the same way, and I made it public that we were asking John Salazar not to undermine the hard work we were doing to improve the correctional system. We had realized that he was not an expert on prison operations and didn't have any positive contributions to the system. In my second administration, when we had the prison riots, Salazar tried to get revenge by going on national television and saying that he knew there were many inequities in corrections here. He represented himself to national television news reporters as a former secretary of Corrections in New Mexico. The reality was that he held that position for only a brief time and left under less than favorable circumstances.

We also took positive action on law enforcement during my first administration. In the 1972 session we resolved a long-standing problem of police jurisdiction in the "checkerboard" area of western New Mexico, just east of the Navajo reservation. In this area, alternate sections of land are owned by different entities: the federal government, the state, the Navajo tribe, and private citizens. There were constant disputes over police jurisdiction and a great deal of lawlessness as people took advantage of that situation.

Representative Leo Watchman and Senator Tom Lee, both Navajos, and State Police Chief Martin Vigil worked out an agreement for Navajo police officers to go through the same training as our State Police. Then we could give them State Police commissions—thus they would have jurisdiction on nontribal lands. That created what could have been a potentially sticky situation, where the Navajo police would operate under two authorities, but it worked out very well, thanks to Chief Vigil on the state government side.

Martin Vigil served the longest of anyone in the history of the state as chief of the State Police. He served under Governor Cargo, then under me in my first term, then under Governor Apodaca, then again under me. Any governor needs a strong State Police chief, and Martin filled that requirement for me. He was a good administrator and he kept the State Police operating on a nonpartisan basis. He worked well with other law enforcement agencies and he demanded that the State Police deal with everyone even-handedly. In my first days as governor in 1971, he was a tremendous help to me as I dealt with the winter emergency. I saw right away the benefits of having someone with so much experience and wisdom in that position, so I didn't replace him with my own appointment, which I could have done.

Chief Vigil was always concerned with the individual officer, and he worked to get them good equipment, adequate protection, and the best training. To that end he pushed to establish the New Mexico Law Enforcement Academy during Governor Cargo's administration. At the time, I was speaker of the House. It was a short 30-day session, when the legislature can only consider bills proposed by the governor. I had to lean heavily on Governor Cargo to get him to send down the academy bill. It carried an appropriation of around $3 million for construction of the academy buildings. Up to that time, the State Police had leased space at the Glorieta Baptist Assembly, some 20 miles east of Santa Fe in the mountains. Because the police could only lease the space in the winter, they were able to train only one class a year, and the facilities really weren't adequate. Since we built the academy, we have had far better training for State Police officers and others in law enforcement from throughout the state, as well.

≋

In 1972, the state Racing Commission began to demand more of my time and attention. This group had oversight responsibility for horse racing in New Mexico. A chief concern was that organized crime would work its way into the state through the tracks. The owners of Ruidoso Downs race track faced bankruptcy when a California bank took Chapter 9 proceedings. After taking over the bank, the federal reserve board found the note from Ruidoso Downs in the bank's portfolio. The federal reserve board was concerned that we had a lot of problems in the racing industry at all the New

Mexico tracks, but particularly at Ruidoso. About the same time, a large racing firm, Kodiak, worked out an agreement with the California bank to take over the loans and buy Ruidoso Downs and Sunland Track near El Paso, which were jointly owned. Kodiak was run by the Alisio family in California.

The Racing Commission, the attorney general, and others made extensive inquiries into the background of the investors and owners of the Kodiak firm. This transaction stirred up a great deal of press comment and concern on my part and on the part of the Racing Commission. Al Rosa, who was related to the Alisios, would be in charge of these tracks, and he was one of the largest shareholders in Kodiak. On the surface, at least, he had a good record. The Racing Commission approved the deal, with many reservations. I had reservations, too, but I still thought the Commission was moving in the right direction. It proved to be a good decision, and Kodiak did build up Ruidoso Downs and Sunland Park. Later in my administration, a group of stockholders bought the two tracks from Kodiak.

As a result of my concerns around the Kodiak deal and its possible effects on horse racing, I submitted a package of new laws in 1973 to strengthen the Racing Commission's position. We wanted to enhance its authority and maintain surveillance over racing practices in the state. I insisted these laws be enacted. We had strong members on the Commission helping push the legislation through. Chairman Drew Cloud was always on hand to testify before the legislature and commission member George Maloof, one of New Mexico's leading business men, testified many times for the proposed legislation, as well. We also had strong support from the press. Bill Hume of the *Albuquerque Journal* was a close observer of trends in organized crime in New Mexico. He wrote that we had watched the racing industry, seen the need for more regulation and oversight, and acted to strengthen the Commission. Backing like that from the press really helped us get this legislation through, and it did pass.

8

Keeping the Plow Straight

A few factors, including sound fiscal management and inflation, combined to make state finances a bright spot during my first administration in the early 1970s. With revenues exceeding expenditures in the state budget, we were able to meet several needs that otherwise would have gone unaddressed. For the Democratic party, however, that period wasn't so rosy. We almost tore ourselves up in the 1972 election at a time when a historically Democratic U.S. Senate seat was up for grabs. Even though I wasn't running for office that year, I got involved by trying to keep our party on track. Another challenge came along when reapportioning the legislature once again reared its ugly head. The 1970 census had shown both an increase in state population and a continuation in the trend of rural population decline. Every time you redraw the legislative district lines, you alter the power structure of the legislature. Someone is going to win and someone is going to lose. I had seen it happen when I was speaker of the House, and I would be involved again in the 1980s, when we also gained a new Congressional seat.

~~~

From my experience as an agricultural businessman, I guess I always had a pretty good head for numbers and finance. During the legislative session in 1971, I would meet just about every morning with the Department of Finance people and Franklin Jones to go over how the dollar package was shaping up for general appropriations, along with the other special projects that had been proposed. I didn't force my ideas on that group, but I liked to show them the direction of my thinking.

One morning, Franklin was covering several blackboards with his figures when I came in with my cup of coffee. I let him go on about fifteen minutes, then I started thinking about all the other things I had to do that morning. I could see he was far from through. So I pulled out a torn slip of paper from my pocket—I had made some notes and figures for the budget the day before—and I said, "Well, gentlemen, this is what I was thinking we need to have for general appropriations, and this is what I was thinking about for capital improvements." It was almost to the dollar what they had up on all those chalkboards. "Why don't you look at that, and you fellows tell me what you think about my idea." It usually ended up working out that way.

New Mexico state government has dealt with both extremes when it comes to finances. We've had years of surplus and years of shortfall when we had to scramble to cover our expenses, since the state cannot by law operate under deficit spending. 1971 began a period when revenue growth outstripped our expectations, which is not the usual condition of state finances. Going into the 1972 legislative session, we had $20 million over and above our revenue estimates for the fiscal year, which ends on June 30.

Though inflation had helped us to accumulate this surplus, the primary reason was that in the preceding two years we had developed a highly effective state Bureau of Revenue in place of what had been a pretty inefficient operation. My predecessor, Governor Cargo, had brought in Franklin Jones to be commissioner of revenue. Franklin revamped the bureau and greatly improved the collection of state revenues. I saw no need to make changes when the bureau was coming along so well and we were able to keep Franklin in that position through the 1972 legislative session. Then he returned to his private law practice.

The question was what to do with this windfall. Some politicians recommended a tax reduction, but I pointed out that we had many unmet needs in New Mexico and I felt we should use the $20 million for nonrecurring expenditures that would help meet them. Those needs included developing better programs for children and youth—both for the gifted and for those in trouble—and strengthening our public education system. Now we had money available to enrich these programs. And working with the legislature, we did succeed in using the revenue surplus to meet such needs, mostly through capital outlays and nonrecurring expenditures.

In 1972, we had a brainstorm to remedy a discriminatory aspect of our tax structure. My administration designed the low-income tax rebate to give fair treatment under our gross-receipts tax, or "sales tax." In New Mexico, that tax is quite comprehensive: it applies to groceries and other necessities of life, as well as to most other goods and services. Although the gross receipts tax was a valuable source of revenue to the state, it was falling unfairly on low-income residents. We were searching for a way to straighten out this inequity without weakening the overall tax structure.

The solution emerged through the leadership of Franklin Jones, Representative Gene Cinelli of Bernalillo County, University of New Mexico economics professor Gerald Boyle, and others. They first presented their idea during the 1971 legislature in a bill to create a "negative income tax." That turned out to be a tough concept for many people to master and the issue carried over to the 1972 legislative session. During the interim, we took great pains to inform the citizens why poor people were entitled to a rebate from the state, even if they hadn't paid any income tax at all. They *had* been paying more sales taxes in proportion to their incomes than any other group. It hit them harder. So we proposed refunding the money to them. In 1972, we changed terminology and called it a "low-income tax rebate," or tax credit, and this time the legislature passed the bill.

We made the tax rebate available to people with incomes below the poverty level, who typically didn't have to file a state income tax return. However, to get the rebate they had to file a state return showing that their income was low enough to qualify. One question on everyone's minds was whether the low-income residents of the state would send in the paper work to claim their share. I was afraid many of them wouldn't, but we had almost 100 percent filing as soon as people realized that by simply filing their return they would get a check in the mail.

In the first year, the state passed back about $3.5 million. I still feel it was well spent. Then we found we had additional monies available and decided that those over 65 who qualified would get a double rebate, which amounted to $80. For the poor in 1972, that was a significant sum—maybe a month's worth of groceries, or more. So when people came to New Mexico and professed to be shocked that our gross receipts tax applied to the absolute necessities—food, medical services, drugs, hospital care, and so on across the board—they hadn't really understood the situation. Far from having a cruel and heartless tax structure, the low-income rebate gave us a model system that I believe was the first of its kind in the nation.

Going into the 1973 legislative session, we again had a surplus. Despite record levels of state spending and the tax rebate, we still had $42 million above appropriations that we could spend, principally to meet capital outlay needs of the state. We used some of that money for parks and recreational areas. I was aware that residents of the Albuquerque South Valley—who had strongly supported me—did not have adequate recreational facilities, so I sought a one-time appropriation of about $300,000 for recreational purposes in those areas. It seemed to me the best way to use those funds was to improve some of the school grounds. I worked with the Albuquerque school board to obtain the land, and the city parks department agreed to maintain the recreational equipment paid for by the state appropriation. This was a first in the United States, for a state to fund such improvements in cooperation with the public schools.

By late 1973, the state had collected $30 million more than we had at the same time in the previous year, so once again the legislature in 1974 would need to decide how to spend the surplus. I felt that it should be used for nonrecurring needs again or a one-time tax rebate for all citizens. Since the budget we were setting in the 1974 legislature would cover the first half of 1975, when the fiscal year ended on June 30, I knew my successor in the governor's office would be saddled with whatever we decided. I wanted to leave the state in good financial condition, which I did, with a $100 million surplus.

During the early 1970s, oil and gas royalties were pouring large amounts of money into the severance tax permanent fund, which my administration set up by state statute. The idea was that our nonrenewable natural resources, such as coal, uranium, and natural gas, were being depleted through extraction, primarily mining. The fund taxed and set aside a portion of the value of these resources, then the earnings from the trust fund would be available to future generations as state revenues. That fund has grown from the initial

$14 million to more than $3 billion today.

The state also maintained a permanent fund that was established by the state constitution. This fund consisted of monies collected from the sale of state lands. Altogether, in 1972 we had some $600 million in the permanent funds and we needed a highly professional financial management staff free of political motivations to supervise them. Robert Mead had been the state investment officer for eight years when I became governor. He was then 78 years old and wanted to retire. Mead felt that his understudy, Robert Short, had acquired the experience to become the investment officer. I agreed, knowing Short's professional abilities, so I appointed him. I also tried to appoint a strong management team to the investment council commission, which had oversight over the funds. Bob Kirkpatrick was one of my appointees and he served for some ten years as a council member. In this way we maintained continuity of the funds during my term, but Robert Short was soon released after I left office.

At the start of my second administration in 1979, these funds had reached about $2.3 billion. As always, I was concerned that we keep politics out of the management of the funds, which by 1983 were contributing 24 percent of the money needed for the ongoing operations of state government. So this time I named a bipartisan committee to conduct a nationwide search for a professional manager. They recommended Hershell Pittinger, who I appointed. However, six months after my term ended the Anaya administration terminated Pittinger, interrupting the continuity I had hoped to set in place.

≋

The 1972 political campaign demanded much of my attention, even though I wasn't a candidate. It was a presidential election year, but my term still had another two years to go. The presidential race greatly influenced our major contests in New Mexico, while the lack of a governor's race deprived the other races of the strong interest it always generated.

U.S. Senator Clinton Anderson had decided to retire, and many people in both parties were interested in succeeding him. Several strong candidates filed in the Democratic primary for his seat. They included former congressman Tom Morris, who had long been discussed as heir apparent to Senator

Anderson, and former legislator Jack Daniels, who run for governor in the 1970 primary. In addition, Lieutenant Governor Roberto Mondragon, Attorney General Dave Norvell, and State Treasurer Jess Kornegay all filed for the Senate seat.

The press noted that all of the four-year elected state officials had filed for the Senate, except the land commissioner, the secretary of state, and the governor. The candidates who were public officials were disrupting state government by not tending the store, and their offices had become campaign headquarters. This provoked much criticism of the four-year term, partly because it was new and still on trial. Today no one advocates going back to two-year terms, but it was under constant discussion during much of my first administration. As president of the constitutional convention in 1969, I had proposed the four-year term and I later found myself as the first four-year governor after the proposal was passed by voters as a constitutional amendment in 1970. Since I had not merely supported the four-year term but was practically its father, I was quite concerned about the poor impression created by the many state officials running for higher office that year. It seemed like they felt they didn't have to be as responsive to the public while they were running for the Senate.

I had to challenge this situation, so I said that if elected state officials wanted to be candidates for other offices, they should resign. Of course, I knew they wouldn't, so I further suggested they should at least take leaves of absence and remove themselves from the state payroll. This went over like a lead balloon with the other state officials, and I wasn't held in as high esteem as I like to be by my fellow office holders for a few days around election time. However, my position did get excellent press and editorial coverage. Even more important, I got strong public support from citizens all over the state, who called and wrote to let me know they shared my views on this issue. After my statement, campaign activity at least moved out of the state offices to some degree, because the candidates were getting a little self-conscious. They had become aware of how strongly the public felt they should resign their offices if they wanted to be candidates.

During late spring of 1972, another issue stirred up the political process. In those days, state law established high filing fees for the major offices in an attempt to limit political contests to serious candidates. The filing fee for the U.S. House and Senate seats was set at $2,500, determined as a percentage of the first year's salary. This fee was challenged in 1972 and the courts struck it down hardly more than a week before the filing date. The courts further ruled that any filing fee whatsoever was unconstitutional and discriminatory because it would prevent people who could not pay the fee from seeking office.

That ruling created havoc among the candidates, the legislature, myself, and all others concerned. Originally, we had about ten announced candidates for the U.S. Senate seat, and these included all the serious, strong contenders, but after the court ruling a herd of new candidates charged onto the scene. I worried we might have a stampede of 50 or 60 by the filing deadline and when the day came we did have 26 people seeking that one seat. A larger number also filed for the congressional seats.

Right after the court ruling, I stated we would probably need a special session to find some other way of controlling the number of candidates. That idea didn't appeal to the legislative leadership, who decided to go ahead with the election. All this created chaos for the secretary of state in preparing the ballot. Since there wasn't any other way for us to hold the election when the courts ruled our system was unconstitutional so close to election day, we had to press on.

I still contend that any serious candidate needs at least $75,000 on hand to *be* a serious candidate. Obviously the filing fee was only a small fraction of that amount. After the election we sought new ways to exclude frivolous candidates. I named a bipartisan committee, which included influential Republicans, Democrats, and public members, and asked them to make proposals. They worked with the legislative leadership and the secretary of state to come up with the requirements for petitions and the primary nominating system, which are still in effect today.

The 1972 presidential campaign helped polarize our Democratic primary election, particularly the nomination for U.S. Senate, and contributed to the splintering of our party. A great deal of money flowed into the state to finance the presidential races, and much of that was spent propping up various candidates for the Senate seat. Who got the money depended on whether it came from a liberal or conservative presidential candidate. The Senate primary campaign began to revolve around the conservative Jack Daniels and the liberal David Norvell and Bob Mondragon. The Daniels wing aligned itself with the more conservative presidential candidates like Senator Scoop Jackson, while the Norvell/Mondragon groups gravitated toward Senator George McGovern at the other end of the spectrum.

Jack Daniels won the primary, and soon thereafter McGovern won the Democratic nomination for president. Seeing dark clouds developing around this liberal/conservative split in our party, I made a strong point that it was going to be very difficult for us in New Mexico to run with Senator McGovern heading the ticket, given his liberal platform, then going on down the ballot immediately to the Senate contest, where we had a conservative candidate, with no race for governor in between to bring the ticket back toward the center. Since it was the first election after we started the four-year governor's term, the absence of a governor's race was upsetting the structure of elections in New Mexico.

As if all this wasn't enough adversity, yet another serious problem developed for the Democrats around the time of the primary election. Bernalillo County Democratic Chairman Rudy Ortiz ran against former Senator Anderson for Democratic national committeeman, and won. Senator Anderson had operated on a broad base, much as I did, seeking the respect and confidence of as many of the citizens of New Mexico as possible. With Senator Anderson retiring and stepping completely out of the political scene after his defeat for national committeeman, and with the much more liberal faction taking over, we were in disarray. The liberals coming on the scene were strong in the Albuquerque area and weak elsewhere in the state. They were too liberal, and the McGovern faction added to that influence, all of which spawned grave problems as we were unable to maintain a balance in the Democratic party in New Mexico that year.

This situation also caused trouble for me with my administrative assistant, Toney Anaya, who later succeeded me as governor in 1983. I needed an administrative assistant beholden only to me, but Toney had been working for the inner group of Rudy Ortiz's wing of the party. Toney's brother, Mike—who was my neighbor at Mike's Friendly Store in Moriarty—was state Democratic chairman. I had persuaded him in 1971 to take that position, and he served well by building harmony among the Democrats and trying to keep the various factions of the party from being too critical of me. My aim was to bring all the people of New Mexico into the mainstream of state government. Mike agreed with this philosophy, and tried to carry it out. But Toney had provided a great deal of help to Santa Fe County Democratic chairman Joe Castellano, who had been successful in garnering the most votes for Rudy Ortiz against Senator Anderson for national committeeman. My loyalties were with Senator Anderson, and this group worked hard to keep him from being our national committeeman.

When the race for committeeman had been developing, I was first at the National Governors' Association conference in Houston, then on vacation in Arkansas, so I was out-of-state for several days at a crucial time. I was relying on Senator Anderson's staff to carry the ball for him, and frankly they didn't do a good job. The impression was going around that my office was openly opposing the Senator because of Toney's support for Rudy Ortiz, which made it difficult for Anderson's staff. With all this going on along with many other things, Toney Anaya and I agreed to part company after the elections. The press asked me if Toney was leaving over an issue at the penitentiary, and I said no, it was over the Ortiz-Anderson contest.

While the Democratic party was tearing itself up, the only consolations I could see were that the Republicans—and my old adversary Dave Cargo— had their own problems. The Republicans fought a hard and bitter primary for the Senate nomination. The leading contenders were Albuquerque politician Pete Domenici, Cargo, and former Lieutenant Governor E. Lee Francis. Cargo, who was much more liberal than Pete Domenici, ran a no-holds-barred campaign, making off-the-cuff remarks about Domenici's problems as chairman of the Albuquerque city commission. He implied that the more influential, wealthier Republicans had much greater influence with Domenici than the average citizens of New Mexico did.

Cargo lost the Republican primary to Domenici. Now Cargo had twice sought to become the Republican nominee for U.S. Senate, and he saw that his future as an elected official and political figure in New Mexico wasn't so rosy. He had been tempted to change his registration to Democrat, but he and I were directly opposed and I was the leader of the Democratic party. He could see that wouldn't work out well, so on August 10th, "Lonesome Dave" Cargo packed up his belongings and moved with his wife and children to Oregon. His departure warmed my heart because he had been a strong critic of mine in the nearly two years I had been governor. He didn't leave without taking several parting shots at me, saying things were not going well the way I was running state government. He also made a few choice remarks about Democrats in general and offered predictions about what would happen to them, and to me as governor, none of which came true.

The primary elections left behind an aftermath of bruised egos and wounded feelings. Labor had strongly supported Dave Norvell for the Senate nomination, and other liberal elements had supported Lieutenant Governor Mondragon. Immediately after the primary we needed to somehow pull together all those different Democratic interests behind Jack Daniels for Senate. That was going to be a difficult task, at best.

The situation was overshadowed by the concern and unhappiness of Senator Anderson, and even more by the unhappiness of his supporters. Many of them felt the Democratic party at the state level had fallen under the control of a small group of liberals, and they chose to support Pete Domenici in the general election. Likewise, the liberals had lost their chosen ones in the primary, the candidates they would have dearly loved to see in the U.S. Senate. Throughout the campaign, I pointed out that we Democrats were going to have to get behind our nominees or we were going to lose our Senate seat for the first time since the Great Depression. We were undergoing tremendous change and our party was in great turmoil. Under these conditions the Democrats didn't have a good incentive in the general election, which developed just as I had feared. In retrospect I am happy that I didn't have to appear on the ticket that year, because it would have been very difficult for a candidate for governor to turn around enough votes to carry the election for the Democrats that fall, when Richard Nixon ran away with it in New Mexico. Pete Domenici won the Senate seat, which he has held onto for more than 25 years. His victory alone caused tremendous rethinking and reshuffling in the Democratic party.

I felt then, and I still do, that if the Democratic party had named Senator Anderson as national committeeman, he would have maintained his firm control over the party and we would have been victorious in the general election in New Mexico. We would not have carried the state for McGovern, but we might have elected Jack Daniels to the Senate.

Two years later, the Ortiz faction backed Jerry Apodaca for governor in the 1974 primary, and they were able to pull together enough of the Democratic party to elect Jerry over Republican Joe Skeen. His election confirmed the change of direction in the party at that time. I think history shows that the pendulum swung then from middle of the road clear over to the more liberal element of the Democratic party. But in 1972 I continued to preach the need to move the Democratic party back toward the center. There was a great deal of discussion about whether that could happen, or whether the party should just go ahead and turn to the much more liberal view.

I realized it was up to me while I was still governor to put together a Democratic group supporting the moderate philosophy I had long espoused, since the older party leaders were gone. They included my longtime friends, Senator Clinton Anderson, former Governor John E. Miles, who was governor in the late 1930s and died in 1973, and Senator Dennis Chávez, who died in 1963. Those moderate Democratic leaders had mentored me and worked closely with me for many years. Senator Joe Montoya and I did attempt to align our thoughts and forces, but there was too much division between the philosophies of the King and Montoya supporters for us to ever function as one organization. Joe was a strong leader, had his own organization, and was more liberal than myself and my followers. The senator was not about to relinquish power to anyone, and likewise I wasn't interested in giving up my own group, either.

After Pete Domenici won the 1972 Senate election, he began taking potshots at my management of state government. I met with the senator-elect and convinced him that the two of us, as the leading public officials in the state along with Senator Montoya, needed to get along together. I thought we would be in a much stronger position if we collaborated on addressing the state's needs and developing a good working relationship between Congress in Washington and the governor's office in New Mexico.

Domenici agreed, and I further agreed to open a Washington office. While Senator Anderson was in office, his staff had operated as a virtual liaison for state government and a governor's staff in Washington. Now that Senator Anderson was retired and all his people were coming home, I felt the need for someone to represent the interests of state government to Congress. I sent Brad Hayes to head this new office. That was the beginning of the governor's office in Washington. It did serve the state's needs, and in my second term Virginia Sears headed this office, which continued as a coordinating center supporting the needs of state government and the citizens of

New Mexico in the nation's capitol. Still, it took funding to operate. I worked with House speaker Walter Martinez and Senator Tibo Chávez, who had been elected to his fourth term as Senate majority leader, to help pass the appropriation for the Washington office.

⁓

In 1972, we were faced with a familiar and agonizing task that came around about once a decade: reapportioning the legislature. I have had more experience with the process of redrawing legislative district lines than anyone else in New Mexico, starting with 1963, then 1972, 1982, and 1992. The first reapportionment I worked on marked the shift from each county having a representative, no matter how small its population, to representation based more strictly on population. Despite having land areas that rival the size of an Eastern state like Connecticut, some of New Mexico's more isolated counties have populations of only a couple thousand people or so, and they're getting smaller. With that kind of low population density, the numbers just aren't there to justify even one representative for the rural counties, while the bigger counties keep on growing and adding numbers to the legislature.

Reapportionment is an inherently divisive legislative necessity. Because it affects every legislator, it is the most intensely political process and the most difficult kind of legislation to pass. Asking a legislator to redesign his own district is like asking the chicken to vote for Colonel Sanders—it goes against his own interest. The shifts in population over the preceding ten years may require him to eliminate his own position. Or his proposed new district may take in a new area where the voters differ so much from his philosophy that he obviously won't be returning to the legislature after the next election. When you are faced with eliminating legislators and commingling districts, all friendship goes out the window. Everyone looks out for himself. Afterwards, you always get strong reminders of the effects of reapportionment because it so drastically transforms the makeup of the legislature. The whole power structure can shift.

Reapportionment seems to naturally provoke lawsuits and intervention by all levels of the court system. Often these suits start in state district court, but the decision there would by no means resolve the issues, and they would go to the state supreme court. The 1982 reapportionment bill wound up in the U.S. Supreme Court, and the federal 10th Circuit Court of Appeals has also made reapportionment decisions for us.

In my second administration as governor, we had to reapportion once again. Based on the 1980 census, we had to redraw all the districts for seats in the state House of Representatives, the state Senate, and the U.S. House of Representatives. On top of that, the state had gained so much population since the 1970 census that we were now entitled to a third representative in the U.S. Congress, instead of just two. New Mexico also had been one of just two states that elected their Congressional representatives statewide, rather than by district.

All in all, this job took a great deal of thought and many, many plans were bandied about in the early 1980s. Syndicated columnist and political consultant Fred McCaffrey and I came up with a plan that proved to be quite close to the one eventually adopted for the three congressional districts. We made Bernalillo County the bulk of one district, and I suggested adding Torrance County to bring it up to the required population figure. When it was finally adopted, this district actually comprised Bernalillo, Torrance, and Guadalupe counties. The other two congressional districts divided New Mexico roughly along a diagonal, creating a northwest district and a southeast district. Some said this would never work, but actually these were quite compatible districts, since they recognized the commonalties within the different regions of the state. We found we had very little criticism. The population totals came out very close to the ideal figures, and almost everyone was pleased with the result.

Then came the job that's never easy: dividing New Mexico into districts for the state legislature. Altogether, I think seven plans were floating around and everyone was reviewing them. This time I had to be responsible for the plan the Democrats presented, which immediately ran into problems with the coalition of Republicans and conservative Democrats that controlled the House in those years. Because they feared losing the House, they made it difficult to reapportion.

All during the summer of 1981 I looked for a day to call the special session for reapportioning the legislature. I tried to bring the legislative leadership together but we always failed to get a quorum of those who wanted a special session. Finally, we wound up enacting reapportionment during the regular 30-day session in 1982, but then early in April the federal court struck down the legislative reapportionment plan we had worked so hard to develop. The court said that the boundaries we had drawn for several districts did not meet the criterion of one person, one vote.

That court decision sent us back to the drawing board, and I had to work with the legislative council and the leadership of both houses and both parties to decide what we would do. I called a meeting and they all came. We concluded the best thing we could do under the court's mandate was to break down the disputed districts in the manner the court had prescribed in the block breakdowns, which were based strictly on population and didn't follow county or precinct lines. We didn't have the census data needed for that step, so Clay Buchanan, the longtime director of the Legislative Counsel Service, undertook to get that information. My staff assistant Brian Sanderoff also did a great deal of work on this. Buchanan worked hard and sped up the process so that I could call a special session, which I set for June 14. Unfortunately, that date threw off the primary election schedule—some House candidates couldn't file for the regular June primary election because their districts wouldn't be determined in time. It turned out they had to file and run by themselves in a special primary election at a later date.

In the special session the legislators worked diligently, overcoming a great deal of contention among themselves to finally pass yet another reapportionment plan, which I signed. The primary election for those House seats was held on August 25. Turnout was light in this unusual election, but there was little complaint about how we handled this reapportionment. When we finally settled on a plan, I felt it served its purpose, although I never believed we reapportioned strictly by the guidelines we were supposed to follow. A major issue was representation for Curry and Roosevelt counties in eastern New Mexico. I felt from the outset that we were not giving minorities in those counties a fair opportunity to select their representatives under that reapportionment plan. I wasn't alone in that opinion, as the plan was taken to the courts in 1982, which ruled the reapportionment was unfair to minorities, and we reconvened to do it yet again. At last, this plan was acceptable.

That struggle over reapportionment was the only problem I had with the conservative coalition in the late 1970s and early 1980s that I was unable to resolve to my satisfaction. Ironically, they did lose control of the House in the 1982 general election, when they lost a number of seats, partly because the reapportionment hurt them and partly because Democrat Toney Anaya had such a strong showing to win the governor's race. But I never had to veto a reapportionment bill, though I had grave concerns about some, and I was always able to convince the legislature to make any changes I considered essential. In the 1982 round I made it clear there was no way I could sign one of the proposed reapportionment bills that looked like it might pass. The coalition leadership understood that I would veto the bill, and they amended it to where I could live with it.

‿

My first term was winding down in 1974. I had completed my major objectives and now only time would reveal what I had achieved. Government was just beginning to function as I had visualized it should. We were in good shape financially, with another surplus developing, but I didn't want to cut taxes permanently and risk forcing the next governor to immediately ask for an increase. I felt our tax structure was well balanced and that we weren't paying exorbitant taxes, so I proposed a one-time rebate. My proposal caused problems in the legislature, because all lawmakers like to go home and campaign on their success in reducing taxes permanently. I had to say many times that I would veto the tax bill unless it was a one-time-only rebate.

In my budget proposal to the 1974 legislature I asked for $364 million of state spending, an 11.8 percent increase over the budget enacted in 1973. I wanted to improve education, meet the needs of the less fortunate citizens of the state, and carry out a strong highway building program. I felt we needed strong law enforcement. In addition, I proposed a $3 million appropriation just to raise state salaries. I recommended a 20 percent increase in funding for the corrections system, where I felt we were falling behind. Though we got some of that money, later events proved we needed all the additional funding I requested.

Generally, I did well with the legislature that year. As it turned out, total 1974 appropriations were within $1 million of my recommendation. And I was particularly pleased with the 1974 school equalization bill, which enacted the new system of spreading state monies fairly across all the school districts. This gave equal funding for all students, whether they lived in a poor or rich community.

I also asked for an open meetings law. I felt that the more openly government operated, the better citizens would know what we were doing. If the press could go in to report, they would do a much better job than if we attempted to operate under a cloak. The bill finally took shape, and in its final version the law applied to most units of state and local government, but not to legislative committees.

The legislature also addressed the issue of preventing excessive numbers of candidates in our primary elections. We had gone through that debacle in the 1972 primary of having the courts rule that our filing fees were unconstitutional, which had left us with no way to control the number of candidates on the primary ballots. So I named a bipartisan task force to study the issue and propose reforms to the election law. Among other things, they suggested—and the legislature passed—that candidates must get the signatures of at least 5 percent of the voters on nominating petitions.

Another issue I pressed was the Commission on the Status of Women. By executive order I had created a panel of 15 members to study the legal and economic status of women, but I wanted to make it a permanent statutory commission so it would endure the turnover of administrations. We wanted to be sure women were treated equally in all respects. Representative Bill Warren of Bernalillo County volunteered to introduce the bill. I worked closely with him and it passed. I named Dorothy Cline to chair this first Commission on the Status of Women. Among the members I named were two from Torrance County: Ethel Floyd, a longtime worker in the Human Services Department out of Estancia, and Povi Bigbee, the balancing Republican member and the wife of my friend, Representative John Bigbee.

The energy crisis of 1974 threatened to drastically reduce tourism in New Mexico, which is vital to the state's economy. That was one emergency we hadn't anticipated, and we had to take hold of it and work our way out. I enlisted the help of former Governor Jack Campbell, who was an expert on energy problems and directed a regional energy federation. He identified some areas we needed to address, including the use of coal and uranium to generate electricity and thereby save natural gas and petroleum for other uses, like transportation.

Nationwide gasoline rationing had reduced the New Mexico allocation by 2 percent. Some legislators felt we shouldn't have to accept that, and the

House passed a bill declaring our independence from that program. I saw that we could not take this stand, especially when people in the East and Midwest were pointing out that New Mexico had gasoline supplies that other areas didn't have. Many experts shared my feeling, arguing that we could live with the 2 percent cut and help other states that were facing shortfalls. Eventually the bill died.

Then we decided to develop an advertising program inviting tourists to New Mexico and stressing that we had plenty of gasoline. I got in the act by riding my horse to work, right up the steps of the capitol building to show we were saving fuel for the tourists. We got terrific press coverage. Governor Stan Hathaway of Wyoming later told me he wished he had thought of that. The tourism business did quite well that year, too.

~~~

1974 was an election year, but I wasn't running for office—not for re-election, because in those days the governor by law could not succeed himself, and not for national office, either. I had always said I would not run for another office while I was governor, but I added that I might run again for governor in 1978.

The 1974 Democratic primary turned into a hard-fought battle between the leading contenders—Jerry Apodaca, a state senator from Las Cruces, against my friend Senator Tibo Chávez. That kind of fight isn't a good situation for a chief executive to get pulled into, so I concluded I would not openly take sides. It's okay to work quietly for what you consider the best interests of the state, but it's dumb to commit publicly to one candidate, because you will be criticized for whatever position you take. Nonetheless, I soon began to work openly for Tibo Chávez.

Apodaca beat Tibo in the June primary, while Joe Skeen, a former state senator, won the Republican primary. Although I wasn't in the race, I had a hard time going about my business during their race for my office. In such a campaign, the nominees are likely to make misleading statements that make it difficult for the incumbent to maintain decorum and run an efficient administration. I had to change strategy a great deal as I lived through their race, staying focused to maintain my progress in office. Of course I hoped my successor would pick up where I left off on the things I was attempting to accomplish. I wanted my cabinet secretaries and top professionals not to be alienated, so they could have a chance to stay with the new administration, regardless who won. I told them to cooperate with the candidates, make information available whenever they were asked, and welcome candidates or supporters visiting their agencies.

After the primary I was on the sidelines observing, and often I had to defend my programs. Maybe toward the end of my first term I was a little too sensitive. In an editorial, the *Albuquerque Journal* said, in effect, look, governor, you shouldn't be so defensive in the governor's office. It's nothing personal, and you'll look back and see that it's customary for the candidates to try to improve on things. They don't want to pick a fight with a sitting governor, but they all want to point out the program they would adopt, and many times it is counter to what the present governor is doing. That advice made sense to me, and I quit being so sensitive. But it is a strange situation, a strange feeling. The candidates have to pick on you, and you learn that the public is tolerant of those accusations and finger pointing. When it was all over, I didn't have any hard feelings toward anyone.

Of course I supported my fellow Democrat Jerry Apodaca in the general election. When he became governor he looked favorably on many of the top people already in state government. For example, Martin Vigil stayed on as State Police chief, Fred O'Cheskey stayed as director of Taxation and Revenue, and Maxine Gerheart stayed with the department of Finance and Administration, although she was demoted from director to deputy. I had named her director, the first woman appointed to that leading position. Governor Apodaca persuaded her to drop back to deputy and Vince Montoya served as director for a year or two, then Apodaca reappointed Maxine to head the department again.

To help ease the transition between my administration and the next, I compiled a governor's manual. I also knew when you move into a new position it is helpful if you can look in one place to see how things are supposed to operate. I knew it would be criticized, because for one thing you can't cover all aspects of the office. That would be impossible. Second, people will disagree with some things that you do put in.

We compiled a thick document anyway, pointing out some pitfalls that I would have avoided if I had received a manual. It advised the chief executive and his staff on interacting with the legislative and judicial branches, and it discussed many jurisdictional problems. The manual had no bearing on policy direction, but it dealt with functional things that the law and constitution provide for. It's like overhauling your car. You can't become a mechanic by reading the manual, but you can learn what the parts are and where they are supposed to go.

Although some said I was trying to direct the next administration, Lee Witt, Governor Apodaca's chief of staff, told me it was a great service to them. When Apodaca left he didn't choose to update the manual, as I had suggested, but I did when I finished my second term after him.

≋

The year 1974 and my first administration wound down together. The staff, the state agency heads, and Alice and I felt we had given four years of our best efforts to New Mexico. We were leaving the state with a $100 million budget surplus and $50 million more in reserves, thanks in part to the severance tax permanent fund we created. My administration had helped create 8,000 new jobs, the Employment Security Commission in-plant training program that we had started was a success in addressing labor shortages, and the prison was running smoothly under Howard Leach and Felix Rodriguez. Our state highways were in much better shape than they were when we started. The new public school funding formula was giving students all around the state more equal access to a good education, while the Organized Crime Prevention Commission was thwarting mob efforts to infiltrate New Mexico. We had taken strong action to protect the environment through legislation, and the Environmental Improvement Board had taken positive steps toward ensuring that future generations would enjoy the natural beauty of our state. All considered, I felt it had been a very productive administration and I was proud of what we had achieved in those four years.

During the two months between the election and the inaugural I enjoyed good relations with the Apodaca administration, though that didn't last very long into the next year. By Christmas, I was about finished as governor. We held a few social events to mark both the season and the end of my term. In late November, Alice held a reception at the mansion for the press and news media from throughout New Mexico. Our first granddaughter, Becky, had been born in October and she was there with her parents, Mr. and Mrs. Bill King. We didn't look for publicity at the reception, but held it as a festivity to show appreciation for the rapport we had enjoyed with the press and their role in disseminating essential information about state government to the public.

After Thanksgiving, we put up Christmas trees in the outer office and celebrated with many of the people who had been with us for those four years—people like Linda Kehoe, Lucille Valencia, Priscilla Cordova, Molly Chávez, and Bernie Baldwin. Alice held several Christmas parties and we ended the year and my term of office with the satisfaction of a job well done. On January 1st, 1975, I handed the reins of government over to my successor.

9

My Style of Governing

Every governor brings a unique flair to the job. During my 40 years of service as an elected official, I had plenty of time to develop my own personal style of governing. Folks seemed to think I had a knack for bringing people together, even around divisive issues, and for building consensus among diverse groups. I worked hard to keep New Mexico headed down the middle path, without swinging too far one side or the other. Extremism tends to favor a small number of people, and I had always believed I was elected to bring the benefits of good government to everyone, not just one special interest group or segment of the population. You might say that my political philosophy grew out of my upbringing on the homestead, where any traveler in need was welcome, whatever their background. My parents never asked a passerby whether they were Democrat or Republican before watering their stock at our well.

When it came to the mechanics of campaigning and handling myself in an elected position, I had spent so much of my life around politics that I had a pretty good idea of how things got done before I ever ran for office. My dad's involvement in politics and his friendships with Governor Clyde Tingley and Governor Arthur Seligman contributed to that education. Then while I was speaker of the House, I worked closely with—and closely observed—two governors who had very different approaches: Dave Cargo and Jack Campbell. Campbell was highly professional, strong on decorum and precise in making decisions. When you went in to see him, he always had a plan, and he would say, "Now this is the way I think it should be." Then you could present your views and work out the problem with him.

Jack Campbell (left), Dave Cargo (second from left), Garrey Carruthers (second from right), Tony Anaya (far right) and I all had quite different styles of governing. Nonetheless, we were able to remain friends despite occasional political squabbles.

Governor Cargo, on the other hand, was more interested in what the press was going to say than he was in the day-to-day business of operating state government. I suppose he knew that as a Republican in New Mexico, he wasn't going to influence the legislature very much. When I was speaker and I would go up to see Cargo, he would always let me in. John Mershon would often go with me, as would Dave Norvell, the majority leader, and Seferino Martinez, the House majority whip. Somewhere along the line, Cargo had concluded the best way to have a good working relationship with the press—and everyone else—was to give them free access to him and his office, even to folks like the artist Tommy Macaione. So we legislators would be sitting there discussing things and trying to arrive at a decision, and his secretary, Grace Evans, would call and say, "The members of the press are out here," or "other legislators are out here." And in they would come: maybe Fred Buckles, Wayne Scott, or Jim Colegrove of the *New Mexican*. They would sit down and start taking notes about whatever was going on. I never had any particular secrets, but a lot of times we would be trying to reach an agreement on a position. If the press heard only part of what we were discussing, their stories would be distorted, as you might expect.

Cargo was always trying to get in the limelight. If you went in and gave him your inside information on the budget numbers, for example, you were barely out the door before he held a press conference and released them as his numbers. I saw that policy wasn't going to work. Larry Prentice, one of Cargo's administrative aides who had worked in the legislature, once told me, "Mr. Speaker, you worked with Dave down here a long time. You know that anything which will make good press coverage, he'll release immediately. You better govern the information you pass along with that in mind." Which is what I decided to do. I told John Mershon, "From now on, we'll put the bills together and then *we* will release the numbers."

During my first 15 to 20 years as a public official, I was able to develop strong working relationships with the press. As governor, one way I maintained this rapport with the media was my policy of working openly, although I wasn't *wide open* like Cargo. Still, I always believed that public involvement and working out in the open were the best ways to guarantee good government, so anyone in state government could talk to reporters. I gave the cabinet secretaries authority to speak to the press on their own, and I encouraged them to tell the media what they were doing if they thought it would advance their programs. Most of them had press secretaries, who would meet with my press secretary from week to week. People working under a cabinet secretary would usually clear their statements with the secretary, but that wasn't mandatory. As a result of my open policy, the media people had confidence in their statehouse sources. Of course, that didn't mean we didn't take a thrashing every once in a while over one controversy or another, but I usually ended up each year in office with positive marks from the capitol reporters, and that was important to me.

Sometimes the media accused me of being too low-key in giving direction to the legislature, but my proposals and the resulting accomplishments showed that I enjoyed great influence there. As a legislator myself, I had learned through the years not to lead too strongly. Excessive direction from the governor can dampen the spirits of the legislators. They are a hard-working body, just as interested in meeting the needs of the people as the governor is. Left alone, they will come up with many initiatives that don't require the governor's involvement, but that he can heartily endorse. So I didn't try to direct the legislature on topics that I knew were going to come out about as I wanted them, anyway.

Not that working with the legislature was always easy. After spending so many years as a member and speaker, I had assumed I would continue my easy-going relationship with the leaders in both houses, and for the most part, that was true. On the other hand, I also found that the separation of powers in the constitution did, in fact, change the nature of my relationship with those leaders, sometimes setting us at odds with each other. Furthermore, the constitution puts clear limits on each branch. For instance, the governor can't spend a single penny of public money until the legislature appropriates it, though he takes the lead in getting his executive budget through the legislature. The legislators, in turn, review the budget requests for each agency, and they are never shy about doing so.

A governor always feels a little friction working with the legislature when it comes to spending money. Legislators each have their home district's priorities in mind, for one thing, while the governor has a statewide constituency to serve, so there has to be some give and take between them. I liked to solve everything before the last week of the session, so we could close out with a unified front. Sometimes, if the legislators weren't able to work out their own internal disputes, they would go with my budget and plan as I had originally presented it.

In my 12 years as governor, I never needed to appear before a legislative committee during a legislative session. A time or two I did consider asking for a committee of the whole of both houses to make presentations, but as it turned out I never had that serious a problem in getting my programs passed. I much preferred to call the leadership of the House and the Senate separately up to my office to go over the problems with them. I almost always got the legislation I wanted, except on rare occasions when they convinced me it wasn't needed. However, my chief people did go down frequently to testify.

The key to all this was having a few experienced people who were intimately familiar with and completely trusted by the legislature. For example, in my first term two of my leading agency heads were Dick Heim, secretary of the Human Services Department, and Bill Giron, secretary of Hospitals and Institutions. Dick Heim had lots of political experience and knew the needs of his department in fine detail. His budget was one of the largest in state government. Bill Giron had wide experience in state government and, like Dick, he was well acquainted with the legislators and enjoyed their confidence. My other agency heads were generally of this caliber. When the appropriations committees of the House or Senate were meeting on those agencies, Dick or Bill would come by my office in the morning and we would spend 20 minutes or so talking over their departmental needs and planning strategy for the hearing.

In my first term, in addition to Bill Giron and Dick Heim, I had Bob Kirkpatrick as head of the Department of Finance and Administration. With Franklin Jones, he coordinated our lobbying of the legislature. I also had two lobbyists working directly between me and the legislators. During this period, Tourism Secretary Fabian Chávez, a former Senate majority leader, and state Banking Commissioner Roy Davidson, a former leader in the House of Representatives, carried the word directly from me to the appropriations committees. If an agency head reported back to me that certain legislators were cool or even opposed to our budget and our approach, or could not understand it, then depending on who the legislator was and who had the best rapport, I would instruct Fabian or Roy to go visit with him or her. Lots of times individual legislators would go directly to one of those two for information, without my even directing a meeting. Fabian and Roy also sat in as staff members on our briefing sessions for legislative presentations and were on hand to meet all kinds of problems. During my second and third administrations, Gary O'Dowd, Kay Marr, and Mike Cerletti filled a similar role, as did my son, Bill, who worked gratis as my chief legislative liaison and was invaluable to me.

I often said that by looking at the name of the sponsor and the title of a bill I could get as good a general idea of its contents as many people would have after reading it. So of course I applied this experience to our briefing sessions. I would comment on the legislators they would be facing. I might tell them that a particular member would view their presentation from a liberal or a conservative viewpoint, and I would coach them on approaches that would appeal to each individual. Afterward, the agency head would go down to the committee hearing and make our official presentation.

We had another resource—the Department of Finance and Administration member who always sat in on legislative budget hearings. These budget people also met in my office with the agency heads to plan strategy, so we had a dual check and a dual presentation. It was a matter of my people knowing their agencies, and the legislature verifying that fact. With this system, I never saw a need to appear in person before a committee during a legislative session. That would have diluted my strength, attracting undue press attention and stimulating legislators to ask a great many more questions than usual.

The legislative leadership knew they could get any answers they needed from me. I met at least once weekly at breakfast during the session with the leadership, and they could take that opportunity to ask anything they wanted. In addition, my office was always open to the leadership and to all the legislators. If they thought they weren't getting proper consideration or the materials and information they were after, those committee chairmen didn't hesitate to come flying up to my office, saying, "Look, governor, you've got people down there saying these things. . ." and we would talk it over and straighten it out.

It was a two-way street. Sometimes I'd be misunderstood. To avoid a stalemate, I would save some of my ammunition, so when the legislators ran up to me I could easily go over their situation and say, "I'll discuss it with the agency head and the Department of Finance and Administration people." Then I would call those people back in and we would compare notes again, and they would go back to the hearings and by that time we would have it straightened out.

The veto is one of the main tools a governor uses to influence legislation. Various reasons could prompt me to veto a bill. I never did it just because a bill had been introduced by legislators who opposed me on some issue or other, even though the media sometimes accused me of doing that. During and after each legislative session I had a number of attorneys going over the bills to determine whether they were constitutional, and what they would *really* do, regardless of the intent behind the bill. If on review it proved to be a good bill, I signed it; if it was a bad bill, I would veto it, regardless of who sponsored it. Many of the bills I vetoed were backed by good intentions, but they were passed in haste. Sometimes my office did the homework for the legislators, after the fact. When we reviewed a bill carefully, it might become clear that as drafted and passed, it wouldn't accomplish the ends that were sought, and would cause more problems than it would cure. Often after my legislative experts like Gary O'Dowd analyzed a bill, we would point out the problems to its sponsors and they would want me to veto it. Then they would go to work and send up a corrected bill. This processes benefited the people of New Mexico, because once you sign a bill, no matter what the intent was, it's what the bill says that counts. As governor I would see an example of that almost every day. People would come up and complain about an existing law, saying, "Well, that wasn't the legislative intent. . . ." The trouble is, years afterward we usually don't know what the intent was, and anyhow we are bound by the language.

Many times a bill would go though both houses and different committees, and by the time everyone put in their little bit, it would be greatly changed from the original intent. In a 60-day session the legislators might consider 1,300 to 1,400 pieces of legislation, and it is just impossible for them to know the contents of every bill. Once the bills have been screened through the legislative process, perhaps some 400 will pass both houses and be sent to the governor for his consideration. Then it is up to the governor to know the exact contents of each bill, as far as possible. For that he needs highly professional legislative analysts on his staff who are interested in the governor doing a good job long after the legislature has gone home and the bills have been printed.

The media commented that thank goodness the governor had the power to veto bills, because otherwise many bad bills would have become law. That didn't mean the legislators always understood why I vetoed a particular bill. At those points, I always called in the key legislators for that bill and told them, "Look, I am going to have to veto your bill." I would have my staff go over the reasons, and I would make it clear that the legislators could visit with me to go over our analysis. Many times they would do just that. Usually, they said, "Well, I knew you were going to veto it," but I remember on one or two occasions I did change my mind and sign a bill I had intended to veto after visiting with the legislator. Generally, I stuck to my reasoning, unless there was something I had overlooked.

One of my vetoes in 1981 caused a great deal of concern—the four-day school week expansion bill. I left the four-day school week in place for the three districts that had been using it—San Jon, Roy, and Cimarron—but I vetoed expanding that schedule to other districts. The school district of the small east-side community called House had begun to pick it up, along with a few other districts, and I really caught heck from those areas for vetoing that bill.

I was fortunate in my 12 years as a governor that I never had a veto overridden, although sometimes I had to do some fast work with my legislative friends to convince them that I was only vetoing legislation that deserved it. I would tell them that I wouldn't look kindly upon their attempts to override me, because I hadn't had any overrides, and I would find it depressing. When I vetoed the first tax reduction bill, also in 1981, I remember the press asking me if I wasn't concerned about the legislature overriding my veto. The bill had passed the House 65-0 and the Senate 42-0. In a quiet, positive way, I said that I had considered that possibility, and I had talked with the legislators, and if I hadn't felt I had sufficient strength in both houses to sustain my veto, I wouldn't have done it. I sent a revised bill back and they passed it.

New Mexico's constitution also allows the governor to veto portions of appropriations bills, while approving the remainder of the same bills. That's a privilege denied the President of the United States until very recently. I used the line-item veto to cut out parts of a bill that I thought would be detrimental, while preserving the parts I thought would work. In 1972, my exercise of this privilege stirred up the Legislative Finance Committee. On May 20, I was still winding up the business left for me by the legislature, and the LFC was meeting downstairs on the third floor of the capitol. Composed of both Senate and House members, the LFC meets year-round to oversee revenues and spending in state government. Along with the Legislative Council, it is one of the most influential interim committees of the legislature. This was an interim meeting, a couple of months after the legislature itself had adjourned. A few of my staff members usually sat in to monitor the LFC meetings, and that day they came rushing up to tell me, "Some of the legislators are saying it was asinine, the way you line-item vetoed things in the House appropriations bill, and they resent it, and somebody is going to have to pay the price."

I knew from my time in the legislature that I had to be careful not to let a situation like this turn negative and damage the rapport I enjoyed with the legislators. So I went down to the third floor, walked quietly into the LFC meeting, and sat down with the witnesses who were making presentations for or against legislative proposals. The LFC members were quite surprised and they paused in their proceedings and turned to me. Some of them expressed their unhappiness about my having line-item vetoed language in the bill that required the State Police to maintain air surveillance of any narcotics trafficking that might be moving up and down the border.

When that bill was under my consideration, State Police Chief Martin Vigil and the State Police Commission had said they could not possibly monitor drug traffic in the way the bill called for. The bill also demanded that the State Police file monthly reports to the LFC on the findings of their drug traffic surveillance. Chief Vigil had said the information in the requested reports would be a matter of record, destroying the confidentiality the police needed to function as a law enforcement agency. Nonetheless, the police were extremely interested in eliminating narcotics traffic along the border. They had said they would continue to combat that traffic and would express this to the LFC, but they couldn't operate under the proposed language. So I struck out those provisions stipulating surveillance by airplanes and the other specific requirements that would have been impossible to carry out, including the requirement of giving complete information to the LFC and others.

When I gave the LFC these views, some of the members still expressed their concern, which I could understand. I said, "We're all interested in one thing, and that's carrying on good government. I'm ready to defend any line-item veto I made and I would like the opportunity to discuss it."

We did discuss it, at great length. My objection went beyond legislative interference with the State Police and other law enforcement agencies doing the undercover work needed to attack the drug traffic. The underlying issue was the separation of powers in government. In this bill, the legislature had taken the position that the law enforcement people were not doing all they could to deter the flow of drugs into New Mexico. They actually wrote specifications for the executive branch to administer. In effect, the legislature was trying to act as the executive director of the State Police Department by assigning specific tasks to them and specifying how to report their activities. I opposed any such infringement on the authority of the executive branch.

I wasn't the only governor to have problems with legislative attempts to encroach on executive power. Often at conferences of the National Governors' Association, my peers would raise similar issues. At such times I would sit back and listen, and finally they would say, "Well, Bruce, don't you ever have problems like these?"

"Not really," I would say. "They passed legislation like that in New Mexico, and I vetoed it."

And they would say, "How do you do that and keep the support of the legislators?"

I said I would go straight to the legislators, telling them how it looked from the eyes of the executive and how in the long run it wouldn't work, and they would see my point. But you had to be sure your timing was right.

The result of that LFC meeting was positive—we parted friends again. I knew I had to handle the problem right there on the spot, before it got into the press that the legislative process was breaking down as it related to the executive branch.

⋙

The key to devoting adequate attention to every aspect of my job was allocating my time properly. From a lifetime of farm and ranch work I had developed the habit of getting up early. So on a typical day during my second term, for instance, I got up around five-thirty to meditate for about an hour while I made coffee. Then I would pick up the morning paper and glance through it. I always carried a little black book, where I wrote my thoughts related to coordinating state government that absolutely had to get done that day or over a longer period of time. The secret was to list the essential tasks. No matter what else happened, each day I made certain I got everything done in that black book before I moved on to the next tasks.

I reached the capitol by seven-thirty and got set for the day. My cabinet secretaries and the other top people in state government knew I would be there. If they had problems or wanted my direction, they came to the office about that time without having to go through staff people to see me, because security and I would be the only ones there. Around eight o'clock when the staff began to come in, I would head for the outer lobby and make a quick trip around and get a cup of coffee and go back through the offices and visit with all the staff for five or ten minutes, just to see if everyone was there and ready to go to work. I really wasn't the office manager, but I did enjoy those brief visits with my staff people who worked hard and made me look good.

Then sometimes I would go back out front and see who else had arrived. The press soon learned this routine, and if they had questions they would come over to drink a cup of coffee and visit with me in a corner of the lobby. Sometimes they wanted to come into my office. I always obliged them, and if they wanted to tape some questions and answers, we would do that.

During my second term, I always met for a half hour at eight-thirty with my three key staff members, Linda Kehoe, Bill Giron, and Brian Sanderoff. We would review my black-book checklist for that day. Some tasks I would assign to the staff themselves and some they would hand off, usually by phone, to cabinet secretaries and other administrators. After discussing my list, these three would bring up their items of business that needed attention. Usually by nine o'clock we would have completed the day's assignments. Then I would call in Jill Marron, my press secretary, and Janet Wise, her deputy, to go over the points they felt we needed to review and any information the media people had requested. I would give them the important things I felt we should stress in trying to get our position into the news media. If reporters needed specific information, the press secretaries would often call them on the phone and I would talk to them personally, or I would give the answers to the press secretaries so they could pass them on. These procedures were highly effective in enabling me to maintain good rapport with the media.

By ten o'clock, I would start meeting people who wanted to see the governor, including officials of state agencies, legislators, and citizens from around the state. I was able to accommodate a great many people every day through that appointment system. All these people flowing through the office kept the security people on their toes, since there would often be someone who acted unusual. I walked around the offices a lot and they didn't want me to run into someone whose behavior they couldn't predict or whose intentions weren't clear. I was never too concerned about my safety, and I loved to sneak off to the ranch without the security people tagging along. But if a potential trouble maker showed up, the people in the reception area knew how to recognize the situation. They would go to Bill Giron, who would then alert security of the potential danger. They would watch the person and in a low-key way escort them out of the office.

Several nights a week, Alice and I went to functions in different communities around the state. We flew in a state-owned airplane piloted by Bob Youngblood, and we usually got back and into bed by eleven or twelve o'clock at night. All that activity made for long days, but also kept me in close contact with state government and with the people. Doing it all successfully came down to setting priorities for the direction where I wanted government to go.

Alice worked hard on every campaign. As the years passed, she became more closely involved in policy issues. (Photograph courtesy Santa Fe *New Mexican*)

Along with this daily routine I held monthly meetings with the full cabinet to review their problems and concerns and bimonthly meetings with key state agency people, whether they came under a cabinet secretary or not. Quite a few were not supervised by a cabinet secretary, including the liquor director, the public service commissioners, the public defenders, and others in a long list.

≋

I've always enjoyed personal contact with the people around New Mexico. In my early years in politics, the nature of campaigning and of working first in the county commission, then the legislature kept me close to my constituents. I felt it was important to keep tabs on their interests and concerns, although a leader can't govern by popular opinion altogether. Through the years, I learned that you have to gain the confidence of the people and be right enough times that they won't be nervous about where you're going. You sure need 50 or 60 percent following you all the time, and sometimes more than that. Try as you might, though, your decisions will always be detrimental to someone.

Once I became governor, close contact with people was harder to come by. As I campaigned for governor the second time, I got many comments from people in different communities around the state who said they liked me as governor the first time, and would support me, but they didn't like the remoteness of state government. They said things like, "Once you guys get elected, you don't come back to see us. Or if you do, it's just a formality, and we don't get a chance to tell you what's on our minds."

I took those comments to heart, and after I was elected to my second term I decided to bring state government out to the people. So in 1979 I started my program of going around the state and holding all-day meetings in various communities. Alice went with me on those trips, and I brought along some cabinet secretaries and other staff members whose jurisdictions had most to do with the local problems in each area. Sometimes legislators would travel with us, as well. Often we would go into the schools, the county courthouse, the senior citizens center, the chamber of commerce, and other public organizations.

We made presentations on what we felt was needed and what we were trying to do in state government, and we invited the people to ask questions and express their thoughts about local needs. We also sought comments about what we were doing in Santa Fe. Then we held office hours and scheduled appointments for all the local people who wanted to come in and visit with us. These local office hours were of great value to the many people who couldn't easily drive to Santa Fe—some communities in the far corners of the state are five or more hours away, by car—but who still needed to get our attention. On top of that, when people do come to Santa Fe, they often don't know exactly which division of state government they should bring their problem to. When we came to their home towns, on the other hand, they expressed their needs directly to the state official who could correct the situation if action was called for. Though our schedules made for hard-working days, my cabinet secretaries and I gathered a great deal of information about local needs in all parts of the state—information we could not have obtained any other way.

At first, much of the press sharply criticized my trips to the outlying areas of New Mexico. They said that we had big problems in Santa Fe, and rather than resolving them, I was taking government to places where the people didn't know about all the things that were going on at the capitol. We impressed on the media people that we hoped they would work closely with us on these visits, and after one or two, they gained a favorable impression and started giving us good advance publicity and coverage of our meetings. For several days prior to each meeting they would announce our coming and give the time and place and the procedure for citizens to be heard.

This program was highly successful and met with such wide popular acceptance that I continued it through all four years of my second administration and my third, as well. Many of the state boards and commissions took notice and adopted their own versions of government to the people, continuing the practice after I left office.

The first time I took government to the people was at Santa Rosa. We had good attendance, and the cabinet secretaries and local officials were enthusiastic about our visit. We met with officials of Guadalupe County, the mayor, and other officials of the city of Santa Rosa.

Their hospital was closed, and we could see they needed help. My staff people were able to study the problem first-hand. Bill Giron met at length with the hospital board and the county officials, and we decided to place a high priority on recruiting the medical staff they needed to re-open the hospital. Many other small New Mexico communities had similar problems. I had gained valuable background about this situation during my 1978 campaign for governor. Dr. Frank Hesse of Albuquerque worked hard on my campaign, and he had the conviction, which I came to share, that we needed to strengthen rural medical services. Not enough doctors and nurses were willing to go into rural areas, and funding was inadequate. So I named a governor's committee on rural health to approach this problem statewide. Dr. Hesse chaired this committee, which later changed names to the Health Resources Committee, and Bill Giron worked closely with him to solve the problems in Santa Rosa and elsewhere. The legislature passed a bill providing grants for medical students, who were obligated in return to provide services to the state after they graduated. In this way we were able to get federal funding to bring physicians into rural areas.

We went back a year later and found the Santa Rosa hospital operating with a good doctor and staff. Unfortunately, the problem wasn't permanently solved, because the federal government later decided that local communities, and not the government, should pay the doctors who come in to practice, which resulted in another round of closing a great many small, rural clinics.

Later in 1979, I took government to the people of Silver City and Grant County. I rounded up my top state officials and we descended on this community for the entire day. By now these visits were creating enough enthusiasm that several state elective officials wanted to go along with us. In Silver City we brought along Attorney General Jeff Bingaman, a native of that southwest New Mexico town. The Bingaman family held a reception at the close of the day for Jeff, Alice and me, and all the other visiting officials, including Secretary of State Shirley Hooper, who had worked in the legislature many years, plus the cabinet secretaries.

That morning, we visited the schools, our group breaking up and going into different classes. Some schools had assemblies and we spoke in auditoriums, where we were well received. We let the students speak and ask questions for about half the time. We also visited the county courthouse and the municipal building and listened to the needs and problems of the workers there. We reviewed our limitations and noted the areas where we could do things for them. Then starting around 2 P.M. we held open office hours for myself and each cabinet member, as we always did. This time we borrowed offices at Western New Mexico University. The lines were much longer in front of my office than in front of the others, but we managed to see everyone who wanted to see us.

During this visit to Silver City, it became obvious to me that we had serious problems with the president of Western, John Snedeker. Although he had led that university since 1962, by 1979 he had lost the confidence of his faculty, who called for his resignation by a large majority vote. Some of the people who came in to see me wanted to keep him, but others expressed great concerns about his administration. This issue had divided not only the Western campus, but the entire Silver City and Grant County area. Enrollment was dropping and obviously would drop further until we corrected the problems. Here was another local issue requiring my attention that I was alerted to through my government to the people program. I saw that I had to do something, but first I needed more information.

I met with the board of regents on the same trip to Silver City, and they agreed we had to monitor the school closely and try to solve the problems to the satisfaction of the local community. I decided to send my staff assistant Brian Sanderoff down there to spend a few weeks on campus looking into the details. This was one of the first assignments I gave Brian after he came into the governor's office as one of my three main staff people. He had done other investigative work for state government, a great deal of it under my immediate observation, but not under my direct jurisdiction. A young man, he had recently graduated from the University of New Mexico and had worked toward advanced degrees. I felt that of all my assistants, he could best relate to the university and to all involved—the community, the faculty, and the students.

I told Brian I didn't want to be divisive or to cause disorder at the institution. Therefore, he should go in quietly, monitor the operation, and let everyone involved know we were trying to help. I asked him to gather information I could use to work with the board of regents in improving the relationships at Western.

Brian did a good job carrying out those orders. Despite our wish to keep the visit low-key, someone on our office staff must have leaked it to the press, because when Brian got off the plane in Silver City he saw a headline announcing his mission. All that fanfare probably added a week to his assignment, but he did work with everyone there, and they were pleased to have someone they could talk to confidentially. Together with the board, we all concluded we should bring in a new president, and we did it in a way that avoided disrupting the university. Within a year or so Western was back on track, expanding its enrollment and thriving.

I am sure that the problems at Western would have eventually landed on my desk in Santa Fe, but by taking government to the people I was able to confront those problems earlier and resolve them more quickly than if I had simply stayed in my office. That was often the case with this outreach program of mine. In other communities around the state, local offices of different state agencies were hardly communicating with one another, much less cooperating to get their jobs done better. In those cases, when the responsible cabinet secretaries visited the local communities together they could readily see the problems and quickly apply remedies. In community after community, as I took government to the people, we were able to get the local state offices to work much more closely together on behalf of the people in their area. The few hours we spent in each community often produced lasting benefits of this nature.

≈≈

Not every problem that came along required me to call out the national guard or dispatch a special assistant on a two-week investigation. One day, several legislative leaders were in my office discussing budgets when my front-desk secretary called.

"Governor," she said, "there is a Mr. Sandoval who insists he has to talk to you immediately. He says he is your neighbor. He has a ranch over on the Rio Puerco next to you." We have ranch land northwest of Rio Rancho extending out toward the Rio Puerco basin in Sandoval County.

"All right," I said. "Put him on."

They did, and he said, "Bruce, this Livestock Board here has tied up my calf. They say the brand hasn't peeled, and they won't give me the money, and they're gonna take my calf. I only had two. What can we do about it?"

"Where are you at?" I asked him.

"Here at the sanitary board," he said, meaning the state Livestock Board on the State Fairgrounds in Albuquerque. From what I could gather, Mr. Sandoval had sold the calf at auction in Albuquerque, but because the brand wasn't deep enough, it hadn't passed muster with the brand inspector. So they were withholding the proceeds from the sale. He just needed to prove the calf was his by going home, getting the cow, and seeing if the calf would suck, but I guess he didn't want to bother.

"Is Lee Garner there?" I asked. So they put Lee on. He was the director under the Board.

"Lee, what about Mr. Sandoval's calf?" I asked.

"Well, yeah, we have the calf tied up here," Lee said.

I said, "Oh, he's a good man. Go ahead and pay him for the calf, and if anything happens about it, I'll make it right, but you go ahead and pay him."

When I hung up, all the guys in the meeting began to smile. One of them said, "Well, that's the personal touch of our governor. Whatever he's doing, he always has time to stop and help a friend."

10

Home on the Range, But Not for Long

I turned over the governor's office to Jerry Apodaca on January 1, 1975. After the inaugural ceremony I talked to him about the great powers and responsibilities of the governor. I told him he would probably wish many times that he had more power. Often he would want to take action but find his hands tied by legislative or judicial restraints, or by the lack of a law empowering him to take actions he felt were needed. And the opposite was true, that some days he would wish he didn't have so much authority. Sometimes he would have no choice but to act in areas that he would just as soon sidestep. We shook hands and when I left the capitol that day, I was a private citizen again.

In the meantime, however, I didn't have to look far for ways to spend my time after Alice and I moved home to Stanley. My brothers and our son, Bill, had been shouldering the load of running the King Brothers Ranch for four years, and I was glad to get back into that business. I spent several months just working around the ranch and reorienting myself. The house my dad built for Alice and me when we were first married was now about 25 years old. We decided to build a new one on the ranch, so we picked a site about two miles south of the old place and got busy building and furnishing a house, fixing up the yard, and generally settling in. Meanwhile, the highway still ran from Stanley to Santa Fe, just like it always did, and so did my car. I followed all the developments in state government and tried to help where I could. I went to the legislature several times and I visited with Governor Apodaca about things that had been pending when I left office. After putting in four years as governor myself, I couldn't just forget about all those issues and projects that I had been so deeply involved in. Besides, I knew I wasn't done with public life yet.

After a couple years, an issue came along that motivated me back into political activity. Although the transition from the King administration to the Apodaca administration had gone smoothly, in 1976 Jerry and I were at odds over a proposed constitutional amendment allowing governors two consecutive four-year terms. At the time, a seated governor could not run for re-election. Jerry began pushing hard for the amendment on the November ballot, which would allow him to succeed himself. At first, I stayed clear of the debate, but as Governor Apodaca campaigned for passage of the amendment, he kept saying, "I don't blame Bruce King for opposing this amendment. He obviously would like to run again in 1978, and he would be my principal opposition if the amendment passes."

After he said this a few times, I decided maybe he didn't have such a bad idea, after all—maybe I should be his principal opposition. So I took up the call and decided to campaign against the amendment. I met with some of my friends in the Albuquerque area, while my supporters kept an office in Santa Fe open for me. We took a pretty simple approach. Apodaca was using "Yes for Two" as his slogan, with "two" being the number of consecutive terms proposed in the amendment. We just turned that slogan upside down and printed a small amount of literature and bumper stickers that said, "No for Two." The Apodaca group pushed their slogan with sophisticated, expensive advertising, which included high-visibility TV ads, and they did a lot of precinct-level work. On my side, we didn't even attempt a strong, organized campaign. All my people worked without compensation or even expense money. The contributions we received covered printing the fliers and bumper stickers, which we passed around to our friends. Pretty soon, we were seeing a good number of "No for Two" signs on cars. Our total budget was about $10,000. By contrast, the Apodaca forces spent around $200,000 for their slick ad campaign and, like us, they took advantage of all the free public time available for discussing the issue.

In our literature, we stressed the advantages to New Mexico of limiting the governor and other statewide office holders to a single four-year term. For one thing, currently an incumbent governor wouldn't assemble a political machine for his re-election, while a sitting governor who could succeed himself might use the resources of his office to build influence for his re-election. Furthermore, a one-term governor feels less pressure to please the politicians because he is not seeking their support for his next race, which gives him more latitude to operate. Finally, if we allowed a governor to succeed himself, many of the talented people who would like to run for governor would have fewer opportunities to serve, since it's usually pretty tough to beat an incumbent.

I found this low-key campaign a lot of fun. I took my usual approach, mostly traveling around and looking up my friends. I was confident that many people would oppose two four-year terms in a row. Support for my position came from many sources. I developed the best relationship I ever had with many of my Republican friends because they shared my views on this issue. Since I had served on the board of directors of the New Mexico Farm and Livestock Bureau, I got excellent support from them, including help in designing the advertising campaign. I also took advantage of all the free TV time I could get. I worked any public debate that came up and tried to meet all the needs that developed for public information. Finally, in the last week I cut a couple short TV ads and urged voters to reserve their right to "turn the rascals out" after four years.

That fall, I went to a football game and many of my friends in the stands hollered up, "We read you loud and clear, governor. We're voting 'no!' " I felt the campaign was working well.

While I was opposing the term amendment, I helped my friend, U.S. Senator Joe Montoya, in his re-election campaign. I also worked for my old friend Governor Jimmy Carter in his presidential campaign. I tried not to commingle these races with the "No for Two" issue, although that proved difficult sometimes. On election day, the proposed constitutional amendment lost by a lopsided margin of some 64,000 votes, with two-thirds voting "no." Jimmy Carter won the presidential race, but Joe Montoya lost to former astronaut Harrison Schmitt.

After the election, Governor Apodaca and I wound up on much friendlier terms. We could both be proud of how vigorously we had campaigned, but we hadn't generated the animosity that many campaigns do when personal issues are involved. Still, the media people began asking me, "Does this mean the people don't agree with the type of government that Governor

Apodaca has been trying to run?" I simply replied that it meant the people of New Mexico didn't want two four-year terms in a row for their elected state officials. I'm sure Governor Apodaca appreciated my not saying the people were against him, which wouldn't have been true, anyhow.

Looking back after all these years, the election on the two-term amendment takes on a new irony, since I was the first governor to run for back-to-back terms after the amendment finally passed in 1990.

〰

Because I knew Jimmy Carter and I had such a strong farm and ranch background, there was quite a bit of talk after the 1976 election about me being U.S. Secretary of Agriculture in his administration. When he was elected, I was out of office and available. That was the only job that could have pulled me out of New Mexico to Washington, D.C. While these rumors were flying around, a few of my friends gave me some advice. From my work with the Western Governors' Association—I was chairman—I knew governors Stan Hathaway of Wyoming, John Love of Colorado, Cal Rampton of Utah, and John Williams of Arizona. They were a mix of Republicans and Democrats, and we were all good friends despite our party loyalties. During this time, they went down the Green River on a two-week raft trip together. Love and Hathaway, who were both Republicans, had held cabinet positions in the Nixon administration and then had fallen on hard times politically. I guess they all got to talking about my fate if I followed in their footsteps. So one night around the campfire, they wrote up a letter to me saying, "Look, Bruce, they don't like us Westerners in those cabinet secretary jobs, so don't you take one. You run for governor instead." I was interested in being Secretary of Agriculture, but President Carter never asked me, so I didn't have to decide.

〰

My campaign against the amendment brought me back into public life. It sure didn't hurt my image and it got me thinking about the future. Until then I hadn't decided whether to run for governor again, but as I campaigned against the amendment, many people told me they would vote it down if I ran for governor. I began to answer, "I'll be glad to," so I was committed to running again and I didn't even have to announce it after the 1976 general election.

1977 was slow, although I traveled a great deal, meeting county Democratic chairmen and mayors. I also attended service club breakfasts and luncheons and dinners and made myself available as a guest speaker. People learned they could have a former governor, speaker of the House, and president of the constitutional convention address their group without expense, so they started inviting me to their functions. I refrained from mentioning politics, unless it was a political gathering. Instead I covered topics that might interest the community where I was appearing, like livestock matters or state government. Word got around that I would not take political advantage of an invitation to speak, say, to the Rotary Club or Kiwanis or Lions, or religious groups, or a homecoming event, or barbecues.

Pretty soon I had a busy schedule, as Alice and I drove all over the state, hitting every county. We spent time at county fairs or whatever the local celebration might be and we stopped in the small communities, most of them mainly a store, post office, and filling station, like Aragon and Pie Town in Catron County, San Jon in the southeast, Capulin and Des Moines in the northeast, Blanco and Ramah in Indian country. We always got a warm reception. Paying attention to these out-of-the-way places paid off. Many months later in the November 1978 election when I was running for governor again, I watched results from around the state and saw that I kept getting large percentages of the vote from those small communities where I might have stopped only for 20 or 30 minutes.

As we took these trips and went about maintaining my organization and keeping contact with our friends, we also took time to relax and see the sites in New Mexico that people should see, but too often don't get around to. I recommend this kind of travel to anyone. Spend six months sometime, just touring New Mexico and seeing all its attractions. Head south in the winter, north in summer. Although it suits the climate best, we weren't always able to follow that itinerary. We did manage to tour all the state parks and museums, but we also went by the local newspaper offices, and the radio and TV stations. Since I was a committed candidate, the press knew why I was visiting them. I talked with them candidly and was able to keep my name before the public without expense.

As the spring of 1977 headed into summer, I still didn't even have a campaign headquarters, but my troops were getting restless and wanted more organization. I told my volunteers we would open offices in Albuquerque and Santa Fe. With my name recognition and the primary still a year off, I didn't feel this step was necessary, but it let my supporters get into the act. Finally in November we opened the headquarters and they ran along for a month or so, when I told everyone to go home for December, enjoy Christmas and New Year's, then come back to work along about the middle of January. Many of my volunteers thought this was an awfully long vacation with the election year coming up, but I finally persuaded them it would be all right.

Early in March, the 1978 campaign picked up steam. Governor Apodaca was backing the candidacy of his lieutenant governor, Bob Ferguson, who was also a former state representative and state senator. Bob and I were old friends. We had served together in the House of Representatives, and then he served in the state Senate when I was governor. I had supported him when he ran for lieutenant governor in 1974.

Bob was strong in his home town of Artesia in Eddy County and throughout southern and eastern New Mexico. He was an outstanding candidate, with excellent qualifications, plus he was well known and highly respected in legislative circles. So I knew I couldn't take the campaign lightly. I would have to work hard to maintain my position.

The first hurdle was the state Democratic pre-primary nominating convention. The process leading to the state convention began in the precincts about the middle of March, followed by county conventions in late March, and the state convention the first day of April. The law that applied that year was quite complicated. It spelled out precisely how a candidate had to go about getting convention delegates and how many delegates and what percentage of the total he would get, given the demonstration of his strength. We held election schools for interested citizens, where we explained the law and generally covered how to participate in politics. I paid the expenses for University of New Mexico professor Bill Byatt to travel around the state conducting election schools. They were open to anyone who wanted to come, Democrats or Republicans or whatever. We didn't check to see if they were King supporters, though I bet most of them were, and we picked up people who were just interested in participating in good government. They came and saw the first-rate materials we handed out, which covered my record and my proposals for the state of New Mexico. This kind of campaigning was very effective for me in 1978. I often attended the election schools with Bill in the larger communities, and we would bring in other speakers, as well.

Meanwhile, of course, Lieutenant Governor Ferguson was working hard to gain supporters, and Joe Skeen and Bob Grant were competing for the Republican nomination for governor. Skeen was far in the lead, so he began to take shots at me, since he could see that I was on track to win the Democratic nomination. He campaigned strongly on a pro–right-to-work platform, which I opposed. He also made a great issue of challenging all candidates to publish their financial statements and publicly declare their personal worth. I wasn't ready for a fight with Joe Skeen just then, so I refrained from taking his bait.

At the state Democratic convention, I got about 78 percent of the vote to Bob Ferguson's 22 percent, but he won enough delegates to get on the primary ballot against me. Now we both went to the people in earnest. I was actually glad to have him in the race. Sometimes you need a primary opponent—it helps you clarify your positions and explain the distinctive elements of your platform. On the other hand, too many primary opponents can hurt your chances because you get attacked from all sides. Also, a tough primary campaign can give the other party ammunition to draw on during the general election, when they pick up on the negative things your primary opponents brought out, as Casey Luna did to me in the 1994 election against Gary Johnson.

Bob Ferguson and I waged a hard but clean competition for the nomination. As expected, he proved quite strong in his home area of eastern and southeastern New Mexico, particularly in Eddy, Chaves, Lea, Otero, and Doña Ana counties. He had represented those people in the legislature for years. With the support of Jerry Apodaca, he ran a fairly effective campaign, but I stayed far ahead in the polls. My big lead made it hard for him to raise money. Ferguson kept challenging me to a debate, but I couldn't see any benefit in giving him the free media exposure. For my part, I sought out as many people as I could, trying to interest them in coming out to work for me. I also cautioned them not to alienate the Ferguson people, since we would need all the support we could get in the general election.

I kept hammering at the basic issues. Right-to-work became a hot topic. Ferguson was all for it and I was against it. I knew how divisive right-to-work could be, so I tried to steer the campaign discussion onto my experience, knowledge, and accomplishments. I also talked about the open-door policy I had maintained whenever I held public office—the people could always get in to see me. My opponents sometimes said I was too accessible and let myself get pulled away from more important matters of governing, but I never felt that way. I knew how to allocate my time carefully, so I could pack a lot into one day.

I also pointed out that I was a businessman, with a strong background in finances. I noted the financial gains we had made in state government during my first administration. We had developed a strong capital outlay program for building schools and other public structures throughout the state and I had left behind a $100 million surplus in the state treasury in 1974, along with a $50 million increase in reserves, for a total gain of $150 million in state revenues when I was governor.

To balance Bob Ferguson's strength in the east and southeast, I had my large bloc of friends in the northern counties of Santa Fe, Rio Arriba, Taos, Mora, Sandoval, and San Miguel. We did have competing Democratic factions in several of those areas, such as Rio Arriba County, with some candidates pushing for good government competing against the more traditional ones. But all their ads strongly endorsed me for governor, which was unusual up there. Of course they weren't so interested in actively helping me, since we came from different camps, but they knew that I had support among their constituents. I also had good backing in the Albuquerque area.

Mac McGinnis, the cartoonist of the *Albuquerque Journal*, was inspired to some striking cartoons by my primary campaign. In one, he noted my ability to remember names: I was shaking hands with men and women, calling everyone by their first names, and he had the roadrunner setting there, saying, "I wonder if he'll remember my name," in reference to my calling that carving a woodpecker back in 1971. McGinnis could be extremely critical on occasion, but his cartoons captured the character and political philosophy of his subjects. I held him in high esteem because I felt he portrayed me accurately to the public, even when he was making a little fun of me.

In the 1978 primary campaign, we had an offbeat candidate for U.S. Senate named Stephen Fox. He was an unusual candidate, without much funding, but he seemed to get around and always made it to political functions. One stormy night we were about to leave Clovis for Roswell. Stephen had also been campaigning in Clovis and was planning to sleep in the bus station. That upset me a little bit—I worried about him—but when we got to Roswell, there he was. I guess he hitched a ride with someone. On a few occasions, I helped him out. I knew he didn't have much chance of winning the Democratic nomination for Senate, but he sure had the drive to keep on campaigning. When the state Democratic convention came around, I even bought him a new suit. Of course, he didn't win and he worked very hard for me in the general election. He went on to become a successful artist in Santa Fe, where he runs a gallery.

When the primary election came around, I beat Bob Ferguson. My old lieutenant governor, Roberto Mondragon, won the nomination for that position again. We would be paired in the general election—a vote for one would be a vote for both. On the Republican side, Joe Skeen won the nomination and my friend state Senator Leo Dow was the nominee for lieutenant governor. They made a good ticket, so we had two strong candidates for both positions.

The morning after the primary election, I had breakfast with Bob Ferguson. In the primary, we had conducted a high-level campaign, with no mudslinging. Even so, I didn't want his supporters defecting to the Republicans. Many Ferguson people felt they had more in common with Joe Skeen than with me. He agreed with Ferguson on a couple issues, including right-to-work, and Skeen was popular in southeastern New Mexico. It turned out that despite my good relations with Bob, I ran into many problems bringing the Democratic party together, more than I had in the early 1970s. Some former Democratic legislators were leading the Democrats for Skeen, and they pulled in a few big Democratic names, most of whom had been inactive in the party for years. These party defectors attracted just about anyone who felt a little disgruntled and hadn't gotten the personal gain they expected from politics. They wanted the old spoils system to work for them the way it used to.

I don't know what these Democrats felt they would gain, but I made their defections work to my advantage in some ways. I knew I wasn't going to get them back, and many of them were known for political patronage, which I pointed out. With tongue in cheek, I said I was sorry I had to represent the people and wasn't able to serve a few of these individuals the way they thought I should. Then I wondered out loud what my opponent had promised them in return for their support. This strategy helped offset the losses from their defections. As the governor's race picked up steam, I pulled more people into my campaign from all over the state, including a Businessmen for King group that produced outstanding results for me.

〰

We focused on a few hot political issues in the 1978 campaign. Reforming liquor laws attracted a great deal of attention. In New Mexico, the state issued a restricted number of liquor licenses—far below demand—and they had become extremely valuable, since they could be resold. When the state did issue a new license under those circumstances, questions of propriety were bound to come up, because so much money was at stake.

Joe Skeen tried to make political hay out of that situation. I touched on liquor law reform, but didn't make it a key issue. I said that if I was elected, I would put a moratorium on any new liquor licenses. I wanted to name a committee to review our liquor laws and a strong liquor director who could take action to curb abuses in the liquor business.

The unavoidable topic in 1978 was right-to-work, which had a tremendous impact on the entire campaign. The press referred to it almost every day. At the same time, television was increasingly influential on campaigning. With its possibilities for media blitzes and its focus on the sound bite, television lends itself to drumming up single-issue campaigns. Right-to-work seemed tailor-made for this approach. Candidates can use TV ads to very effectively pound one issue over and over. In 1978, Joe Skeen made a great pitch for right-to-work. He suggested it would solve every evil, and that anyone against it would obviously oppose motherhood, as well. That kind of ad is powerful, but the impact of TV can be felt not only through paid advertising, but also through news coverage. Reporters tend to throw a saddle onto some subject that draws attention, then ride it for the distance. That can be frustrating when you're running for office, and since TV news stories tend to be shorter than a newspaper article, for instance, you don't get as much chance to explain your thoughts on a subject.

I could see that right-to-work was taking over the campaign. Though an important issue, it was hurting the candidates by diverting attention from our other positions. I felt it would be much better for the voters to resolve it themselves, rather than having it bog down every legislative session and gubernatorial campaign, so I proposed we place right-to-work on the ballot in a referendum and let the people of New Mexico decide directly. That way I sidestepped having to come out strongly against it, even though the Republicans were pushing me to make a stand. By advocating a referendum, I avoided campaigning strictly on my opposition to right-to-work, which would have alienated the more conservative voters in eastern and southern New Mexico. It had been on the ballot once before, in the 1950s, and had failed then. I had a hunch it would fail again if the people had another vote.

I got some unexpected help when Ronald Reagan visited New Mexico to speak on behalf of Joe Skeen. In his prepared remarks, former Governor Reagan said right-to-work ought to be placed on the ballot so everyone could vote on it. A newspaper cartoon the next day showed Joe Skeen looking pretty low, and Reagan saying, "What did I say wrong?"

Although right-to-work grabbed headlines, it wasn't the only issue generating press coverage in the 1978 campaign. Some people were concerned about the turnover at the top levels of state government that usually follows a change of administrations. The *Albuquerque Journal* said in an editorial that it would be a shame to lose some of the most able cabinet secretaries in state government when a new governor came in to replace Jerry Apodaca. I got quite a bit of mileage by pointing out that those top administrators of proven ability in state government had no need to worry about their jobs if I was elected. Many of them knew that already, since Governor Apodaca had retained several of them from my first administration.

I also campaigned on restoring the independent status of the State Police. The Apodaca administration had heavily reorganized state government, moving the State Police under the Criminal Justice Department. The police were unhappy with the department head, Charles Becknell, and their nominal boss was John Ramming, who had been convicted of a felony earlier in his career. The police viewed this with much concern. They felt the reorganization wasn't working well for them and they stirred up a great deal of publicity. I jumped on the issue, saying that if I was elected, I would move the State Police out of Criminal Justice and restore them as an independent agency.

In the area of taxes, I talked about my long experience with the state tax structure and promised not to raise taxes. I said I would look over the revenue situation and although I might make some adjustments, I thought the existing revenues would meet the needs of state government without any drastic changes.

As the campaign drew to a close, the Highway Department came into the spotlight. The highway people were always interested in who was going to be the new governor, and they were active in campaigns. Now in 1978, the media pointed out that the highway people were being much more active than usual. The press claimed I wanted to go back to the old way of running the Highway Department by moving out the professional staff to make room for my cronies, who would then prioritize road work on a political basis. None of that was true. My intent was to have a professional highway department, and I said so. Like the Republicans, I planned to keep Highway Department Secretary Fred O'Cheskey in place as the top administrator.

≋

In the 1978 campaign, a regular parade of public figures from out of state rolled through New Mexico to bring attention to the candidates in their party. Arkansas Senator Dale Bumpers, an old friend of mine from the days when we were both governors, came to speak at one of my fund-raisers. He brought his wife, and they also visited some of their family in Albuquerque. Senator Bumpers made an excellent speech for me, and I think it boosted my campaign. Other Democratic national figures came and helped me, including Morris Udall, the staunch Democratic Congressman from the Tucson area, and Governor Bruce Babbitt of Arizona, who had friends around Clovis, New Mexico, and sought their support for me. President Carter sent his mother, Miss Lillian, who also helped me.

On the Republican side, former President Gerald Ford came to New Mexico a few days before the election to speak for Skeen, when it looked like our governor's race was extremely close. Before that, former Texas Governor John Connally came to stump for Skeen, as did Governor Reagan. Those big Republican names drew many supporters and loosened pocketbooks, and allowing the Republicans to run a well-financed campaign. The news media covered these visiting dignitaries heavily.

For in-state support, I found I could count on Jerry Apodaca, even though we had had our differences. Jerry had supported Ferguson in the primary, returning the favor to me from four years earlier when I backed Tibo Chávez against him in the primary. But after the primary back then, I had supported Apodaca, and now he came back and worked for me, making many appearances for my campaign. He did it in a manner that was humorous, not heavy, and I appreciated his help.

We took a caravan of Democratic candidates around the state. One day Toney Anaya, who was running for Senate against incumbent Republican Pete Domenici, issued a press release expressing concern about whether all the Democrats were supporting him. He and I weren't the best of friends since we had that falling-out over his opposition to Senator Clinton Anderson becoming our national Democratic committeeman. The media made a big fuss about Anaya's claim that we were divided, insisting it was true and claiming we couldn't work in harmony. So Toney and I took great pains to show togetherness and persuade people that we were supporting each other, which in fact we were.

≋

I ran my usual people-to-people campaign in 1978. We didn't use consultants and we hadn't developed the highly polished media campaign that would come to dominate politics in later years. Even my own campaign workers wanted me to adopt more sophisticated strategies, like hiring consultants and using more technology. Some people said I couldn't win by just shaking hands and visiting mines and manufacturing plants, but I kept my emphasis on traveling around the state and meeting everyone I could. The roots of a campaign start with people—and I like people. I have always gotten great satisfaction out of going out and talking to the citizens of New Mexico, working my way through a room, introducing myself and shaking hands, and letting folks know they would have a friend in the capitol if they elected me. I take that approach not just to get votes, but to meet my constituents and find out who they are and what they need. I feel that I can find something to like in every person I meet, which I try to keep in mind when I'm talking to them. Even if I have problems with someone, I always look for the positive side.

In addition to traveling the state, we put on many large barbecues in Albuquerque, in Santa Fe, and at our Stanley ranch. Our friends would see to it that our beef was cooked, and they would get the beans and slaw and potato salad. These events were well-attended and gave me a chance to speak about my record and platform and what I would like to see done for New Mexico in the next four years.

In 1978, I could feel major differences in campaigning compared to my 1970 run for governor. Things had really changed since my early experience with Santa Fe County politics back in the 1950s, or even further back in the 1930s and 1940s when my dad was active in the Democratic precinct. In those days, politics started at the community level and was based on relationships. You met as many people as you could—that's how I learned to do it. I have always practiced personal campaigning, seeking out voters and talking directly with them. This year was no different. One time I visited a little cafe in Anthony, a small town in the southern Rio Grande valley that is half in New Mexico and half in Texas. I shook hands all around, even with some Texans who had stopped in for their coffee break. One man said, "That's strange. I live in Texas and I've never seen a Texas candidate come by, and here this makes the fifth one from New Mexico that's been in here." Of course, we have a much smaller population than Texas, but I think New Mexico politicians are exceptionally outgoing because of our strong tradition of personal politics.

Nobody campaigned harder or with a more personal touch than I did. Here, I chat with a young voter during the 1978 campaign against Joe Skeen. (Photograph courtesy Santa Fe *New Mexican*)

By the middle to late 1970s, however, campaigning was becoming more marketing and less relating face-to-face with people. Candidates were being packaged and sold through the media like any other form of merchandising. With television now playing a much stronger role, the costs of mounting a serious campaign for statewide office had increased tremendously. TV also brought a certain slickness to campaigning. Back in 1974, Jerry Apodaca and Joe Skeen had each campaigned this way, using highly professional media advertising. Apodaca once said that the TV spot where he was jogging in a sweatsuit, saying, "Vote for the man nobody owns," gave his campaign a great boost. I tried to stay one step removed from this new, highly polished approach. I kept hard at work, getting around the state and visiting with people to discuss the issues with them. I ran a low-budget operation, even by the standards of 1978. My opponents, however, were going all-out with the "package and sell" approach. While our total expenses were under $200,000, my opponent spent at least twice that much, and Senator Domenici put around $1 million into his run for re-election against Toney Anaya.

In the final weeks of the campaign, Joe Skeen and I debated a couple times on TV, and the Skeen people heavily advertised that face-off, urging voters to make their choice based on the TV debate. For the occasion, I even got a new hair style, making me look a little more contemporary. Most people felt the first debate ended in a draw, so I didn't lose any ground there, and the Republicans backed off their advertising of the second debate, apparently thinking they were not gaining an advantage with that tactic. In contrast to the debates, another aspect of the media campaign was actually effective for me, as my supporters wrote numerous letters to the editor of the newspapers—unbeknownst to me—pointing out my strengths and the errors of my opponents.

The rise of media impact on politics was accompanied by the diminishing influence of the once-powerful local party leaders, or *patrones* as they're known around New Mexico. In the early 1950s, a candidate for governor could go into a half dozen of the larger counties, see two dozen people, and come away with a pretty good idea whether or not he would carry those areas in the election. That had changed completely by the late 1970s. Voters had become too well informed to be led to the polls by a local boss. I would have to say it's a change for the better, because it's more democratic. It also suited me well, because my style of campaigning—getting around, mingling, introducing myself directly to people, getting to know them, and asking for their vote—hadn't ever changed much. It worked well in 1978.

I read the World Almanac to a Hereford bull on the King Brothers Ranch at Stanley, 1979. This photo was taken as publicity for the *Albuquerque Tribune*, which was marketing the World Almanac at the time.

The most exciting thing that happened to me during the 1978 campaign didn't have anything to do with politics. It was a case of mistaken identity getting a little out of hand. A couple weeks before the election, Alice and I were flying in a two-engine airplane and our son Gary was driving the car so we could get around once we landed at the various community airports on the east side of the state. We had campaigned in Roosevelt County, then with some of our staff and a newspaper reporter we flew down to Carlsbad for a big evening meeting. That's about as far south as you can go in New Mexico and still draw a crowd. Afterwards, we went out to the Carlsbad general aviation airport to take the plane to Alamogordo. It was pretty late by then and it was raining cats and dogs. Gary and the Eddy

County workers who helped load the baggage into the plane were in a hurry to get us off.

We hadn't much more than lifted into the air when the pilot said, "Oh, my goodness, somebody didn't shut one of the doors on the baggage compartment. We've got to land." So he immediately circled back to Carlsbad and landed at the far end of the long runway, quite a distance from the terminal. The whole outfit sits out in the middle of the desert a few miles from town. The pilot got out in the rain and shut the baggage compartment door. After he got back in the plane, it wouldn't start. It was too hot and I guess it had vapor-locked. The pilot said we would have to wait for it to cool before we could take off, and we sat there about 30 minutes. Then just as he got the plane started, lights came on from all around us on the runway. We heard voices on bullhorns hollering, "Don't move that plane."

One man stepped forward wearing a trench coat, with a cigar stuck in his mouth and a submachine gun in his hands. "All of you guys come out of there with your hands up!"

The pilot went to the door and said, "We've got Governor King in here."

"I don't give a damn who you got in there," he said, apparently not believing the pilot. "You come out with your hands up!" We could see men outside pointing guns at every window of the plane, right at our heads.

I knew this was probably a drug raid and I said, "Boy, I don't blame you guys for being so cautious. When you start arresting people for running narcotics, you have to be very careful."

When the trench-coated leader heard my voice, which I'm told is very distinctive, he said, "Doggone, it *is* the governor!" He was obviously a little embarrassed. "Governor King, I want to apologize. . . ."

"No apology needed," I said. I was never so happy to have someone recognize my voice. "But what are you people doing out here?"

"We've been setting a net for people running drugs, and we thought tonight was the night, and we thought we had them."

With all this straightened out, we tried to take off again, and again the plane wouldn't start, so we had to sit awhile and let it cool. Finally, we got up in the air and headed to Alamogordo. By the time we reached the hotel, it was about 3 A.M., and the phone rang. It was the drug agents calling to ask us not to report what had happened so they could set up their sting again tomorrow. I told them the only people who knew about it were those riding with us, but that included the reporter. He had already written the story, but agreed to talk to his editor. They held the story with the understanding that when the sting took place, they would get an exclusive on it, which they did. In fact, the agents caught the drug traffickers a few nights later.

≋

Election night was a madhouse. Up until one or two in the morning we still didn't know who had won. I just sat there as we got calls from all the counties with their results. Brian Sanderoff was keeping a running total and he would say, "Oh, this is bad. . . . Oh, wait, this looks pretty good." The returns went back and forth that way. Roosevelt County came in and we had lost it, and I started to get a little worried. But then the indicator precincts started coming in from Albuquerque's Northeast Heights, a traditionally Republican area, and although we weren't winning, we weren't losing too badly. I still remembered how Gene Lusk lost the election in 1968 because Dave Cargo carried the Heights. We only lost Bernalillo County by maybe 3,000 votes, and staying close there helped me win the election.

When the final count was in, I had beaten Joe Skeen by about 4,000 votes, a much smaller margin than I was used to. But a win's a win, and I felt fortunate to bring it off against all the forces that I had battled. One reporter wrote that with Senator Pete Domenici and Congressman Manuel Lujan both scoring big victories for the Republicans, I was lucky to win. Skeen was a strong candidate—he did finally go on to the U.S. Congress— and the Democratic defections stole away some of the party's voting base. As I look back on it, I see that my reputation worked for me in that election. Also, my position of putting right-to-work on the ballot so people could vote it up or down probably helped save me the election, since I didn't have to turn off a large segment of the voters by campaigning on strong opposition to it. Right-to-work is a classic example of how a single issue can dominate a race and make it much more difficult to campaign. It's hard to get across all your strengths when everyone wants to know your answer to just one question.

Offsetting these drawbacks were my volunteers, who represented a wider range of citizens' interests than my volunteers of 1970 had. People came in to work for me because they felt I had managed government well in my first administration. Many of them had never even met me, but had followed the news media during those first four years. Along with this volunteer activism, the weakened state of the Democratic party machine gave the general electorate more room to get involved, which I think was for the better.

11

Back in the Saddle Again

The top floor of the Roundhouse in Santa Fe felt like home. I settled into the governor's office like I was sliding a leg over a comfortable, broke-in saddle. Yet as I have found over three terms in office, each administration is a totally new endeavor: times change and people change, and you can't predict the events that will define your time as governor. In January 1979, I was ready to take on the tough issues like right-to-work and liquor law reform, and I knew we'd have another round of debate on how to spend the state's revenue surplus. I also knew we had to somehow improve the situation in our Corrections Department and at the state penitentiary, but I don't think anyone expected that problem to blow up into such a horrific nightmare as it did in 1980.

Things started off pretty easy for me. Although a new governor is not sworn in until January 1st, his administration starts gearing up immediately after the election. On November 9th, we opened a transition office on the third floor of the capitol. Working here was a complete turnaround from the pressures of the campaign. Right away, long lines of people who wanted to talk to me started forming outside the door. That was fine by me. I had the reputation of being willing and able to see many people, and I let each one know I appreciated their interest. I also had to tell them that not many jobs would be available, and not many applicants were going to be placed in top positions.

The transition office also gave me a great opportunity to become familiar with the current needs of state government. Now that the campaign was over, the professional people working in the various departments and agencies came forward to share their knowledge, not only with me but with my staff and cabinet secretaries, which I started naming by the end of November. I wanted to put together my permanent working staff and get them oriented before we took over on January 1st. This was complicated by the fact that I was dealing with a different structure of government than I had worked with in my first administration. Governor Apodaca had reorganized the departments, and it still needed a great deal of fine tuning, so I was looking for people with experience and stature to fill the twelve cabinet positions. I also had to consider many candidates for the exempt positions. They were political appointees who lay outside the personnel system and were not under any cabinet secretary.

I began by mentioning which of the cabinet secretaries in the Apodaca administration I would ask to remain. I also let those who had campaigned for my opponent know they need not report for work on January 1st. I kept Bill Huey as chairman of Natural Resources, Fred Muniz as secretary of Taxation and Revenue, Bill Stevens as secretary of Agriculture, Fred O'Cheskey as secretary of the Highway Department, Dr. George Goldstein as secretary of the Health and Environment Department, and Reuben Miera as secretary of Transportation. Another holdover was Charles Becknell as secretary of the Criminal Justice Department, with jurisdiction over the penal institutions. I asked Martin Vigil to remain chief of the State Police.

During the campaign, I had been criticized by some who thought I would fire Fred O'Cheskey, but I kept him on, like I said I would. I also found satisfaction in retaining Reuben Miera. I had been attacked for cronyism when I appointed him to a position in my first administration, but he had worked out well and Governor Apodaca had made him Transportation secretary. I was glad to keep him on. In fact, each of these carryover secretaries had served in my first administration, except for Dr. Goldstein. I knew their abilities. By staying, they gave me a nucleus of proven skills that helped immensely to maintain continuity in state government.

Maxine Gerheart was secretary of Finance and Administration for Governor Apodaca, but her health was poor and she wanted to leave, so I appointed my nephew, David King, to fill that slot. I also named Larry Ingram secretary of the Human Services Department. I brought in Larry Kehoe as secretary of Energy and Minerals and John Salvo as secretary of Commerce and Industry. Salvo was controversial at the start, but he gave a good account of himself. To take on the changes I wanted to see in liquor laws and enforcement, I named my former press secretary Jim Baca as liquor director.

By the middle of December, I had all these appointments out of the way. I also addressed some organizational issues. I told the news media I was going to remove the State Police from the Criminal Justice Department, something I had promised during the campaign. It hadn't worked out well for the law enforcement agency to work under those in charge of the justice system and penal institutions, so I was restoring the independent status of the State Police. I also intended to move the Employment Security Division out of the Human Services Department and establish it as a department of its own.

≋

The day after my second inauguration, I went to work preparing for the upcoming legislative session in January. With the House of Representatives in great turmoil, I began to work on legislation with Senators Aubrey Dunn, C.B. Trujillo, and Ike Smalley, the established leaders of the Senate. The legislature convened on January 17th, and the House would decide its leadership then. A coalition of some Republicans had joined with the conservative east-side Democrats to revolt against the previous House leadership. The new coalition divided the ranks so closely that no one knew whether the House would re-elect mainstream Democrat Walter Martinez to a fifth term or pick the coalition candidate, Gene Samberson. After a brief delay while the legislators signed the register, the secretary of state conducted the election for House speaker and Samberson won. This was the first time in New Mexico we had a coalition speaker, and it completely changed the organization of the House, since the speaker appoints the committees and heavily influences the fate of legislation. Yet the coalition hadn't been confident of winning, so they weren't prepared to take charge. They hadn't decided who would chair committees or how they would assign members. After the speaker election, we held the usual joint session with the Senate about three hours late, when I delivered the State of the State address. Then they recessed for the afternoon and took a day or so to select the committee chairmen and work out their procedures. The day of the election, the Democratic caucus censured the dissidents who had joined the coalition. Cartoons around the state showed the big elephant hugging the coalition Democrats, while the regular Democrats stood off to the side.

There was much short-lived speculation about whether I could work with the coalition. A cartoon in the *New Mexican* showed me with a juggling act, trying to hold the show together. Right away, I took steps to make sure I could do business with them. During the second week of the session Alice and I invited all the legislators to the executive mansion, and virtually all of them came. That pleasant evening helped a great deal in building good relationships between the legislators and me as the session progressed. Much credit for my success with the coalition also goes to Jim Otts of Eddy County, a Democrat coalition member who remained a loyal friend of mine. Jim worked hard to keep the executive and legislative branches working together.

Feeling at home at the House Speaker's podium in the Roundhouse, I delivered my 1979 State of the State address to the New Mexico Legislature. (Photograph by Barabarellen Koch, courtesy Santa Fe *New Mexican*)

The executive budget I submitted to the legislature called for appropriations of around $750 million. I worked with Aubrey Dunn, Senate finance committee chairman, and John Mershon, who was once again House appropriations chairman, on getting the budget through. I also brought in my son, Bill, to lobby for me. He had grown up around the legislature and knew most of the members, so he was able to effectively communicate my position to them. We felt that state revenues were sufficient to allow a $75 million tax reduction. I wanted to do away with the gross receipts tax on food, but many legislators including Senator Dunn were concerned about how that would affect the state's tax structure, so we compromised on a $45 per person tax rebate, and a double rebate for citizens over 65 years old. The legislature reduced our proposed $45 rebate to $40, kept the doubling factor for those over 65, and passed the bill. That rebate went to every resident of the state, reimbursing them for sales tax they had paid for food, and it was a first in the nation.

Although I fought a few times over revenues with the coalition, I found I was able to work with them on the budget just fine. When the smoke cleared after the session, total appropriations for general fund operations in fiscal 1980 were $753 million, just three million over the budget I had sent to the legislature. About half that amount went to the on-going operations of public education, plus another $9 million in capital outlays for schools. We also earmarked $5 million for a new agriculture building at New Mexico State University in Las Cruces.

Considering how hot an issue right-to-work had been during the 1978 campaign, I wasn't surprised when a right-to-work bill passed both houses in the 1979 legislature. To avoid any unnecessary wrangling, I vetoed it unceremoniously and sent it back the same day it came up to me. However, the speaker and a few others questioned whether I had imposed the veto properly. Evidently my staff had sent the original copy of this bill back to the legislators along with my veto message, which obviously was sufficient. But the enrolled and engrossed copy was sent to the secretary of state with the veto message, which was an unnecessary step. The speaker and others contended that this copy, as well as the original bill, should have been sent back to the Senate. They raised quite a flap, contending that the bill had become law because of this supposedly faulty submission of the veto message. Finally, Attorney General Jeff Bingaman ruled that the manner of transmitting the veto message was sufficient, that the veto had been given wide publicity, and that it was common knowledge that I had vetoed the bill. So my veto withstood the challenge.

Crime and law-and-order issues came up during the 1979 legislature. I had campaigned hard in favor of the Crimestoppers program. Started in Albuquerque by police officer Greg MacAleese, it provides reward money for anonymous tips that lead to an arrest. Crimestoppers had proven very successful in Albuquerque and I wanted to expand it statewide, so I was pleased to sign the bill that created and funded a New Mexico Crimestoppers program. We later hired Greg to run the state program. He established the national Crimestoppers in every state that requested it, and he helped the New Mexico Game and Fish Department establish Operation Game Thief, which worked exactly like Crimestoppers. He worked with the Human Services Department to develop a similar program for reporting fraud and abuse in human services. Before we were done, Crimestoppers and its spinoffs became one of the outstanding accomplishments of my second term.

To strengthen our efforts against organized crime, I signed a bill giving subpoena power to the Governor's Organized Crime Prevention Commission. This bill also allowed the commission to release information they had collected in secret, so they could keep the public informed about attempts by organized crime to enter New Mexico. I felt that public exposure of these attempts by the mob to infiltrate our state would help discourage them before they had established operations here.

〰

A couple national issues stirred up discussion in New Mexico in 1979. Because of gasoline shortages around the country, President Carter had authorized the states to allocate their supplies. I didn't feel we needed to—we had enough gas. The Energy and Minerals Department kept close track of our gas supplies, and we were able to drive our cars as usual. In a state with very long distances between many towns and little public transportation, rationing was a hardship I was happy to avoid.

About the same time, the Pentagon was pushing the MX missile. The idea was to play a kind of shell game with many missiles, moving them around so the Soviets would never know exactly where one was. Of course, it took a lot of open country to do this, and western states were the top candidates. One of the prime locations, at least in the Pentagon's collective mind, was eastern New Mexico. I asked Brian Sanderoff to be my special representative on this issue. After he studied it and reported back to me, we concluded it would be best for New Mexico to base the MX in Nevada or Utah. Those two states didn't take kindly to my suggestion, and their governors said, "No, thanks, you guys take it," to which I replied, "No, you guys go ahead."

On one of my trips to Washington, D.C., the Air Force gave me an enthusiastic briefing on the MX. They made such a hard sell I felt like I had a target stitched onto my suit coat. They explained the advantages of deploying the missiles on the eastern plains near Clovis, where they already had a base. Then at one point they pulled out some large-scale maps of the area, and I mentioned that I often bought cattle in that area. I went over and studied the maps for a while and pretty soon I got oriented so I could pick out the individual farms and ranches where the missiles would be based. I explained who lived in each one, calling them by name. I could easily visualize exactly how it would disrupt the way of life over there. I guess it was obvious I knew what I was talking about, since I had such detailed knowledge of the area. From that point on, their briefing was considerably more subdued. I told them it would be a better idea to place it on rangeland, and not on our irrigated farming lands, which supported intensive agriculture and were a vital part of the economy.

As it turned out, no one got the MX missile. The Pentagon eventually abandoned the notion, much to our relief.

≈≈

During my first administration, our youngest son Gary was finishing high school and Alice kept her energies focused on our home. She was involved in all of the things a First Lady has to do, like caring for the mansion and keeping it open to the public. She also worked on many children's programs in the early 1970s. Then in my campaign for a second term—with Gary now in college—I had said that Alice was going to be involved in my administration. The state would get two public servants for the price of one. After I was elected, for all practical purposes she became a member of my staff as the state's number one volunteer, devoting her full-time energies to helping young people and the elderly. She also promoted volunteer activities.

We set up Alice in her own office in the governor's office suite. Now she had the clout and prestige to travel around the state looking at youth and senior citizen programs and trying to boost the interest and enthusiasm of the volunteers and paid workers in those programs. It would have been impossible for me to get to all these communities, but people accepted Alice in my stead, which gave us double coverage in many areas. In fact, some people felt more comfortable approaching Alice with their requests than me or my staff. She gave them an avenue into the governor's office that hadn't been there before. Then she would pass the information or request on to me or my staff, although as time went on, she handled more and more things by herself.

Alice became a public figure in her own right during my second administration, and she carried that role even more strongly into my third term as governor. She had a constituency all her own. People in education, health care, and child care considered her one of their leading champions. She worked behind the scenes, starting with my inner circle, but she also testified before legislative committees and appeared before many public groups, carrying her message that the children of New Mexico needed support.

At first a few people, including some cabinet members, thought she was meddling, but soon they liked having her help. Alice worked closely with the cabinet secretaries in her areas of interest, particularly Larry Ingram of the Human Services Department, George Goldstein of the Health and Environment Department, and my chief of staff, Bill Giron. With these folks she would travel to the rural areas of New Mexico and investigate their needs related to health and services for the handicapped. We didn't have much health care in the outlying areas, and Alice worked hard to coordinate state services for them. She also helped set up health clinics and food distribution centers. She worked extensively with the Navajo Nation to address health and housing needs through joint state-tribe programs.

Starting in 1979, Alice worked on the proposed new juvenile code relating to young offenders. This attracted a great deal of interest and attention.

Alice chaired the committee I appointed to review and suggest recommendations to the juvenile code. That committee included Jeannie Stover, wife of Albuquerque Police Chief Bob Stover, David Schmidt of the Council on Crime and Delinquency, Sally Evans of Santa Fe, Judge Joe Caldwell of Taos, Senator Caleb Chandler of Curry County, and Representative Frank Horan of Bernalillo County. This group traveled all over the state, holding hearings to get public input and to publicize their efforts.

Some people felt we should design a juvenile code to lock up offenders and throw away the key. Instead, our approach called for good rehabilitation programs aimed at diverting young people away from paths that eventually lead to adult penal institutions. We also wanted to keep juvenile offenders separate from adults. Spending money on prevention can actually save the state money by reducing the need for additional detention facilities and correctional programs. Unfortunately, prevention and rehabilitation can be expensive and it was tough getting money out of the legislature, where the juvenile code was discussed at length. We never quite got the funding we needed, but we were able to make some constructive changes that protected children while ensuring they received punishment that fit their crimes.

This revised code set down guidelines about how law enforcement agencies and the courts would handle juvenile crimes such as truancy and petty theft. It established prevention and treatment programs and set time limits on how long children could be incarcerated at the Springer correctional facility. It increased the role of the Youth Diagnostic Center in Albuquerque regarding evaluation of the needs of delinquent children. The code also spelled out a child's right of privacy and protection from the news media in reporting crimes.

From 1979–1982, Alice worked with the state Youth Authority, an agency that dealt with juvenile justice programs, and she chaired the Juvenile Justice Council, which oversaw the expenditure of those funds. The council included about 25 people from social services agencies, law enforcement, and the juvenile justice agencies. We used the federal funds to run programs for improving the conditions of juveniles and to create legislation separating children from adults in the justice system.

Also in my second administration, Alice chaired the New Mexico committee of the International Year of the Child in 1979. This group held hearings all around the state to find out what children needed, then developed a state plan that we submitted to Washington for funding. The next year was the International Year of the Family, and we did the same thing for family issues. I appointed a Family Policy Task Force, with representatives from the Human Services Department, the Hospitals and Institutions Division, the Youth Authority, the courts, and the general public. They met monthly and put together a plan to better coordinate, connect, and deliver state services to families. This plan demonstrated the benefits of putting all these services under one roof, an idea we took one step further in my third administration, when we created the first state Children, Youth, and Families Department in the nation.

Alice's other great interest was volunteerism. We used my office and funding from the national ACTION committee to create the Office of Volunteerism in New Mexico, which supported volunteer issues at the state and community level. I hired Pat Powell to run this office, which eventually grew large enough to move out of the governor's office as a private, non-profit corporation. Its purpose was to help local communities develop their own cadre of volunteers through training and other support. Unfortunately, the Office of Volunteerism didn't survive the Anaya administration, which succeeded my second term. It often happens that a new governor doesn't share the interests of his predecessor, and many times a worthy program just dries up and withers away.

≋

I had campaigned on a stand of reviewing and, if necessary, reforming liquor laws. I backed that promise with action early in 1979. I was pleased to sign a liquor control bill that took some initial steps to reform the state Liquor Division, although we all knew they were just a start toward liquor reform in New Mexico. Meanwhile, I was taking drastic action within the existing law to correct the state's chronic problems regulating liquor—for instance, sales to minors were rampant and bars were violating the blue law against selling package liquor on Sundays. Not many people thought we could make headway against abuses of the law. One newspaper editor, Ralph Looney of the *Albuquerque Tribune*, wrote that I had about as much chance of reforming liquor laws as food prices had of dropping 50 percent. His predictions were half right.

During the transition after the election, Jim Baca had been writing a report on organized crime. He saw that we had problems in the area of liquor control and he came in to talk to me about it. "We've got to make changes in the Liquor Division," he said. "The public just doesn't have confidence in that agency." I knew Jim was a bright, capable young man, so even though he didn't know all about liquor laws, I made him liquor control director. I didn't ask him to reform the laws. I just said, "Go straighten out the Liquor Control Division."

Jim took me seriously and showed he was a strong leader. With Attorney General Bingaman, he began carrying out the intent of the law and the rules and regulations administering the Liquor Division. That was a good start. Right after the inauguration, he ordered some weekend raids. The agents were excited because until then they hadn't been allowed to do anything. They busted a bunch of bars for selling package liquor on Sunday. We let the press know, and the next week we got big headlines saying the Liquor Division was already turning around after only three weeks under the new administration.

We ran into plenty of resistance. The Democratic party had deep ties to the liquor industry, and many people from that line of business were politically active. Every time Jim issued a citation, someone would call me up or even visit me in person and say, "Baca's going crazy!" I would tell them, "Well, you fellas got to obey the law. Jim's over there to do what's right, you know." I never once asked him to back off. And we went through some sticky situations.

A key element of our reform plan was to reduce the market value of liquor licenses. Although the state issued licenses for a $50 fee, after that they could be resold on the private market for hundreds of thousands of dollars because of their limited numbers. This situation was made worse by the fact that you couldn't transfer a license from one county to another, or even from the unincorporated parts of a county into a municipality in that county. These restrictions further limited the supply of licenses and artificially increased the demand. Many people were manipulating those licenses for profit. They weren't in the liquor business, they were in the liquor *license* business. We projected that licenses would reach $1 million apiece in ten years. It was a wide-open opportunity for corruption in government. We also found organized crime was involved. As Jim started investigating these characters, they put a lot of pressure on him, breaking into his car, stealing files, and so on. Jim never bowed to that intimidation, and he helped put some of those folks away.

After this went on awhile, Jim came to me and said, "Governor, we need to reform these liquor laws. Let me have a crack at it and work with the legislature."

"Okay," I told him. "You handle it, and I'll help you where I can." It was a huge task. The liquor lobby was so strong and so many legislators were being supported by liquor people that no one thought we could do it.

In 1981, Jim finally felt he was ready to introduce legislation rewriting the state's liquor laws. As we expected, it was a major issue in the 1981 session. Jim and Jeff Bingaman kept the topic before the press and got big play in the papers and on television, so that no legislator could face the voters back home and deny how they had voted on liquor law reform. After some brilliant maneuvering in the legislature by Albuquerque Senator Les Houston, who worked untiringly day and night to design the legislation and get citizen support for it, the legislature passed the bill. Now I needed public input before I signed it. The day I was deciding whether to sign or veto, a line of lobbyists stretched outside my door and down the hallway toward the elevators on the fourth floor. We had pressure from all sides, not just from the liquor industry. For instance, the churches were hesitant to support the bill, but they felt it was better than the law it replaced.

After careful review, I did finally sign the liquor reform bill. Public reaction was immediate and favorable. People were getting the beer and wine licenses they had so long been denied, and I think everyone was glad we were more closely regulating the liquor industry. I stated to the press that we were at last turning in the right direction with liquor control, after decades of building on the wrong policies. Without a doubt, liquor law reform was a high point of my second administration. The prevailing wisdom had been that it was impossible in New Mexico, and we certainly could not have achieved it without such a high level of support from the public and the press.

〜

In my second administration, I realized the correctional system had deteriorated dangerously. We needed to move quickly in developing a long-term
plan to turn that situation around. In my 1980 state of the state address
opening the legislative session, I devoted several paragraphs to across-the-
board improvements in Corrections. I asked the legislature to adopt a ten-
point plan that we had taken a year or so to develop. It stressed the need for
capital outlays, better training and pay for the guards, an improved prison
industries program, and an improved recreational program. I also called for
a direct line of authority from the warden and the director of the Santa Fe
prison to the governor and legislature. I asked the legislature to restore the
powers of the state Correctional Commission, which had once been in charge
of the day-to-day operation of the penitentiary. Under the Apodaca
administration's reorganization of state government, the commission had
been reduced to merely advising the Criminal Justice Department.

When I had left in 1974, our correctional system had been in good
shape, but over the years since then it had deteriorated. While everyone—
the legislature, previous governors, myself, and the public—knew it was bad
off, the pressure and population had built gradually over the years. Now it
was clear we had overloaded the correctional system, and many people who
worked there had resigned. The state penitentiary just a few miles south of
Santa Fe was a particular hotspot, troubled by almost weekly incidents. Then
on December 10th, ten hardcore prisoners—in supposedly maximum security—escaped. I was alarmed and we immediately began to look into the
unrest at the pen and the entire correctional system. I was leaning heavily on
Corrections Secretary Charles Becknell to solve those problems. About this
time, I needed more facts, so I asked Attorney General Jeff Bingaman to
conduct a thorough study of the situation, and he began carrying out this
request. Then as we got ready for the upcoming legislative session, Becknell
decided to bail out, resigning about a week before the session began. I appointed Adolph Saenz to replace him. He had to move his home and family
from back east to New Mexico, so he was not able to report to work for a
month or two.

Meanwhile, I had brought in a new warden, Jerry Griffin, who had been
doing a good job running the correctional institute at Roswell. In hindsight,

that was probably a difficult time to appoint this young man as a new warden, with many clouds gathering on the horizon, but none of us predicted the severity of the storm that was brewing. While we were addressing the needs as we saw them, we stumbled onto different problems that had not been apparent before. We were trying to act on the recommendations of the attorney general—such as adding more cells and more guards—but even those efforts added to the friction and compounded the problems at the penitentiary. We had set aside part of the institution for remodeling and the contractors were working in one of the cell blocks. It turned out their tools and equipment contributed to the trouble ahead.

Finally, the pen just boiled over. About two in the morning on Saturday, February 2, the emergency phone beside my bed in the mansion rang, startling me awake. It was Chief Martin Vigil of the State Police, and my stomach knotted up in apprehension.

"Governor, we've lost contact with the penitentiary," he told me. "When we call there, we don't get any answer. I thought I'd better alert you. It's possible we have a serious problem."

My first thought had been that, whatever the precise nature of the situation, we didn't want to risk losing control at the pen and having the inmates take over. With the recent escapes on my mind, I could imagine the devastating effects we'd have now if the inmates began a mass escape.

"Did you call out the SWAT teams?" I asked Martin, and he confirmed that he had. I told him to keep me informed, then I called General Frank Miles, commander of the New Mexico National Guard, and ordered him to call out emergency troops to the penitentiary so we could be certain to contain the prisoners there. My initial concern was protecting the civilian residents who lived in the rural neighborhoods near the penitentiary. I could imagine prisoners cutting through the fence and scattering throughout the community. So I called Linda Kehoe and Bill Giron, two of my trusted staff members, and instructed them to begin alerting every household near the prison. I wanted those people to know that we were having problems and that they should take extra precautions.

Within 20 minutes, I got a call telling me the penitentiary prisoners were rioting. The guards had lost control of the prison, although they still held the towers and controlled the perimeter. SWAT teams were already on the scene, their members drawn from the State Police, Santa Fe city police, the sheriff's department, and other law enforcement agencies in the area. No prisoners had escaped yet, but I still didn't know how aggressively the prisoners would try to break out. I fretted over that prospect until I received word within an hour that the National Guard had arrived. A couple hours later, Guard units were setting up a protective shield around the penitentiary. By daylight, around six-thirty that cold winter morning, all the units were in place and I began to rest a little easier about protecting the citizens who lived in that area, but those fears were soon replaced by my concern for the safety of the guards and the welfare of the prisoners.

About 7:30 A.M., I went to State Police headquarters, where they were in contact with Deputy Warden Bobby Montoya and Deputy Corrections Secretary Felix Rodriguez, who were at the penitentiary. They had gone in the front gates and up to the cell blocks, where they were attempting to persuade the inmates to give back the penitentiary. The prisoners were demanding to talk to the governor, among other things. I felt no hesitation about negotiating with them to resolve the problems. I hoped that, given the rapport I had established with the inmates in past years, I could convince them to return the prison to the Corrections officials.

The first prisoner who got on the line said, "Is this the governor?"

I told him it was.

"Well, Governor, we've been having problems out here and we want to visit and make some corrections," he said in a conciliatory tone. "We want to get attention."

Chief Vigil and several others were listening in on our conversation. I went very slow, but I did let the inmate present the position of the rioters, since he was representing himself as being their leader. Then someone else at the other end of the line must have heard my voice, because I could hear him say, "Well, that *is* the governor." Then he grabbed the phone away from the first inmate and began to make *his* presentation. I realized that no one was in charge out there. Finally, after two or three of these exchanges, one man did seem to have more authority than anyone else in the prison ranks. He maintained the conversation, saying "Governor, we're unhappy because the guards have been treating us like a bunch of kids and they were trying to make us shut off the TV and go to bed early, and the food hasn't been as good as it should be."

I could tell this fellow must have been doing time at the prison for a number of years, so I took a new approach. "You know, I thought we worked pretty well in the early 1970s, when I was governor before. We did a lot of things to improve the inmates' quality of life. We had good educational programs, good work-training programs, and good recreational programs."

To this he said, "Yeah, that's right, you did. And that's the reason we're just going to have a peaceful takeover. We're not going to destroy any of the facilities or harm anyone. We're going to turn everyone back over this afternoon, but we wanted to bring our problems to everyone's attention." His tone was becoming more belligerent.

"Well," I said, trying to calm him down. "I'm glad you felt we had a good prison system in those years."

"Yeah, but you've been there a year now and nothing has improved. We're impatient, that's the problem, and nothing is happening," he said.

Then he demanded that we send Bobby Montoya and Felix Rodriguez to negotiate with the inmates and that we not try to retake the prison by force.

"We're going to give you just one hour for those negotiations to start," the inmates said. "We want a table placed out in the corridor and Bobby Montoya and Felix Rodriguez will know where they should be."

I told them it would take us an hour to get our negotiating team together, and they agreed to that schedule. So with that I went out and talked to Felix and Bobby, who had worked with the penitentiary for several years and were game to meet with the inmates. After these two officials made contact with the prisoners, they began trying to work out guidelines for returning the prison to the authorities. One of their demands was access to the news media. In particular, they wanted Ernie Mills, the veteran capitol radio reporter and newspaper columnist, to come in and listen to their grievances. He immediately agreed.

Meanwhile, the rioting intensified. As always happens with mob rule, especially if the mob is out of control at a penal institution, there was no clear direction to the demands and activities of the inmates. Even while they were negotiating with us and insisting the takeover would be peaceful—and I believe they were sincere—others had unlocked the maximum security wing, home to about a dozen of the worst, most hardened offenders. Now these men gained control of the institution. Many of these hardcore criminals were vindictive and bent on revenge against those inmates—mainly in protective custody in Cell Block 4—who they suspected to be snitches, or informers.

These hardcore leaders from maximum security took over the control center by breaking through a set of glass windows that were supposedly unbreakable, according to the architect's specifications. Then they brought in acetylene torches that were being used in the prison remodeling work and began cutting through the bars that housed the suspected snitches. I can only imagine the cold terror gripping those inmates as they watched their attackers grimly cutting into their protective cells. Once inside, the maximum security inmates went on a killing spree, murdering the other prisoners in horrific, barbaric ways. It must have been a hellish scene. A few others were murdered elsewhere in the penitentiary, as well, while the other prisoners were negotiating with the Corrections officials.

During the morning, I had moved in closer and set myself up at the warden's house on the prison grounds where I could confer directly with the National Guard commanders on the scene and with the State Police officers. I had ordered that the line of authority go through Felix Rodriguez and Martin Vigil as the codirectors of the operation, with General Miles included in making decisions. Then Felix delegated command of operations on the scene to Bobby Montoya, and Martin delegated to State Police Captain Bob Carroll. We all stayed in such close contact that we had no problems with the chain of command.

It was about 10 A.M. when we received word that 14 prisoners had been killed. I was devastated. About the same time, the inmates released a few guards and prisoners who needed medical attention, and they confirmed that it was becoming a bloody riot. As the gravity of the situation began to sink in, we discussed retaking the penitentiary by force. We had enough strength assembled by now, but we had to weigh both the consequences and the timing. The inmates had at least two guns and all the riot equipment of the guards. They would unquestionably put up stiff resistance if we advanced, and in the ensuing battle we were likely to lose the lives of at least a few police officers and National Guardsmen. In light of that scenario, we decided to establish as much control as possible without force. We had sharpshooters in the towers who could prevent the bloodshed from moving outward into the grounds below them. At least we had contained the riot to a central area of the prison.

By midday, the situation seemed stable, even if it wasn't resolved. I was confident the commanders on the spot could best decide how to retake the cell blocks, so I headed back to the state capitol. I felt it was important to tell the legislators what I knew about the riot, since I had already reported to the media that at least 14 inmates had died. The riot had become a national news story, with the press flying in from all over the United States as rapidly as they could gather. And it is amazing how rapidly they can gather. When I left the prison, at least 150 news reporters had arrived at the riot scene.

At 1:00 P.M. I reached my office. The inmates had set fire to the gymnasium at the pen and we could see the smoke from all over town. It was particularly visible from the upper floors of the capitol when I brought the leadership of both houses and both parties to my office. I also invited all the legislators who had been involved with the correctional system and the correctional study committee, which was a 13-member interim committee made up of legislators from the House and Senate. Altogether about 40 legislators packed into my office, and I briefed them on the latest developments of the riot, the number presumed dead (by now, 14 murdered and perhaps another 10 dead from smoke inhalation), and the arrangements to provide medical help to those guards and prisoners released by the rioting inmates. The warden was getting them into the yard area, but we still had no shelter or food for them.

The legislators were as concerned as I was and extremely supportive. That's one thing about our state government: until then, minority members had tried to pick holes in my programs whenever they saw an opportunity, but now all the legislators immediately expressed their 100 percent support of any decisions I would make. I appreciated that, but I wasn't exactly sure what decision we needed to make. Then Chief Vigil interrupted our meeting with a phone call.

"We have reliable information that they have now killed four guards and we think that we better move in," he told me.

"Then we had better move in," I said, but then Felix Rodriguez got on the phone and said, "Listen, Governor, I probably have better contacts inside than the State Police or anyone else. I have reliable information that we haven't had any more lives taken in the last couple of hours and no guards have been murdered. I think that given another two or three hours, we can negotiate with them and regain control without further loss of life."

Because I had such great confidence in Felix and his knowledge of the institution, I decided to wait until later in the afternoon to make the decision.

All the nationwide news coverage prompted various national "experts" on corrections to call me with advice. One such caller urged me to go ahead and storm the pen, even though we would lose a few police officers and National Guardsmen. "You're going to lose them anyway," the caller said. "You won't be able to take the prison back without bloodshed. The quicker you do it, the fewer you'll lose."

"What about the prisoners?" I asked him.

"Just disregard the inmates," he said. "You have to go right in with guns blazing and take charge."

I disregarded that expert advice.

Instead, we did it Felix's way. By nightfall, he and Bobby Montoya were negotiating with some of the inmates and getting concessions by giving additional news coverage to those who had gotten somewhat in command of the inmates. They secured the release of 3 or 4 guards who were hostages, out of about 18 who were inside at the time of the takeover. Some other guards had been released earlier, as well. The negotiations continued to drag on into the night, but we never saw an opportunity to move in. About two in the morning, we began to get more guards out, including a number who needed medical attention, and the inmates were cooperating. They began to say there had been too much killing already—in the end, 33 inmates died. When the riot had started, a few inmates rampaged through the entire penitentiary, unlocking everything, so everyone was running loose on the inside. Now those with apparently better judgment than the murderous gang had taken control and were negotiating with us to release more guards and prisoners who needed doctoring. In the meantime, inmates had begun leaving the prison of their own volition in a steadily increasing stream, and they kept coming out into the night to surrender themselves in the yards.

By the wee hours of Sunday morning, we had custody of most of the inmates. Inside, the fires set by rioters in the living areas had pretty much burned themselves out. Felix and the other negotiators were exhausted. None had slept to speak of, so with things quieting down I suggested they all get some rest until daylight while other officers filled in for them and for our commanders on the scene. We had turned on the floodlights in the towers, so the yard and fence were brightly lit, allowing the tower guards to keep up their surveillance of the entire grounds. I spent most of the night on the phone with the commanders, reviewing their various decisions. When dawn came, I headed back out there. Negotiations had resumed and more guards were released.

Naturally, the media jumped on the story like a mountain lion on a mule deer. We had so many inquiries that we stopped taking individual requests for information and I fell back on a press release. Much of the early press coverage distorted the facts—not surprising, considering the chaos and confusion that swirled around that first night, with false reports circulating even among our officials on the scene. I wanted to keep the press informed so they wouldn't compound the problem, but even with our best efforts, we saw stories on the ten o'clock news Saturday night claiming that 80 people had died in the riot. Reporters passed on other distortions and errors as fact.

Sunday morning I met with the press as I entered and left the prison. I also met with relatives of the inmates, who were more concerned even than the press about what was going on. With smoke curling up from the inner living quarters and the rumors of high body counts, it certainly didn't look good from the outside. The relatives had swarmed onto the scene, setting up a tremendous encampment at the outer perimeter of the penitentiary grounds, and they pressed in as close as we would let them. Whenever I came through, they came running up to me, begging me to protect their husband, or their boy. Of course, I wished I could give them those assurances, and I told them we were doing everything we could to save lives—and that included the lives of the guards who were still held hostages. Their families also had assembled. It meant a great deal to me that we brought them all out alive.

The guardsmen and police officers had sealed off the area. As the prisoners gave themselves up, the guards held them in custody within that sealed area, but they were all outside. I was concerned about the weather, although we were blessed with fairly mild temperatures for early February at 7,000 feet. If we had had the zero-degree weather that we've experienced many times before, we would have faced a huge problem. Nature spared us that weekend. We got every prisoner a blanket, gave them firewood to burn, and fed them box lunches.

By midmorning Sunday, we had gotten out all but a few guards, and we knew they were holed up. One was in the old gas chamber, and the others had likewise found sanctuary. They couldn't get out, but at least they were safe. The negotiations were going well and by early afternoon, we got out the last prisoners who weren't still involved in the rioting inside. Now the cell blocks were held by those who wanted to keep up the mayhem. We had everyone else in our custody, out in the open. Although they were gathered in big groups in the prison yard, at least they were isolated from the cell blocks and from the rioters. I gave orders to bring food in, but when we made the first drops from National Guard helicopters, the prisoners tore things up pretty well because they didn't want to divide the rations amongst themselves. To prevent any more fights, I ordered the Guard to bring enough bread and lunch meat and wienies so there would be a loaf and meat for everyone. We got that done and it calmed the prisoners down.

By 3:00 P.M., Chief Vigil called and said it was time to retake the cell blocks. Our people had worked it out with the prisoners so we could go in without a violent confrontation. They wanted me to come, so Alice and I went back on out to the prison. As we arrived, the officers and troops were moving in rapidly through the main gate. I was nervous about their loaded guns—what if a prisoner got a hold of a rifle?—and there were a few skirmishes, but they got the remaining prisoners out and regained control relatively peacefully within half an hour. The riot was over.

With nightfall it began looking like a storm was blowing in and I was concerned about the plight of the prisoners in the open and also of the guards who were watching over them. We had a couple cell blocks that were still fit to house prisoners, and we let some of them back in. But before we could do much of anything, we had a tremendous problem just identifying all 1,100 inmates, who were thoroughly commingled, the hardened maximum security prisoners mixing with the rest. We had a long, long way to go before we resolved that problem, but the National Guard and the law enforcement officers did a terrific job maintaining order throughout the night.

We set up a communications system to inform the relatives of the prisoners we could identify about their status, and we had to notify next-of-kin for those who were dead—the number had climbed to 33 by that time. Meanwhile, Felix Rodriguez and my staff assistant Bill Giron were steadily bringing order back to the situation, and they were doing a great job. In fact, Felix was later honored by a national correctional association for performing beyond the call of duty during the riot. We kept hot food coming for the inmates and set up medical assistance teams with medics from around the state. As the next few days passed, the tensions gradually subsided. We continued identifying the prisoners. Many of their records had been burned, which made the job difficult. We were also working on where we could place them in other facilities. I had plenty of offers from fellow governors to use their prisons, and the federal system was accommodating, as well.

When I got back to the legislature, I found they had been working overtime during this calamity. Speaker Samberson, Representative Russ Autrey, and Representative John Mershon—all members of the coalition—had taken it on themselves to see that we had ample funding to meet the penitentiary's needs, which everyone now recognized. Finance Secretary David King and the House appropriations committee had concluded that we needed about $80 million for refurbishing existing facilities and for a new building program so we could house those inmates we had just sent out of state. Bill King and Gary O'Dowd helped draft that bill.

The legislature unanimously approved the funds. That was one of the quickest-passing bills I ever saw rip through the legislature. Because of the emergency situation, the bill gave me authority to oversee the expenditures without legislative approval. They also requested that Bill Giron oversee the expenditures, which was fine by me. As it turned out, we spent only the money necessary to complete a renovation and addition to the correctional facility at Los Lunas, which amounted to about $12 million. I kept a lid on the spending because after things had settled down a bit I realized we didn't have to move so rapidly. I thought it better to carefully study our construction needs, get architectural plans, and give the legislature a chance to review them.

Our new secretary of Corrections, Adolph Saenz, was dedicated to designing a good system, and I felt he had the administrative ability to pull it off, even though it was a nearly impossible situation to resolve quickly and to everyone's satisfaction. I gave him a great deal of leeway. He moved rapidly as he tried to bring order to Corrections, but it wasn't too many days before the *Santa Fe Reporter*, a weekly newspaper in the capital, published a

254 ~~ *Bruce King*

story saying we had not adequately investigated his background. They claimed he had been in the CIA and had left under pressure amid accusations that linked him to torture down in Uruguay. Adolph immediately denied the story, but many in state government were extremely critical of his continuation as secretary of corrections. With all the turmoil we'd been through, that story sent major repercussions throughout the state correctional system.

In the meantime, about two weeks after the riot Attorney General Jeff Bingaman approached me about creating a blue-ribbon citizens' council to help us develop correctional policy. I agreed, and named a representative cross-section of citizens to the panel. I wanted them to be the focal point for all information and suggestions that were coming in. I told Adolph to work with them, although he would remain in charge of Corrections. Well, he worked at it quite hard, but it wasn't long until he got into a big hassle with David King and the Department of Finance and Administration over Adolph's handling of monies in the state financial system. For his part, Adolph felt David was trying to run his department. Everyone was still under intense pressure, and we were all tiptoeing around the issue of the penitentiary. People developed short boiling points and tempers were flaring as strong accusations flew around.

Now the Legislative Finance Committee got on my back for appointing the citizens' panel. The LFC claimed it was infringing on their legislative responsibility—they wanted to be left alone to review the needs and the competency of Adolph Saenz. One exception was Senator Alex Martinez, a new member of the LFC, who supported me strongly and bought me some time with that body while we regrouped and reviewed the prison situation again. The trouble was, the *Santa Fe Reporter's* accusations made it difficult for Saenz to maintain the stature he needed to do his job effectively. Within two or three months it became obvious that he faced an impossible challenge. Finally in June the LFC requested a meeting with me on a Saturday afternoon. I consented, and when we got together they asked me to fire Adolph Saenz. I had already decided to replace him—with all the criticism, we just couldn't pull the operation together. In his defense, I have to say that no matter who might have assumed that responsibility amidst all the confusion of the riot, no matter who might have tried to bring order out of the chaos under such intense media scrutiny—that person would have been doomed from the day he started. So I explained all this to Adolph, and he resigned. To fill the slot for the time being, I named Bill Giron as acting secretary of Corrections.

We had begun working with the National Institute of Corrections, which had sent us the assistance of several experts. That collaboration had been quite successful. I have learned that you need the support of these professional organizations to help you through much of the decision-making related to prisons, including the hiring process. The day Adolph Saenz resigned, Jerry Yamamoto came on assignment from the institute. He had been California secretary of Corrections. Right away, he began working closely with Bill Giron and Felix Rodriguez. Together, they managed to quickly restore a great deal of order and to rebuild confidence in the Corrections Department. Soon it was time to hire a permanent secretary. Unfortunately, a few nationally broadcast news stories on television had painted an inaccurate, unfair picture of our situation. Probably as a result, we didn't receive a single application for the open position of secretary of Corrections, so we continued a couple more months with Bill, Felix, and Jerry running the system. Then we advertised again and finally hired Roger Crist from the Montana correctional system. That same year, he had been honored as the outstanding correctional official in America. I felt he was the one who could best manage our riot-torn prison system. Hiring him proved to be a turning point, as we made very rapid progress in reforming Corrections.

Before the legislature met again in 1981, we got our ambitious capital outlay program and training program underway. Roger Crist naturally put a great deal of his own philosophy into the effort. By the end of the 1981 legislature, we were able to show them substantial progress and lay out a clear plan to meet our needs for the future. They demonstrated their approval by reappropriating much of the unspent $80 million from the 1980 session.

Our plan was to complete the 488-bed unit at Los Lunas first. It would alleviate pressure at the Santa Fe penitentiary. We further decided to build a medium security facility at Las Cruces, a new classification intake system at Grants, and two modern facilities at Santa Fe to replace much of the old pen. With the legislature's backing, Roger Crist dove into this building program and most of the facilities were completed by the end of my term in

1982. In addition to all this construction, I pushed for a good community corrections program, a job facility within the prison, and an educational program for inmates to support their rehabilitation. We were soon able to bring back the prisoners we had sent out of state after the riot, mostly to Arizona and Texas.

We went a long way in a short time toward developing a model prison system in New Mexico, and I became the spokesman for modern corrections at the National Governors' Association conferences. From the knowledge I had learned the hard way, I was able to warn my fellow governors about the danger signals, and many of them later told me I helped them avert similar catastrophes. I always promoted good basic staff training and a solid rehabilitation program for any youth who might be in trouble. Alice and I have always believed that one of the best ways to solve prison problems is to keep people from ending up there in the first place—such prevention starts with youth. I preferred youth training programs in communities, so that kids wouldn't even be incarcerated. If they did get into the correctional system, I wanted to see a strong classification system and separate facilities to keep them from mingling with the hardened criminals. I wanted to educate those young people who came into the system, rehabilitate them, and turn them away from the life of crime so they would never end up in the adult criminal justice system. For those who did wind up there, we needed a safe, controlled environment. Furthermore, we needed to assure that the small number of dangerous inmates in whom destructiveness was deeply imprinted would never return to the streets where they could endanger the public, nor would they have the opportunity to attack their fellow inmates.

After the riot, a group including the American Civil Liberties Union and representatives of the penitentiary inmates filed suit against me as governor. They demanded improvements at the penitentiary. In addition, the plaintiffs of the already pending Duran v. King lawsuit eventually wanted me to testify in the trial, but I claimed immunity as the chief executive, though I did finally answer a 92-point questionnaire submitted by the ACLU and others. My answers satisfied the judge and that was the end of that.

On July 21st of 1980 I felt we had progressed to the point in cleaning up Corrections that I could sign a consent decree with the plaintiffs of

Duran v. King. The consent decree named Judge Campos as the supervisor from the court system, and we agreed on a model plan for improvements at the penitentiary. Among the stipulations were limits on the number of prisoners at the penitentiary, regulations governing the number of prisoners in a cell, and so forth. Judge Campos would review our progress and once all parties were satisfied that the requirements of the decree had been met, it would be lifted and the court would relinquish supervision of the prison. However, to this day the decree remains in effect.

For nearly two years after the riot it seemed like everyone was investigating it: Congressmen, the newspapers, the FBI, the New Mexico State Police, the Santa Fe district attorney, and so on. Responding to constant inquiries just absorbed too much time and energy and diverted us from the daily tasks at hand. Finally I got sick of these endless investigations, which never seemed to turn up any new insights into the circumstances surrounding the riot. Eventually we were able to take some action to fend off these groups, but the issue of the riot and the prison system even dragged into the 1982 governor's primary campaign. It seemed like it would never go away, with the lawsuits heating up and the plaintiffs insisting I testify, so I was gratified when a grand jury reported after I left office that we had made positive improvements in the prison system.

Over the next three years we poured an awful lot of time and effort into the prison system. The State Penitentiary riot of 1980 had been the worst public emergency of all my years as governor. Probably no other event focused so much national press attention on New Mexico. Although several of the news reports tried to assign blame for the riot, it really resulted from a combination of circumstances, including years of inadequate funding. A major deficiency at the penitentiary that we didn't know about was the plate glass that had been installed around the control center. It had been specified by the architect with the understanding that it was unbreakable, but the rioting inmates smashed through it in about seven minutes. Then they were able to gain control of the penitentiary. On subsequent settlements with the insurance companies and others, the glass companies were held accountable and did contribute some 40 to 45 percent of the monies paid out by the state. Finally, I still believe that if the ten-point plan my administration had created in 1979 had been put in place, the riot never would have happened.

∼

Even with as much time as this corrections mess took, we were able to accomplish big things in other areas. Besides reforming the liquor laws, we almost doubled public school funding, and we built new roads or improved old ones all around the state, which directly benefits the average citizen and makes a clear contribution to their daily lives. Another area with direct impact on citizens is taxes. Once again, state government revenues were on an upswing in the early 1980s. As I prepared for the 1981 legislature, I saw that we could afford a large tax cut, somewhere between $180 million and $200 million. That was unheard of in the history of New Mexico, but the state was in a strong financial position, with additional monies in the general fund, the permanent fund, and the severance tax permanent fund. We had increased the state severance tax in the 1980 session, and we ended fiscal year 1979–80 with a $75 million surplus, which was $68 million more than we had projected. So I knew we could afford a tax cut.

Tax reduction, however, takes some careful thought. In 1980 I had vetoed a tax relief bill passed by the legislature because I felt it hadn't been sufficiently studied and didn't give homeowners the breaks they needed. It gave more relief to large utilities than to small business owners, and I thought that was unfair. So my administration worked during the interim to develop a tax reduction plan to submit to the 1981 legislature. It removed property tax at the state level, helped out the homeowner and small business owner, and also gave a break to the utilities and oil and gas industry. Our proposal would also reduce the state income tax and gross receipts tax.

We faced a hard, drawn-out fight in the legislature. Republican Representative Colin McMillan chaired the House taxation and revenue committee and was a staunch Republican member of the ruling coalition in the House. He had been particularly critical of me for vetoing the 1980 tax reduction plan they passed, but when it came to the actual work in 1981, he and all the rest worked closely with us to pass the new package. In fact, the press and others called it the "Big Mac" tax cut and Colin deservedly got some of the credit for getting it passed. However, many times if we weren't watching, he would push in and try to make it look like he was the only one promoting tax reduction. That's par for the course in politics, and we countered by making it known that we were the original authors of that tax cut.

What pleased me most was not the tax reduction, or the revenue surplus behind it, but the fact that we had appropriated money to meet the needs of the state and its citizens. We had set aside $80 million for developing new correctional facilities, and we still had ample money for education, including pay increases for the school teachers and for the personnel in our colleges and universities. We also funded a strong social program for those in need, including the senior citizens and youth, although we weren't as successful as I would have liked in addressing the needs of young people. Alice had worked on developing these programs, giving a great deal of time in attempting to improve the lot of adolescents and teenagers who got into difficulties and needed help and guidance, rather than punishment by the law.

12

Building Trust and Border Crossings

Growing up in the farm and ranch country of northern New Mexico, I had always felt close to local Hispanic culture, so I was naturally drawn to Mexico. As the governor of a state with hundreds of miles of international border with Mexico, I made it a priority through all three of my administrations to build up New Mexico's relationship with that great republic to the south. I enjoyed few activities more during my tenure in office than becoming friends with the Mexican people and their public officials.

Of course, New Mexico has old cultural and even political ties south of the border, but I felt we needed to develop stronger economic and diplomatic bonds for the benefit of everyone. Whenever the issue of foreign trade came up, it seemed a bit misguided to make a hard run at opening up Japan or other Asian markets for our products without first doing all the business we could with Mexico. The world had become a global market place, all right, and our front door to that market opened into our immediate Mexican neighbor, the state of Chihuahua.

I came at this issue from a couple directions—developing relations between our state government and that of Chihuahua, and working with the governors from the American Southwest and northern Mexico to address issues that affected us all. I worked hard on concrete things, like border crossings and promoting the North American Free Trade Agreement, and also on building friendship, trust, and cooperation.

The governors of Texas, New Mexico, Arizona, and California had common opportunities and problems with the six adjacent Mexican states. I took a leadership role in bringing us together to tackle these concerns. During the 1970s, we focused on questions of law enforcement—particularly in regard to the flow of drugs across the border—immigration of undocumented workers into the United States, education, and the arts. The discussion about undocumented workers included the fact that, since it was not illegal to employ them in the United States, they were then eligible for the same benefits as American workers—social security benefits, in particular. Although employers withheld money for social security and other insurance from the wages of these undocumented workers, they rarely collected these benefits. This greatly concerned Mexico. Governor Bill Clements of Texas and I worked hard on this problem, making several suggestions for legislation introduced in Congress. Later, in the 1980s, our emphasis shifted somewhat to common economic development for both sides of the border, an issue that reached a high point with the signing of the North American Free Trade Agreement.

Alice and I laid the groundwork for these future collaborations when we traveled to Chihuahua in June 1971 for our first meeting with Governor and Mrs. Oscar Flores. We needed to work out the details for the Anapra port of entry near Sunland Park, New Mexico, and El Paso, Texas. I wanted a port to expedite the flow of goods between New Mexico and Mexico. We didn't have a major border crossing that could handle a large volume of trucks. We also lacked a way to connect trucking with rail service, so our goods had to cross into Mexico from Texas. I felt that hindered our state's economic growth. Anapra was just off Interstate 10 and Interstate 25, the region's major east-west and north-south transportation arteries. Our proposed site was also only a stone's throw from El Paso, which together with Ciudad Juárez across the line in Chihuahua forms the largest border metropolitan area between our two countries. The Anapra port would give us direct access to a major gateway into Mexico.

When it came time to set up the meeting with Oscar Flores, I got directly involved. For governors to get together they just about have to deal with one another personally—there are too many details to run through someone else. So I first spoke with Governor Flores when we were setting up this conference over the phone. I had picked up enough Spanish working around the ranch to hold a conversation, but I immediately told Governor Flores that I spoke Spanish poorly, saying "*Yo no hablo Español. Yo hablo poquito, pero nado lo mucho.*"

He listened a minute, then without hesitation said, "Well, then, governor, why don't we just talk in English? I understand English." My assistant, Linda Kehoe, was on an extension prepared to translate for me, and she broke up laughing over that. Obviously Governor Flores spoke better English than I did, so I well remember that exchange. It set the tone for our meeting, and in Chihuahua we felt we were friends the moment we met.

I brought down a plane load of New Mexicans. Right off, Governor Flores said, "Governor, I've got some of my key people and we've got two buses. We better have some of my people get on the bus with your people. You and I had better ride on the front bus, and let's have your lovely wife Alice and my wife go in the car." He had a nice chauffeur-driven car, so they got in. I didn't know where they would wind up, or when we would see them again, but Alice was courageous and delighted to be with Mrs. Flores.

I thought passing up the private car to ride with our staff people on the bus said a lot about Governor Flores' character. As we rode along, everything we saw was a conversational enticement. It turned out we were both ranchers, and we developed an enduring friendship from that initial meeting. I didn't know where we were going, but we soon reached the governor's quarters, where they had a beautiful reception waiting, with mariachi bands and all kinds of hors d'oeuvres and refreshments. We got there about 10 A.M., and this went on until about noon. Then Governor Flores said, "Bruce, we do things differently in Mexico. You better go rest a couple of hours, and then we're going to have lunch. Then we'll get into business after lunch."

"Okay," I said, "if that's the way, we'll do it." So we went and rested for a couple of hours, and then we came back and had about a two-hour lunch. I thought, "Boy, we're getting the red-carpet treatment, but I don't know if we're going to accomplish much in the way of business." Despite those thoughts, I was so pleased with the good feelings developing between us and Governor Flores and his wife and the Mexican people that I wasn't worrying about it.

After our siesta and lunch, we met at four o'clock sharp back at the capitol building, where we began at once to discuss the port of entry. We worked out exactly where it would be, with maps and documentation. All this went extremely well, and by evening we were close to agreement on Anapra, embodying many details that we had already worked out. We retired for the night and met early the next morning. At 7 A.M. they brought in breakfast and by ten o'clock we had settled everything. We gave the details to the professionals to type out. My staff was having a hard time getting the office equipment they needed, and Governor Flores' staff was translating, and it was going pretty slow.

Governor Flores said, "Governor, this is getting to the point where we will have to do something."

He took out a table and wrote down all the points we had agreed on, in beautiful Spanish longhand, and he said, "Here, you sign it, and I'll sign it, and they can get all that other stuff together and we'll sign it some other day." So we did, and I still have that handwritten draft somewhere. We then joined the other members of the party, had a nice lunch, and departed.

Our agreement resolved many of the obstacles in the way of opening the port. U.S. Senator Joe Montoya took care of the needs at the federal level for establishing the customs facility. He was chairman of the Senate subcommittee that handled those areas. Governor Flores worked quite successfully on the corresponding problems with the government of Mexico. The cattle growers associations in both countries assisted a great deal, as did the New Mexico Department of Agriculture at New Mexico State University. The press also went with us and gave our visit excellent coverage. They were interested and they shared our feeling that we would succeed in opening the port of Anapra.

In spite of all our efforts, though, somewhere along the line we lacked just a little bit, and the port never became a reality. If Governor Flores and I had each had longer terms of office, we probably would have succeeded. Mexico did build a connecting road and got within half a mile of the port, and we built a crossing that was needed on our side, but when Governor Flores and I left office, the drive to create the port of Anapra went with us, since our successors on both sides of the border didn't show interest in the project. Maybe they didn't want Governor Flores and me to get the credit. Opposition developed and the project dropped by the wayside, although we did manage to open a large livestock crossing at Columbus. Unfortunately, despite its importance to agriculture, Columbus is just too far from a major city and from transportation arteries to serve as a large port of entry.

Several years later when I came into office for my second administration in 1979, both sides of the border were debating whether the crossing should be at Anapra or nearby Santa Teresa, New Mexico. By that time, a developer on our side of the border name Charlie Crowder had gotten into the act. He had land at Santa Teresa and was willing to work with the state. That location had better security than Anapra, more room for development, and an opportunity to link the highway system with the railroads in an intermodal facility, which would greatly enhance our ability to ship goods throughout the U.S. So we all got behind Santa Teresa at that time, but we didn't get too far along before I left office again.

On the positive side, my collaborations in Chihuahua opened up a new era of friendly relations between Mexico and New Mexico. Our meeting with Governor Flores was the forerunner of the Bi-national Border Governor's Conferences that we started in later years, which became an important, ongoing forum for resolving issues common to both nations. That first visit also began my friendship with Governor Flores, who opened many doors for me in Mexico. When he became attorney general of Mexico in the late 1970s, he arranged for me to meet with President López Portillo, which led to productive meetings with Mexican presidents.

About the same time that we were developing the Anapra agreement, Senator Montoya was also working hard to make the Albuquerque airport an international airport. When it opened in 1971, Alice and I went with a group of Albuquerque businessmen to Chihuahua to invite the Governor and Mrs. Flores to Albuquerque for the ribbon cutting. They agreed and we held a friendly ceremony at the airport, with many other dignitaries attending. Afterwards, Governor and Mrs. Flores stayed over and came to the executive mansion in Santa Fe. Alice and Mrs. Flores toured the many attractions of Santa Fe while the governor and I toured the King Brothers Ranch at Stanley. We relaxed and enjoyed the occasion in New Mexico, just as we had earlier in Chihuahua.

In September, I went to Columbus, New Mexico, and cut the ribbon that opened the livestock facilities on both sides of the border, with some cattle pens in Chihuahua and some in New Mexico. Governor Flores and I continued to clear out much of the red tape involved with importing and exporting livestock, particularly in cattle transfers across the border. It was a complicated process up till then, because from either side you had to drive to the crossing, unload your cattle, dip them in vats as a treatment for parasites, have them inspected by a veterinarian and a brand inspector, and then load them up again and drive across to the other country. The facility we built at Columbus streamlined all this, so that by the time you were done with the process, the cattle emerged in pens on the other side of the border without ever getting back in a trailer. Columbus is still one of the largest cattle crossings between the United States and Mexico.

Late in April 1972, I lead the New Mexico Amigos on a visit to Mexico. This time our two New Mexico congressmen, Harold Runnels and Manuel Lujan, came along, as did Senator Montoya. We started in Juárez, meeting the mayor and Governor Flores on the bridge spanning the Rio Grande, which is the international border at El Paso, Texas. They gave us a wonderful reception. We attended a banquet and had audiences in Juárez with President Echeverría, who was a friend of Senator Montoya and the late Senator Dennis Chávez. Then we traveled on to Mexico City, with its 10 million people. All five major newspapers ran front-page headlines about Governor King and the New Mexico Amigos visiting on a goodwill tour and honoring the republic of Mexico and the capital city with their presence. It was quite a warm welcome.

President Echeverría was not in Mexico City when we arrived but he arranged for us to meet with former President Miguel Aleman, then director of the national tourism office in Mexico. He received us exceptionally well, and we also met with the governor of the state of Mexico and the mayor of Mexico City. They received us royally, beyond any expectation we could imagine during our three-day stay in Mexico City. Police escorts took us everywhere, driving down the opposite side of the street with lights flashing in heavy traffic—it would about scare you half to death. We visited various business people and government officers and were treated to the finest in Mexican theater, dance, and music. From there, we went on to Guadalajara, where we met with the governor of the state of Jalisco and spent a couple of enjoyable days discussing ways to improve tourism between our two countries. We also discussed improving air transportation and tightening our drug enforcement activities, which I already had been proposing. In return for this trip, many of our friends from Mexico came to see us in New Mexico. On one such visit, four Mexican citizens from the state of Sonora, headed by Rafael Cavalarjo, came to make a presentation to their counterparts in New Mexico.

All these visits during my first term as governor were just the start of our work with Mexico. We were beginning to establish New Mexico as the leader among the U.S. border states in public relations with that nation. When I was re-elected for a second term, I used our Southern Governors Border Commission—which was made up of the governors of Texas, New Mexico, Arizona, and California—as the structure for working with our counterpart governors of the neighboring Mexican states. Dr. Gerald Thomas, president of New Mexico State University at Las Cruces, agreed to serve as chairman of the commission. As a prominent resident of southern New Mexico, he had a good grasp of the needs and problems of the region.

The commission met at Brownsville, Texas, in April 1979. When our discussion came around to undocumented workers, governors Jerry Brown of California and Bill Clements soon got at loggerheads over that issue. This was one of the first meetings of mostly new governors, and our commission almost fell apart right then. I had to work carefully with them to keep the group from adjourning and heading home before we even got started that first day. However, once we got underway and began to work, we all wound up good friends, even though we didn't agree on the exact direction we wanted to pursue in some respects. We also developed good rapport with our friends in Mexico.

After my 1978 election to a second term as governor, I also re-established my role as goodwill ambassador to Mexico. In the spring of 1979, Alice and I accepted an invitation to visit with President López Portillo. My friend Oscar Flores was now attorney general of Mexico, and through him I was able to secure an appointment with the president. Fabian Chávez and Leo Griego, then the state personnel director and my main contact with Mexico, worked for me to set up this meeting. Alice and I and Gerald Thomas stayed in Mexico City with the United States ambassador to Mexico, Patrick Lucy, who was a former governor of Wisconsin and a longtime friend of mine.

President López Portillo met with us for an hour and showed much interest in working out our mutual problems across the international border. After the meeting, we held a press conference with a crowd of reporters from throughout Mexico, particularly Mexico City. They asked pointed questions about American treatment of undocumented workers from Mexico, who they felt were entitled to humane treatment. I agreed with that point of view, and I told them that in New Mexico we were considerate to foreign workers and treated them fairly. I pointed out that if those workers were to receive their benefits, as the Mexican government wanted them to, then at least we had to identify the workers for that purpose. This was a difficult problem, one we aren't any closer to solving today than we were in 1979. But the Mexican reporters and officials did understand our need to identify workers so they could receive their benefits, after we explained the reasoning to them.

Late in September 1979 I was elected chairman of the Southern Governors Border Commission by my fellow governors of Texas, Arizona, and California. We were all working well together and with our Mexican peers. We started developing sister-state relationships across the border, which was easy for me, given my history of working with Governor Flores of Chihuahua in the early 1970s and later with his successor, Governor Manuel Aguirre. I persuaded the governors of the Mexican states to establish their own border commission, and Governor Aguirre was elected chairman of that group. He and I, as co-chairmen, developed a good working relationship.

I soon announced that I wanted a meeting of the governors along both sides of the border. I got tremendous support from Governor Clements, who had visited and cultivated friendships with the three Mexican states across the Rio Grande from Texas. Bruce Babbitt and Jerry Brown had also visited their neighboring Mexican states and established good relations with them. They all backed the idea and we pulled together the first Bi-national Border Governor's Conference, which we held in Chihuahua. As co-chairmen, Governor Aguirre and I communicated daily with our respective national governments.

Organizing the conference took a lot of work, and it turned out to be an outstanding meeting. The media in both nations were good to us, giving the conference wide coverage and repeating many times that we had improved working relationships across the border. We all became good friends and I was proud of my fellow governors from both nations. We began the international dialogue on a variety of subjects, including building roads, establishing ports of entry, improving communications, trading petroleum products, exchanging agricultural information, trading breeding stock, and so on. We encouraged Mexican students to come study here. We also discussed water issues and our state Game and Fish Department developed a collaboration to help their counterparts stabilize wildlife management in Mexico.

Perhaps the most important outcome of this conference was the precedent it set. The work of these border conferences became more and more substantive as the years passed, and they helped change our nation's attitude toward Mexico as a trade partner and as a neighbor. We all gained a more accurate understanding of each other, an understanding based in reality. We also found that we weren't much different—for instance, in the ranching communities on both sides, we faced the same kinds of problems. When a Mexican rancher got a hole in their fence, they just put their cows back and fixed the fence, the same as here.

I believe the good relations we were establishing, based on open dialogue and mutual respect, helped lay the diplomatic groundwork for the North American Free Trade Agreement and other policy initiatives pursued by our national governments, particularly by my friend President Clinton in the mid-1990s. I'm proud of my role in getting the ball rolling.

In April 1980, we called a joint meeting of the New Mexico Border Commission and the border commission of our sister state, Chihuahua. Jorge Alona coordinated the plans for the meeting for Chihuahua, and David King did the same for New Mexico. We had excellence attendance from both sides of the border at the conference in Deming, New Mexico.

When we were in the Deming area we toured the stock facility at Columbus, New Mexico, and Palomas, Chihuahua, which former Governor Oscar Flores and I had opened in my first term. Until then it had not been possible for cattle to cross the border there. We found on this visit that more cattle now crossed at Columbus than at any of the other crossings up and down the entire border with Mexico. The facility was paying its way, operating as we had hoped.

We were also working with the Chihuahua officials on developing the twin plant, or *maquila*, concept, which encouraged American manufacturers to build assembly plants in Mexico. Items such as clothes or even machinery would be partially assembled in Mexico, where labor was cheaper, then imported to the U.S. without the heavy taxation of a finished product. The final work was completed at the factory's American twin. Both countries benefited from this economic development activity: American companies were able to manufacture a product less expensively and their plants brought good jobs into Mexico. We toured the factories at Palomas before we crossed back over at Columbus.

Once again, the most important accomplishment of that meeting was establishing rapport, this time between Governor Manuel Aguirre of Chihuahua and me, with our staff people likewise working closely together and understanding one another. Governor Aguirre met with us at Deming, then we went on with him to Nuevas Casas Grande to continue the meeting. Our security men went with us on the 150-mile drive, and on the way back to New Mexico, Governor Aguirre and Jorge Alona rode with us. It gave me a chance to develop my friendship with the Chihuahuan governor, which continued throughout the remainder of my term in office.

In October 1981, we held the second annual Bi-national Border Governor's Conference, this time in the El Paso area. Governor Clements was co-host. Jerry Brown and Arizona Governor Bruce Babbitt also attended. So did Manuel Aguirre, who had been newly elected in Chihuahua, Governor Roberto de la Madrid of the state of Baja California, and the governors of the other border states of Mexico. We passed a resolution praising Presidents Reagan and López Portillo for working with us for better relations between our two countries. All the governors were deeply involved in the conference. As the newspapers covered the proceedings, I often received credit for occupying the peacemaker's role at our meetings. I did have a good feel for unity and how to resolve problems that came up, and I was happy to exercise that ability at these and other meetings.

Later that year, I met in El Paso with President-elect Miguel de la Madrid of Mexico, with virtually no fanfare. This meeting came about at the suggestion of his cousin and my fellow governor, Roberto de la Madrid. I had been a good friend of the Republic of Mexico, and Governor de la Madrid called me and said, "Bruce, it would be nice if you could come and meet our new president and get to know him from the start, so you will have a friend there when he takes office." I was pleased to accept the invitation and we kept the media coverage low-key. During our meeting, we discussed the need to improve the working relationship between our countries.

The last border conference I attended during my second administration was in 1982 at Tijuana, chaired and hosted by Roberto de la Madrid, who was still governor of Baja California. We paved the way for this conference in

February. When the New Mexico legislature was winding down, Bill Clements and I met in El Paso with Roberto to discuss our border problems and settle on a location for the next Bi-national Border Governor's Conference. In his statement after the meeting, Roberto said that friendship would resolve the problems along the border, and we did have excellent relations and good feelings among us. We set the next conference for later that year in Tijuana, Baja.

At the Tijuana conference I received a great reception and I found I enjoyed esteem among the Mexican people. I respected the customs of Mexico, just as I have always respected the customs of the diverse cultures in New Mexico, and I guess the Mexicans recognized that, because they treated me a little different from the other U.S. governors. One time the Mexican governors gave a cocktail party for the U.S. officials, and I was the only American governor who showed up. After that, whenever there was a meeting, the Mexican governors would come up and give me an *abrazo,* the big embrace where they throw their arms around you. They didn't do that with the other Americans.

In early December, when my term as governor was drawing to a close, Alice and I went to Mexico City for the inaugural of our friend, Miguel de la Madrid, as president of the Republic of Mexico. We were royally received. President-elect de la Madrid had run as the candidate of the PRI party, which held a large reception with dignitaries representing countries from all over the world. I was pleased when they chose me to represent the United States. I had been a great friend of Mexico and had contributed as much as I could to the good relationships we had developed between Mexico and the United States. Alice and I were honored when they seated us with the high dignitaries at the inaugural. I acquired many new friends, including the former president of Costa Rica, an acquaintance that led Alice and me to visit Costa Rica immediately after I left office in January 1983.

≋

When I came back into office for my third administration in 1991, we still had not developed a significant border crossing between New Mexico and Chihuahua, but I found that Governor Garrey Carruthers and Governor Fernando Baeza had renewed the attempt. Garrey Carruthers was from Las

Cruces, which is only a half-hour drive from the border, and he took the idea of a crossing very seriously. He and Governor Baeza had decided to open both Anapra and Santa Teresa because there was so much division they couldn't settle on one port. So that's where it was when I came back. The original Anapra site near Sunland Park had its loyalists, but Santa Teresa had gained considerable support with its plentiful land for development. Though a bit west of Anapra, it was still close to the metropolitan area of El Paso-Juárez-Las Cruces, to the interstate, to utilities, and to other critical aspects of the infrastructure. I favored Santa Teresa—I had made that decision back in the early 1980s—but regardless of where it was going to be, I was determined to keep this effort alive and finally build a full-scale port of entry.

Whether it was Anapra or Santa Teresa, we needed a crossing that was strategically located relative to domestic and international transportation arteries. A crossing like Columbus just didn't measure up. Lacking such a well-placed port of entry, we were losing border trade business to other states, primarily to Texas at El Paso. Furthermore, we hoped to develop a multimodal facility, one that brought together air, rail, and highway traffic, and Santa Teresa offered that possibility. With a multimodal port of entry, we could then attract manufacturing and warehousing firms, which would significantly boost the economy of southern New Mexico.

In the first three or four months I was in office, I worked very hard to get back in with my Mexican friends. I met with Governor Baeza to convince him we couldn't build both ports at the same time. Neither side had enough money. So I suggested taking one at a time, and he agreed to go with Santa Teresa if we would help him continue with Anapra. I went along with that, so in the spring of 1991, Governor Baeza and I signed an agreement to open the border crossing between Santa Teresa and San Geronimo, Chihuahua.

After that, we charged after it pretty hard. The entire New Mexico Congressional Delegation supported us—Congressmen Bill Richardson (who became the U.S. ambassador to the United Nations in 1997), Steve Schiff, and Joe Skeen and Senators Pete Domenici and Jeff Bingaman. As chairman of the Senate Budget Committee, Pete Domenici was particularly helpful working the federal funding. It was a truly non partisan effort, and we didn't have much trouble with the federal government. However, at the local level we did run into some opposition—although it was never *open* opposition—from leaders in El Paso and Juárez, who thought it would drain off business from their crossing. They had helped kill the idea in the past. I argued that they were already overcrowded and that the bridges crossing the Rio Grande, which forms the border there, made it hard to move goods back and forth. Santa Teresa didn't need a bridge—it's west of the river, which runs north-south as it leaves New Mexico at that point. The geography gets a little confusing down there: for maybe a dozen or more miles, the border between New Mexico and Texas is defined by the Rio Grande, which runs north-south right there. Then after the river leaves New Mexico, it hooks eastward and makes the border between Texas and Mexico. At Santa Teresa, which is several miles west of El Paso and the river, the international border is just an imaginary line across the mesquite desert. I finally persuaded the Juárez people that Santa Teresa would benefit them by easing their congestion.

Once rivals for the governor's seat and always members of opposing political partes, U.S. Senator Pete Domenici and I became good friends who often collaborated on projects benefitting New Mexico. Converting political enemies to friendly supporters was a trademark of my political style. (Photograph courtesy Santa Fe *New Mexican*)

We also helped work the national government on the Mexican side. In fact, with Congressman Bill Richardson and members of my cabinet, I met with President Salinas to discuss the new border crossing. All together, we met three times, and on the last visit he said, "Governor, we're going to go ahead and put that port in from the Mexican side—I know it doesn't even need a bridge. So let's not talk about that. Let's talk about other things today, because we're going to get that done."

The truth of the matter is, the Mexican national government did a much better job on their side of committing funds and building a permanent structure. We had to do it piecemeal, because even though Senator Domenici got us $12 million for the structure, they wouldn't release the money until we had secured all the clearances of title and so on from the developer, Charlie Crowder, and it took a while to get a title without any liens. While we were waiting to clear all that up and receive the federal funds, we freed state funds from the General Services, Highway, and Environment departments. With that money, some help from the Atchison, Topeka, and Santa Fe Railway, and in-kind contributions, the various state departments all worked together and built a temporary structure. We did finally get the title to the land and it all worked out in the end.

With Governor Baeza (left) of Chihuahua, Mexico, and Sam Adelo, who often interepreted for me, I signed the historic accord to open the Santa Teresa border crossing, 1992. I had worked since the early 1970s to create a port of entry between New Mexico and Mexico.

In 1992, we got the Santa Teresa port open to where you could drive across, even though the buildings on our side were temporary. We even developed a runway that could land large jets, like 727s. The next year, we officially dedicated and opened the big port of entry. Dignitaries from Chihuahua, Juárez, and New Mexico led the dedication ceremony, which capped off two decades of work on my part to open a major border crossing with Mexico. I had the feeling you get after a long day herding cattle from one pasture to another, when you finally push that last cow through and stretch the wire gate shut: it's the satisfaction of knowing you've done your job.

People, livestock, and trade goods began moving through the new crossing early in 1992, creating a major opportunity for economic development related to border trade. In the years since then, we built permanent structures on our side and Santa Teresa has become an important international port of entry. By the end of my administration, we had boosted our trade revenues with Mexico by nearly 50 percent, thanks in no small part to the economic stimulation of Santa Teresa.

≈

In the early 1990s, the notion of a North American Free Trade Agreement was generating a heated debate at the national level. President Bush and President Salinas were both in favor of it. The idea was to open up Canada, Mexico, and the United States into one barrier-free market by eliminating the tariffs on all trade goods, thereby giving businesses in each country equal access to customers in the other countries. The treaty would create a huge consumer market of more than 360 million people. However, NAFTA had its share of detractors in the U.S. Some people feared losing jobs to Mexico, while others felt we would basically be exporting our polluting industries south of the border, where the environmental laws were more lax. However, I believed it would solve more problems than it would create. For years I had contended the only way to get a handle on illegal immigration was to create jobs at home for Mexicans, and NAFTA would do that. I also felt the environmental concerns could be addressed. We wouldn't lose jobs to Mexico because better employment opportunities in Mexico would keep immigrants at home, so they would not be taking jobs over here in the United

States in the first place. It would all balance out. So I came out for NAFTA.

1992 was a presidential election year, and my old friend from the National Governors' Association, Bill Clinton of Arkansas, won the Democratic nomination. Bill Clinton was a bright young man and an astute politician. I knew from our many breakfast conversations at National Governors' Association conferences that we held similar views on a wide variety of subjects, and I had been one of the first governors to back his candidacy in the primary. When the general election race against President Bush took off, I campaigned with Governor Clinton around the west. During this period I also led a New Mexico delegation to Mexico City for another meeting with President Salinas. Alice, Congressman Bill Richardson, Economic Development Secretary Bill Garcia, Tourism Secretary Mike Cerletti, and others went with me. At these meetings, we would review our accomplishments on matters like the port of entry, NAFTA, and other areas of common interest. The first two years of my third administration coincided with the last two years of the Bush administration, and this was our first visit with President Salinas since Bill Clinton had won the presidential election.

As a congressman from New Mexico, Bill Richardson worked closely with me on many issues, including the opening of a port of entry between Mexico and the United States at Santa Teresa. President Bill Clinton later appointed Richardson to serve as ambassador to the United Nations, then Secretary of Energy.

Naturally, the Mexican president was quite eager to find out how Bill Clinton would deal with Mexico. Congressman Richardson explained to President Salinas that I was an inside friend of President Clinton, that we had a lot of rapport from working together as governors, that I had a lot of influence with him, and so on. Well, at that point I wasn't even sure where President Clinton stood on NAFTA, and I didn't want to be held responsible for things that might not happen. I explained that what Bill Richardson said was true, I had been good friends with Bill Clinton, we had worked together in the National Governor's Association, and I had flown with him all over the western states trying to get him elected.

"Yes, that's friendship," agreed President Salinas.

I hesitated for a moment, then added, "But he may not do what I suggest after the election. Once he's president, he may not be nearly as responsive to my ideas. I already have a much harder time making contact and having input than I did in the primary campaign," I told him. "I can't even reach him."

Sizing up the situation like an old hand, President Salinas replied, "Well, that's politics."

When Bill Clinton came to New Mexico in the fall before the election, of course I accompanied him on his appearances around Albuquerque. After his jet landed at the airport, we had the usual press fanfare that accompanies a presidential candidate. Right there on the runway, Governor Clinton answered a few questions and we all got our pictures taken, then we drove off in a limousine. We chatted a bit in the car, then Bill asked me, "What about this NAFTA, Bruce?" Bill knew about my rapport with past and present Mexican presidents and he wondered how the treaty would affect us border states. He hadn't yet taken a stand on the treaty, and the public-opinion polls were leaning away from it.

President Bill Clinton and I have been friends since we met at a National Governors' Association meeting. We always enjoyed each other's company, as we did in this private moment during the 1994 gubernatorial race in New Mexico.

I told him he'd have to decide, then I quickly sketched the positives and figured I'd let him worry about the negatives himself. I pointed out that my view was influenced by how I thought NAFTA would affect New Mexico, but a president has different concerns than a governor. I hated to be even a little bit responsible for something as big as NAFTA, though of course I knew he had thoroughly researched the topic, because that was his way.

He pressed me for my opinion, saying, "Where do you stand? Tell me what you think. You always figure out what's in the best interest of the people."

"Well, Bill," I said, "I'm all for it. I think it would benefit people on both sides of the border down here."

He took down some notes and we moved on to other topics, then we made our first stop, which was at Sandia National Laboratories on Kirtland Air Force Base. After he toured the facilities, we went on to the University of New Mexico. When Bill got up in front of that student crowd to speak, he came out for NAFTA, which was a position he never wavered from after that. I know he had been studying the issue before we talked, but it's nice to think I had a little influence on that policy decision.

From my life in politics I've learned there's a whole lot of territory between a campaign promise and enacting a law. Even if you're in favor of something, you've got a legislative body to convince. So even after Bill Clinton beat George Bush and became president, NAFTA was far from being a done deal. I did what I could to support the treaty and continue building good relations with Mexico. Texas Governor Ann Richards, who was also a friend of mine, shared my interest in further developing business partnerships between the United States and Mexico, so she arranged for President-elect Clinton to meet with President Salinas in Austin, Texas, before Clinton even took office. Because I was friendly with the presidents of both nations, I was able to help get them together.

Both men felt very comfortable with me. That day in Austin, Bill Clinton arrived first, and I met with him privately. He asked if I would join in the meeting with the Mexican president, and I agreed. Then President Salinas arrived and we also visited awhile. He, too, said, "You are going to be with us, aren't you?" So we had a very congenial meeting. Both men felt much more comfortable meeting under those kinds of informal terms, rather than an official state visit. That was the key to establishing rapport on the same terms that Congressman Richardson and I had established with Mexico, and it did work out just as we hoped it would. We visited about the problems along the border, and by then President Clinton was sold on NAFTA.

The April 1993 Bi-national Border Governors' Conference in Monterey, Mexico, focused on the issue of free trade. I gave a speech in favor of NAFTA, as did Mexico's secretary of trade and economic development, and others. It seemed that we border governors from both nations were all of one mind, so we decided as a body to support the treaty and wrote up a joint communiqué addressed to President Clinton. We all signed the letter, which called for quick passage of the free-trade agreement. We said that the economic benefits of open markets would allow the United States, Canada, and Mexico to improve environmental and workplace conditions. We also wrote that NAFTA would positively impact education, the environment, tourism, transportation, and investment. We all pledged our support of joint projects in high-tech training, developing a master transportation plan along the Mexico-U.S. border, and creating conservation parks, for example.

President Clinton signed NAFTA later in 1993. By 1997, Mexico and the United States were trading almost $100 billion a year in goods and services, and the dire predictions about lost jobs and increased pollution had proved untrue.

⁓

While the federal government was debating NAFTA throughout 1993, we weren't sitting around waiting for Congress to make a decision. We were busy with Santa Teresa, of course, and we also set plans in motion to open a trade office in Mexico City. I had decided I wanted to do this when we were on a trade mission to Asia and Taiwan. They asked us to open a trade office. I couldn't see having one in Taiwan but not in Mexico, and we couldn't afford both, so I decided we'd better open one with our neighbors first. I felt we still hadn't come near developing the full potential for trade with Mexico. The office would help New Mexico businesses make the appropriate contacts in Mexico—it would be something like matchmaking businesses with markets or business partners.

We ran this project out of the Economic Development Department, and Secretary Bill Garcia worked hard on it. The legislature appropriated funding for the Mexico City office—we didn't want anything extravagant, just a place that conveyed we meant business. I even flew down to inaugurate the office and bring attention to our new presence in the Mexican capital. Bill hired a bright young MBA from New Mexico named Jerry Pacheco to run the trade office, and he did an outstanding job. Even though it takes a while to get deals in the pipeline—some of the opportunities pay off, and some never go anywhere—we began to see results before I left office in 1994.

At the end of my last four years in office, I could look back over my career as governor and feel proud of what had been accomplished with Mexico. The port of entry had been a long time coming—that's politics!—but it finally came, while NAFTA had redefined the way we did business with our south-

ern neighbor. In addition to these economic advances, we had also continued to build on our long-standing cultural ties. In 1991, Governor Baeza
and I had signed an agreement that included cultural exchange through a
New Mexico-Chihuahua Commission. Through it we intended to bring
goodwill and continue the wonderful friendships we had made. It provided
for monthly contact between our respective economic development staffs, a
joint effort on health and environmental issues, an agreement to work together on common agricultural issues, education exchanges, and tourism and
cultural contacts. It formalized the initiatives I had been pursuing since the
early 1970s, when Oscar Flores and I gave each other tours of our own
ranches and came to realize that life on one side of the border wasn't so different from life on the other side. That's what being a good neighbor is all
about.

13

Running Again

When I handed the reins over to Governor Toney Anaya in 1983, things were going pretty well in state government, although we knew by the end of 1982 that revenues were starting to drop off our projections. The Big Mac tax reduction had cut too much revenue, but the vast increases in the permanent fund and severance tax permanent fund, along with a much larger state investment portfolio, gave New Mexico plenty of reserves. These were Governor Anaya's concerns now, anyway—I moved back to the ranch and took up my place helping run the outfit, though of course I always kept one eye on the goings-on in Santa Fe and the operation of state government. Because they were having such a difficult time identifying the revenues they needed, I thought I might run for governor again and help straighten things out. Being governor was now my first and only choice of public office. I never had any intention of running for U.S. Congress or Senate.

The next opportunity for me to run came in 1986. Obviously, I would have been one of the front runners, but my good friend Ray Powell wanted to run, along with several other strong Democrats. It seemed like it wasn't good timing for me. I didn't want a hard primary, especially against Ray, followed by a hard general election. Yet when I decided not to run, all the others dropped out, too, and Ray ran unopposed in the primary—a first ever in the Democratic party. I worked hard for Ray, helping to raise funds and otherwise pitching in on the campaign. He was a strong candidate, but he lost to Republican Garrey Carruthers of Las Cruces. After that loss, Ray became state Democratic chairman and in 1989 he told me, "Bruce, you've got to run, because we have got to win the governor's office back."

Paul Bardacke already had a running start. He had been attorney general from 1983–1986, and now he was a very strong opponent for the 1990 primary nomination. He campaigned on environmental and economic issues and even brought up the 1980 penitentiary riot in an attempt to hurt my standing with the voters. All this blew over after the primary election, when Paul immediately came over to my side. He also helped me considerably when I faced lawsuits over Indian gaming in 1992. But for now I was in a rough primary race. The other Democratic contenders took off after me, too, since I was the front runner, but I still managed to win the nomination in June. Although I got Bardacke's support from then on, the Republicans went back and picked up some of those complaints against me—that's how a hard primary can hurt you in the general election.

Casey Luna won the Democratic nomination for lieutenant governor, so he would be my running mate. The Republicans nominated a sharp candidate to oppose me in 1990: Frank Bond, a very honorable gentleman who was quite knowledgeable about state government. Frank was a Santa Fe lawyer, and like me a member of a pioneer ranching family in New Mexico. He had won a seat in the state House of Representatives back in 1975, when he conducted an aggressive door-to-door campaign in a heavily Democratic district. He also helped run Senator Domenici's 1984 re-election campaign, and in 1987 Governor Carruthers named Frank chairman of the Commission on Higher Education. Now 47 years old, Frank easily won the 1990 Republican nomination for governor, so I didn't take him lightly. He obviously would have made a good governor.

I knew Frank's family. The King Brothers had bought the Alamo Ranch, which covers a large tract northwest from Rio Rancho to the Rio Puerco, from his mother. That shows how New Mexico politics remains a fairly personal affair, despite the huge changes in mass media communications, our large population growth, and the overall shifts in the structure of society. I respected Frank, and he respected me. It was a pretty clean campaign. Even so, Frank didn't waste any time tearing into me. He accused me of pardoning criminals and claimed I was responsible for the riot, but I quickly corrected him. I told him he didn't understand the parole system and how it works. Then he got onto other things he didn't feel had gone right in my previous administrations. One time we were in Española, where I had really been taught politics in the old school during my early campaigns. That area where the Chama River flows into the Rio Grande is the heart of Rio Arriba County politics and one of my old power bases in the north. I was talking to a group and I said, "I'll tell you one thing. This young whippersnapper isn't going to come in here and tell us all the problems we've had and the mistakes we've made when he doesn't even know the cures." Well, that term "whippersnapper" stung him a little bit, so the next time I saw him I explained that I wasn't trying to be negative.

He said, "Well, I didn't care much, but my mother sure didn't like it." His mother and I were the best of friends, so I felt bad about that. Then the next time we faced each other on TV, he asked me, "Just exactly what does 'young whippersnapper' mean?"

"Well, Frank, it means you're a nice young man but there are a lot of things you don't know," I said.

That got him for a minute, but later he said, "I know Bruce is a nice guy, but how old will he be if he completes eight years in office?"

I would have been 75. Real quick, I countered, saying, "I'll be exactly the same age as President Bush," who was running for re-election. "Do you think he's fit to run the country?"

This was much more the kind of campaign I love to run. I don't mind that back and forth banter. It was fun and it never got mean. I was able to distinguish myself from my opponent and make my points clear, unlike in my final campaign in 1994, when I had my former Lieutenant Governor Roberto Mondragon on the left with the Green Party and Gary Johnson far to the right with the Republicans, and I got stuck in the middle with very little room to maneuver. When you've got three candidates, it's hard to run an issues-oriented campaign, partly because you just don't have time to zero in on your platform when you share the stage with two other people.

Running against Frank Bond, I campaigned on my ideas for stimulating the economy and creating jobs, providing more training for workers, and improving trade relations with Mexico. A big part of our economy is tourism, and I planned to create a new Tourism Department to stimulate growth in that sector. My campaign also included the slogan, "Two for One," referring to the outstanding contributions that Alice would make in my next administration. I promised to make education a top priority with Alice's help and to focus on the needs of families and children by creating a new cabinet department in that area. I also promised to give increased attention to the environment by elevating the Environmental Improvement Division to cabinet-level department status.

When the November election came, I beat Frank Bond by a safe margin of about 20,000 votes. I never felt any hard feelings toward him. Frank had been an ally of mine when he was House minority leader and I was governor in my second term, and he remained one after this race. In fact, I appointed him to the Game and Fish Committee.

≈≈

After the 1990 election, Alice and I took a brief vacation, then came back to closely review the condition of state government. I discussed all this with Alice, telling her that in those departments and agencies that were going well with professional people leading them, I didn't want to upset the operation. I would leave them in place. Garrey Carruthers had been an honest, concerned governor who had tried to run a professional operation. To keep New Mexico moving forward without any lost motion in the transition of administrations between parties, I thought we'd try to hand off the baton like a pair of 880-relay runners, so we could stay at full speed. I met with Governor Carruthers and of course he loved the idea. He was exceptionally helpful.

The transition went especially smoothly between Republican Governor Garrey Carruthers (left) and my third administration. (Photograph courtesy Santa Fe *New Mexican*)

Chief Justice Joseph Baca performed the swearing-in for my third term as governor at midnight, January 1, 1991. Alice and my granddaughters looked on. My son Bill's oldest daughter, Becky King, held the Bible, flanked by Stacy King on the left and Jenny King on the right.

However, I didn't want to keep *everyone* on, and in a couple cases I needed to find successors for people I *did* want to retain. I was sorry I needed to name a new State Engineer to replace my old friend Steve Reynolds, who had died. In Corrections I had expected Secretary Lane McCotter to stay on and he initially agreed, but then his personal circumstances changed and I was looking for a new head of Corrections. I also wanted a new secretary of Public Safety to oversee the State Police. A few cabinet secretaries from the Carruthers administration knew that I would replace them, so they vacated their positions. For instance, the Highway Department had gotten so controversial that I had known since the campaign I would have to move out the current secretary and put in someone new. For all the new appointments I made a concerted effort to find qualified, professional people. I had taken heat during the campaign from critics who claimed I would appoint only politicos, which wasn't true. To counter that impression I worked especially hard to name cabinet members who had backgrounds largely outside of politics.

The first appointment I made was State Engineer, mostly because Garrey Carruthers had lined up somebody and I wanted to nail down a successor for Steve Reynolds—who had died while serving in that office—before a good candidate got away. In New Mexico, the State Engineer oversees all issues related to water rights and water use. Water is a scarce and incredibly precious resource in arid New Mexico, so the State Engineer has tremendous power. He adjudicates all disputes over water allocations for any purpose, whether it's domestic use, farming, or recreation. You can hardly drill a well or bulldoze a check dam across the barest trickle of a stream in an arroyo that runs only in July without the State Engineer's approval. You might call him the water czar—and Steve Reynolds was the czar among czars. He had enormous impact on water law not only in New Mexico, but in the entire Southwest and Rocky Mountain regions, where he was recognized as the leading expert. It reflects on his stature that in my second administration, I let him go to Phoenix for a few months after Governor Bruce Babbitt asked me if he could borrow Steve to help write water law for Arizona.

Steve had been State Engineer since Governor Mechem appointed him in the 1950s, but I'd known him even longer than that. When I played football at the University of New Mexico in the 1940s, Steve was the line coach and I was a tackle. We got to be friends right then and we became reacquainted when I first entered the legislature in 1959. That year the Farm Bureau asked me to introduce a bill creating a water board to replace the function of State Engineer.

Steve came over to me and said, "Hey, Bruce, are you sure you know what you're doing?"

I said, "Well, no, not exactly, but the Farm Bureau has this policy and they want me to introduce it."

"That would eliminate my job completely," he said. "That's no big deal, but I don't think we need a board setting water policy." He went through it all and he convinced me to pull back the bill. We became very good friends after this. He was always interested in professional management of water, which is so valuable that whoever has the right to say where it goes must be absolutely nonpolitical.

When I was campaigning the first time for governor in 1970, some of my friends in the lower Pecos Valley—Chaves and Eddy counties in southeast New Mexico—felt they weren't getting a fair shake from Steve. Basically, they wanted an increased allocation of water because they felt the Roswell area in Chaves County was holding back too much. Steve wouldn't see it their way, so they wanted me to publicly commit to fire him. I told them I couldn't do that because he and I were good friends, but more importantly, I thought we really needed his expertise in that field. Then they said that Pete Domenici, my Republican opponent, was going to fire him if he were elected. For his part, Domenici was too bright to come out publicly and promise to fire Steve Reynolds, and nothing ever came of this attempt by the lower Pecos Valley farmers to oust him.

Feeling at least as comfortable in the saddle as at the governor's desk, I was proud to be a true cowboy governor and a horseman. (Photograph courtesy Santa Fe *New Mexican*)

A different challenge to the State Engineer's autonomy came along under Jerry Apodaca's administration, which immediately followed my first term in office. Jerry massively reorganized state government, and with some justification he moved the State Engineer's Office under the Natural Resources Department, so that Steve no longer reported directly to the governor. When I came back for my second term right after Apodaca, I planned to keep on Bill Huey as Secretary of Natural Resources. I called him in and asked him where he was having the most problems.

"You're going to have to give me some help on the State Engineer," Bill said. "Steve Reynolds doesn't relate to me much. He just does what he wants!"

I told him, "Bill, I've got to be honest with you. Steve and I go way back, and he is a great State Engineer. His job really doesn't lend itself to someone being over him other than the governor, and even the governor isn't much over him. I'm not going to be any help to you in that situation— we're just going to let him do his thing." And that's what we did. Then in 1983, when Toney Anaya became governor, he restored the State Engineer's Office to its cabinet-level status, so Steve reported directly to the chief executive again—although, in reality, the State Engineer has to be outside even the governor's purview when he's making water judgments. Along with secretary of Corrections, it's one of those purely professional positions in state government that should never be tainted by politics. State Engineer is a truly apolitical position, and Steve Reynolds had the personal integrity to pull that off.

Now, as I took the baton from Garrey Carruthers in 1991, I needed to replace Steve with someone of comparable stature and impeccable reputation. After Steve passed away, Garrey had done a comprehensive search for a successor and finally identified a 20-year veteran of the State Engineer's staff, Eluid Martinez, as the best candidate. Since I was coming in so soon, they let me go ahead and appoint him to the position.

Back in 1971, the winter emergency had taught me the value of forging an immediately productive relationship with the National Guard and the State Police. From the 1980 penitentiary riot I had learned the critical importance of having a well-managed Corrections Department under professional corrections people. This time, before I took office I wanted to settle these three key agencies that you had to have in place to handle an emergency. My trusted friend General Frank Miles was still head of the National Guard. I had appointed him in my first term, and of course I kept him on. Next I turned to Corrections. Lane McCotter was secretary. I knew that he had run a highly professional department and I wanted him to stay, so I immediately made friends with him. We talked it over and he agreed to remain in the position, but then a personal matter forced him to change plans, and he moved to Utah.

Lane told me that we had two trained professionals already in the department who could run Corrections: Eloy Mondragon and Herb Maschner. Lane and I both evaluated Mondragon and Maschner and came to the same conclusion independently that Mondragon should be secretary, with Maschner as his deputy. I knew Eloy Mondragon from my previous administration, when I had moved him up after the riot. He had gone on to Puerto Rico, then had came back to New Mexico. I was delighted that he was in line for the top job. Lane and I held a press conference where we announced we both thought Eloy Mondragon was the man for the job of secretary of Corrections. That showed we were serious about having a very orderly transition in that department.

I knew I needed to make a change in the leadership of the State Police. They were now under the Department of Public Safety, with a military style of leadership that didn't really fit their civilian mission. I wanted to change that. Meanwhile, the police officers and patrolmen were very dissatisfied over various internal issues, so I decided to find someone new to lead them. I started looking around for a secretary of Public Safety who could lead the State Police, too, but I couldn't find anyone with the experience I wanted. At that time, a former state chief who I had a lot of confidence in, Richard C de Baca, had retired from the State Police and was running his lumber company in Santa Fe. He was the son of Richard C de Baca, senior, who had worked for me back in my Santa Fe County Commission days. I talked to Richard and said, "Look, you've always wanted to be in charge of the State Police. Why don't you come in and be secretary of Public Safety? You've got your sons who can run the business while you're gone and you'll still be living in Santa Fe."

"Oh, well, if you really need me, I'll do it," he said finally, even though he lost his retirement by taking the job.

The Highway Department likewise needed a change at the top. The department had lost both its focus and, along the way, public confidence in its ability to maintain the roads. Accusations had flown around about officials taking advantage of their position for personal gain, and it was all a big mess. I felt the department had a sound professional staff, which I planned to keep intact. Wanting to move someone up from that group to be secretary, I named Lou Medrano, who had been the department engineer in Roswell. He did good work, but left late in the term for personal reasons, so I appointed Carroll Young to replace him. Having worked his way up through the department over 30 years or so, Carroll really new the operation inside and out. I was pleased to move him up to the top spot.

Part of my campaign in 1990 had been the notion that voters were getting two for the price of one because Alice worked so closely with me, even though she was not officially in the cabinet. In my second administration, Alice had shown how valuable she was to the state when she emerged as a leading champion of family issues and volunteerism. This time around, we arranged an office for Alice and her staff in the governor's suite on the fourth floor of the capitol and she got to work right away, once again on a strictly volunteer basis. She focused on a few key areas we had identified during the campaign as being top priority: creating the Children, Youth, and Families Department at the cabinet level, improving and reforming the state's educational system, developing a drug-free campaign, and drafting the Children's Agenda Budget that would bring coherence to the state's delivery of services to children.

Alice and I teamed up on nearly everything during my 40 years in politics. In my third administration, she lobbied hard for legislation to improve education and the general conditions of children and families.

Alice was busy, to say the least. Some people muttered about the "meddling first lady," while others questioned whether she was eroding the governor's authority, but they never understood how closely Alice and I worked together. We both had the same vision of what we wanted to accomplish for children and families. I saw the only way to get there was for me to turn that whole area over to someone very knowledgeable who had the abilities to work it through the legislature. Alice was the perfect choice. She came to be recognized statewide as the leading advocate of these issues. In fact, Alice was so prominent and influential during my third administration that one Santa Fe newspaper even suggested she might run for governor herself next time. That was never really in her plans, but it shows how much respect she commanded among the press and the public.

While I campaigned in 1990, I had pointed out that a lot of people weren't paying their taxes. In some cases it was unpaid gross receipts tax, income tax, or even oil and gas royalties, and they amounted to significant lost state revenues. I planned to correct that situation. I brought in Dick Minzner to lead this effort as secretary of the Taxation and Revenue Department. Dick had been majority leader of the House of Representatives and he had chaired the House tax and revenue committee. He was now a practicing attorney in Albuquerque. Dick kept the department's professional staff, and he talked the legislature into giving him 80 new positions. In the first calendar year, the department collected $40 million in delinquent taxes. It soon became widely known that you couldn't get away with dodging your taxes, and people started paying up.

I kept on Anita Lockwood from the Carruthers administration, where she had been deputy secretary in the Energy and Minerals Department before Garrey moved her up to head the department. I was so impressed with her work that I kept her as secretary. I also left Dennis Boyd as secretary of the Health Department, but he took another job in Houston after about a year, so I moved up Mike Burkhart to fill that post. After we created the new Environment Department by pulling it out of Health in the 1991 legislative session, I appointed Judith Espinosa as secretary.

We wanted a top-grade professional to lead the Economic Development Department, and I found just such a person in Bill Garcia, who had been with the New Mexico division of USWest. Under Bill's direction, the department brought in thousands and thousands of new jobs to New Mexico. Existing businesses expanded their operations—most notably the Intel plant at Rio Rancho, which eventually hired Bill away from me—and new companies opened their doors around the state. When Bill went to Intel in 1994, I moved up my deputy chief of staff, John Garcia, to fill the open secretary slot at Economic Development.

Tourism is closely related to economic development—it remains one of New Mexico's top few industries and contributes huge tax revenues to the state's treasury. When I took office, it was already a $2.2 billion industry in New Mexico and the state's largest private sector employer. I felt tourism was important enough to merit its own cabinet-level status. Bill Garcia and the legislature agreed, so we pulled it out of Economic Development in 1991, though the new Tourism Department shared staff and resources with its old parent. Now I needed someone who could really move the industry along. Santa Fe hotel owner and manager Mike Cerletti filled the bill. He had vast private sector experience in the state, but I had to work hard to persuade him to go to work for the government. Under his leadership, revenues from tourism increased tremendously. Mike went after foreign tourists with innovative approaches. For instance, in one very successful program he trained minimum security penitentiary inmates to answer tourism inquiries. During these years, New Mexico and Santa Fe gained international status as a favorite destination.

To lead the General Services Department, which does everything from tracking our inventory of vehicles to running many of the state's computer systems, I needed someone of spotless reputation who was absolutely honest and sincere, yet independent minded. Laura Threet fit that description to a T. She had been director of the Albuquerque Community Foundation and had worked with United Way. Laura was reluctant to come into the cabinet at first, but I finally persuaded her, and she brought a great deal of prestige to my administration.

Another strong professional who agreed to join my cabinet was Dick Heim, who I appointed secretary of Human Services. That tended to be a very controversial job, but Dick had performed well in the same position in my first administration. In the meantime, he had been chief administrator at St. Joseph Hospital in Albuquerque.

As secretary of Labor, I brought in Patrick Baca of Sandia Pueblo, a former Sandoval County commission chairman who had worked in industry and had a strong background in setting up training programs. Kay Marr agreed to be secretary of Finance and Administration and my longtime friend Judy Basham assumed the post of state personnel director.

My key staff members included press secretary John McKean, who had been a news director with Channel 13 TV in Albuquerque, chief of staff Jim Lewis, and my assistant Elizabeth Martin. Caroline Gaston, a former high school principal from Albuquerque, came on as my educational advisor, and I brought back my former personnel director, Chuck Spath, to help on education projects, as well—once again on loan from the U.S. Department of Energy. I asked my son, Bill, to return as my legislative liaison. He had practically grown up in the capitol, so he was very effective in lobbying for my programs.

Lieutenant Governor Casey Luna participated in cabinet meetings. I also invited state Superintendent of Public Instruction Alan Morgan to attend even though he was not an official member. The state superintendent is appointed by the state Board of Education, which consists of ten elected members and five appointed by the governor. Education is so interwoven with other state agencies that it only made sense to have Alan join us at the table, where he made a great contribution and helped us coordinate education initiatives with other activities related to children.

This cabinet was a very congenial group that enjoyed working together. We held monthly cabinet meetings at the governor's mansion. Alice and her crew would get breakfast ready and we would start about seven-thirty and run till noon. If one of them had a particular problem, we would let them make a presentation. If not, we would present a program on something we were stressing. It made for a very cohesive group, and an unintended effect was to promote competition among them in reporting accomplishments. That was healthy. During these meetings we worked on some of our larger, interagency projects, like the Santa Teresa Intermodal Crossing at the border with Mexico, which involved the Highway Department, the General Services Department, and the Economic Development Department. I also created teams of four among the cabinet members and asked them to come up with ideas for improving the operations of government.

I also met weekly with each cabinet secretary, and of course they could come in and see me any time they were having trouble. I made it known that I preferred to get a jump on talking a problem over so we could begin working out solutions before it reached the boiling point. Everyone knew that I started work at seven-thirty, before the rest of my staff except a security person, so they could always get me without an appointment before the official work day started—and they often did. As long as things went well, I left them to run their own outfit. I believed that if I gave overall direction, they generally would do a good job. Mike Cerletti once said, "Bruce King is the best boss I ever worked for. He's always around if you need him, but if you don't, he stays out of your way." I took that as a high compliment.

It always seems that the crowds have hardly gone home from inauguration when the state senators and representatives start checking into their motel rooms for the January start of the legislature. Fortunately, my cabinet came together quickly with a unified front and I immediately began work on my state of the state address with their input. Bill King coordinated our legislative program and always kept me fully apprised of what the individual cabinet members were taking to the legislature, too. Also, my son Gary was now a state representative, so he kept an eye out for us in the House. When January 17 came around, we were ready to champion our programs in child and family issues, economic development, the environment, and fiscal management.

14

In the Best Interests

I came into office in 1991 with what I thought was a straightforward philosophy. I wanted to increase the overall prosperity of New Mexico for the benefit of all our citizens. To do that, we needed to create new wealth in the state. Much of our economy at that time was based on the service industries, and often that meant money simply changed hands among our own people. We needed to bring new dollars into the state—through new manufacturing facilities, increased trade outside our borders, and expanded tourism. Then we could invest the tax revenues generated from that new business in social programs, especially education, children's health, and crime prevention. If you neglect to spend some of that new wealth on helping people to pull themselves up out of poverty or to otherwise improve their situation, then you end up with a widening gap between the "haves" and the "have-nots." That gap severely strains the social system. We also had to make sure that increased industrial activity did no harm to the environment. New Mexico remains a very pristine state in many areas, and I wanted to keep it that way.

This program might be simple to explain, but carrying it out was another matter. Few people argued with increased prosperity, although some opposed growth for its own sake. But when it came to deciding how—or whether—to spend the tax revenues generated from that new wealth, I knew I could count on resistance. Beyond that, we had some disagreements about what constituted appropriate economic development, especially in the area of gambling on Indian reservations. Despite these potential sore spots, I had been elected by a broad cross-section of voters from both sides of the political middle, a loose coalition of the urban middle class, people with ties to farming and ranching, Native Americans, labor, the old-line Hispanic communities of the north, environmentalists, youth advocates, educators, and so forth. It was my old political base. If my administration could avoid the political land mines that I knew were out there—and Indian gaming was especially explosive—then we could accomplish what I had in mind.

≋

Alice and I both felt strongly committed to the families and young people of New Mexico, where one-third of the population was under 21. The programs and services that affected them—child care, family preservation, health care, drug-abuse prevention, and education—defined the arena where Alice had her greatest impact. We wanted children to grow up well-rounded and able to contribute positively to society. We also wanted to see fewer kids entering our correctional system. Some critics have called us soft on criminal youth because we emphasized prevention and helping at-risk children make positive choices in their lives. However, we have always felt that the 1 percent who commit crimes are overemphasized. They certainly need to be punished, no doubt about it, but the basic problem is to keep the next generation from reaching that point. At the same time, if some kids do end up in the correctional system, we're not going to disregard them, but rehabilitate them to lead productive lives. As a society, we can't afford to let an early mistake derail someone's entire life.

Instead of focusing only on punishing the relatively few who strayed onto the crooked path, we felt it was much more constructive to increase our investment in all the other children. Our first major step in this direction during my third administration was to create a new, consolidated agency: the Children, Youth, and Families Department. Alice rode point position on this entire initiative, starting in 1991, and we accomplished a great deal over the next few years. Our work for children and families became a model for other states who wanted to take a similarly holistic approach to providing family-related services.

The roots of the Children, Youth, and Families Department ran all the way back to my second administration, when I had appointed a Family

Policy Task Force, which was chaired by Alice. They had developed a plan to coordinate state support aimed at families and children. Support services were scattered among several departments, chiefly the Human Services Department, the Health and Environment Department, the Department of Education, and the Department of Public Safety, which dealt with the juvenile justice system. Law enforcement agencies and the courts were also involved. We had seen how much more effective we could be in this area if we consolidated those services in one department. By pulling these together and restructuring our delivery of services, we could spare people the trouble of going to so many different offices and agencies. They would get better help, while on the state side we could provide that help more efficiently.

Early in my third administration, I again asked Alice to lead the charge. Starting in 1991, she chaired the task force I appointed to study the concept of a unified department and to make recommendations for implementing it. The task force included the secretaries of my cabinet whose departments would be affected and representatives from the courts, children's advocacy groups, and providers of children's services. They all took an active role. The task force traveled the state and conducted hearings to find out from the people what they needed, then the group would come back and study ways for a new department to effectively address those needs. The task force also cooperated extensively with existing state agencies to figure out how the current system worked and how all those pieces would fit together in the new department with the least disturbance to the families we were already serving. The final design for the department combined a restructuring of the service delivery system with coordination and policy-setting that cut across all state agencies whose work affected children. The task force also developed a Family Policy for New Mexico, which was endorsed by many organizations, a service delivery philosophy, a continuum of needs for children, and an analysis of current state spending on children. It was the most comprehensive picture ever created of child- and family-related issues in New Mexico.

House Speaker Raymond Sanchez carried the bill to create the Children, Youth, and Families Department in the 1992 legislature. Alice testified whenever they asked her, and the bill passed with hardly a dissenting vote. Republicans and Democrats alike were for it. State Representative Bob Light of Eddy County even gave $100,000 in private funds to get the department off the ground immediately after the legislature adjourned, since the funding wouldn't take effect until July 1, the start of our state's fiscal year. That kind of support shows how strongly people felt about the direction we were taking, and it was heartwarming.

I was very pleased to sign the law creating the nation's first state-level Children, Youth, and Families Department in 1992. Looking on as I sign the bill were Isabelle Eylicia-McGehee, an aide in the Office of the First Lady; Dick Heim, secretary of the Human Services Department; Caroline Gaston, chief of staff to the First Lady and my education advisor; Nancy Jo Archer, director of Hogares; Alice King; David Schmidt, director of the Council on Crime and Delinquency; and Jeanette Miller, who spearheaded my anti-drug programs.

I appointed Wayne Powell as secretary of Children, Youth, and Families. He had come up through the Human Services Department, where he was currently serving as deputy. I also named an advisory board of cabinet members and representatives from the courts, law enforcement, Health Department, and governor's office to monitor the new department as we rolled it out. They met monthly to plan and coordinate the various agencies' efforts for children and families. It was exciting to see interagency collaboration replacing the old turf battles, and shared strategic planning replacing the old hit-or-miss approach to solving problems.

The Children, Youth, and Families Department was the crown jewel of the third King administration, the very heart of our vision for improving the status of children in New Mexico. It was one of those deals you always hope for but hardly ever pull together. Once we achieved that goal, however, we didn't stop there. In 1992, we developed the Children's Agenda, which established a comprehensive framework for the services New Mexico provided to children and families. It included specific goals and ways to measure the effectiveness of our services for children and families. We used this document to guide the work of all state agencies providing family-related services during the second half of my administration.

The agenda started with good prenatal care for expectant mothers, quality health care, early diagnosis of health problems and disabilities, an immunization program, pre-primary education, and so on for children in their first years of life. It also spelled out family support services, such as child abuse intervention, family preservation programs, and intensive, community-based services for vulnerable families. We used the agenda to develop the nation's first Children's Agenda Budget. It gave a unified picture of the funds we would need in every relevant state agency to address all children's issues. The budget was a much better way to go than the previous approach, which had been every agency developing its own budget and going to the legislature with independent requests. Now we had brought coherence to the appropriation requests in this crucial area of state services.

At this time, with George Voinovich of Ohio I was vice chairman of the Action Team on School Readiness of the National Governor's Association, so we were pushing the same theme on the national level, as well. The Action Team issued a report that outlined benchmarks for states to measure their progress toward the first of the National Education Goals—that every child will be ready for school when they first enter the education system. We also wanted to see communities and the private sector share some of the responsibility for meeting the needs of children and families. To meet this national education goal at the state level, Alice spearheaded the development of a New Mexico plan for readiness to learn, which focused on increasing both the availability and quality of child care and child development programs.

Education was a theme of every King administration. My enjoyment of people naturally extended to children, like these who gathered around to hear me read a story in a school library in Santa Fe.

Alice and her staff initiated so many programs to support the readiness goal and other objectives of my administration that it's hard to know where to begin when I talk about her work. She started the on-going Early Immunization campaign, with help from former First Lady Rosalyn Carter and Betty Bumpers, the wife of Dale Bumpers of Arkansas. This program raised public awareness of the need to protect youngsters from early childhood diseases. The Alice King/Lovelace Immunization Van program took free immunization services to more than a dozen small New Mexico communities where health services are minimal or absent.

With her staff, Alice also helped 33 school district communities develop local plans to improve the health of school-age children. Our philosophy in this program was the same we took with education, that the whole community needs to get involved. Everyone has got to pitch in, in a coordinated way, because the resources required to solve many of the challenges facing communities are beyond the means of any single agency or group. So we wanted to empower communities and build their capacity to help themselves by partnering with the state, with local government and community leaders, and with their schools. For instance, 25 counties developed comprehensive plans to meet their own unique needs for pregnant women and young families under the Department of Health's maternal and child health program.

We hired Jeanette Miller to direct our drug abuse programs, which operated throughout the year. Under Alice's leadership, we kicked off our annual Red Ribbon Campaign against drugs in 1991. We also set up Drug-free Committees in 123 communities and Navajo chapter houses, helping them get a handle on their drug problems and come up with a plan—and funds—to solve them. The New Mexico National Guard was involved in the anti-drug effort, too, by letting kids use their facilities in the small, outlying communities and conducting their own "Guard Against Drugs" program. We also started the Drug Abuse Resistance Education program in our office.

In 1992, we asked basketball star Michael Cooper to chair the October Red Ribbon Campaign—he had played on the world champion Los Angeles Lakers basketball team after leading the University of New Mexico Lobos to some great victories in the 1970s. Because he was such a strong role model among the youth in our state, we felt he lent great credibility to the Red Ribbon Campaign. On another front, during the State Fair in 1991, the Indian communities helped organize the Indian Red Ribbon Run against drug abuse. That year, runners from the Navajo Nation and the western pueblos ran from the Arizona state line to the Fairgrounds in midtown Albuquerque. It took them several days. The second year, we added runners from the Colorado border, so all the northern pueblos could participate. The two groups of runners joined up at the Indian Village of the Fairgrounds for a ceremony. Indian leaders felt it was a very effective way to raise their people's awareness of the dangers of drug abuse.

≈

Along with working to increase the effectiveness of our social services and health programs, we also poured a great deal of creative energy into improving education. Again, Alice carried the banner. We took the approach that we had good teachers—and I worked on getting them better pay—but the system needed an overhaul. Our kids weren't achieving as well as we wanted, dropout rates were high, and some of our schools weren't safe.

The buzzword was "systemic change," which basically meant you had to reorganize the whole education system: the way teachers teach, the material kids learn, the way parents and other community members get involved, and the way the state Department of Education interacts with the local school districts. We wanted to see parents, business people, and others participating in decision making at the schools because we felt local communities knew best what they needed. Our teachers had to update their skills and catch up to the research that promoted using different teaching strategies to reach different kids. Not everyone learned well from the lecture method, for example, and we needed a lot more hands-on instruction, particularly in science and math. We also needed to tie school more closely to work for many of our children.

The state Board of Education had already taken steps toward reforming and improving our education system through a comprehensive plan that laid out a vision for schools. The ground was ready for our seeds of change. In the first year of my administration, we convened a Summit on Education to get ideas from teachers, parents, business leaders, and others across the state. The people who came endorsed the National Education Goals, later named Goals 2000, which had come out of earlier National Governors' Association meetings. At the Summit on Education, we came up with ways to meet those goals in New Mexico. To hear the concerns and get input from people beyond the Albuquerque-Santa Fe corridor, we went on to hold eight regional summits with a similar agenda. We also convened a Governor's Youth Education Summit to hear from the students.

Later in my term, I appointed the New Mexico Education 2000 panel, chaired by the outstanding school superintendent David Chávez of the tiny southeastern community of Loving. The panel wrote a state plan to meet the national goals, submitted the plan to the federal Department of Education, and received funding for local school-improvement projects. The main thrust of the state's Goals 2000 plan was for communities to start long-range planning for their schools, then figure out what they needed to improve in areas like curriculum or teacher training to reach their goals.

Alice also organized a Governor's Forum on Education in 1994 with special guest Richard Riley, who was then Secretary of the U.S. Department of Education. During this session, educators and others participated in roundtable discussions about the progress of New Mexico toward the National Education Goals. It also gave Secretary Riley the opportunity to see what we had accomplished and take that information back to Washington.

Early on, Alice and her staff—particularly my education advisor, Caroline Gaston, David Colton of UNM, and Chuck Spath—took the lead in pulling together a broad group of educators, scientists, parents, state Department of Education staff members, local school board members, and so on to write a proposal for reforming science and math in all our schools across the entire state. The plan they came up with addressed every aspect of math and science from kindergarten through eighth grade. It called for true systemic change. In 1992 we won a $10 million grant from the National Science Foundation to implement it over a five-year period. The planning effort for that grant broke new ground by involving such a broad spectrum of people in the process—we had scientists from Los Alamos National Laboratory sitting at the table with parents, and professors from the University of New Mexico beside museum staff workers.

The way we tackled writing that grant reflected what we tried to do in all our education and family-related programs—we wanted to coordinate resources that hadn't been coordinated before, and involve every group that had a stake in the outcome of a proposed program. We also wanted to make sure the local communities had a say not only in the planning process, but in the way a new program was rolled out in their hometown. We used a similar approach during the last year of my term to develop a statewide School-to-Work initiative, which was intended to help the schools come up with courses that would prepare students to enter the job market after graduating from high school. We called together a steering committee, then held meetings around the state to share information and get input. We didn't finish this process before I left office, but we left enough in place for my successor to continue building on our efforts. Maybe the best thing to come of this project was the unprecedented collaboration between business, labor, several departments of state government, and education.

We backed several individual school-improvement and systemic reform projects. A group called Re:Learning New Mexico was helping schools form committees to write long-range plans based on a thorough understanding of their own needs. Re:Learning helped teachers upgrade their skills and provided a framework for carrying out reforms in every part of the school— curriculum, communication, teacher development, and so on. Alice's staff became strong advocates of Re:Learning and we helped them get increased funding from the legislature and the State Board of Education, as well as from private foundations. With this support, the number of schools involved in Re:Learning jumped by a third, and students in those schools scored higher on achievement tests than students in other schools.

A major theme in systemic change in education across the nation was linking health and social services closely to the schools. New Mexico became a leader in this area, as schools became Medicare providers to increase health services for students. The Communities in Schools project, which we started in 1991, brought schools and families together with health and social service providers to reduce dropout rates—and they did decline during my administration. We presented a series of regional conferences to help local communities make their own plans for involving schools, health providers, and the community in the health of students. We also saw the benefit of making services more accessible and cost efficient.

One key to improving schools was to pull in the business community, so I named the Governor's Business Executives for Education to advise me on education matters. Lee Bray of Sandia National Laboratories was chairman of this group of CEOs of businesses in New Mexico. As their main approach, they decided to introduce into the school system the principles of Total Quality Management, which was so popular in the business world then. They called the initiative Strengthening Quality in Schools, and established a pilot project at three public schools in Cibola County. A team from the state Department of Education went through training in total quality principles and started expanding the program to other schools. Strengthening Quality in Schools carried on well past the end of my administration, with good results in improving student performance and keeping kids in school.

Alice and her staff also were strong advocates of volunteerism. They established the Governor's Office of Volunteer and Community Service, which helped communities come up with strategies to expand volunteerism locally. Alice's people also won a federal grant for a state operation of the AmeriCorps program started by President Clinton as a kind of domestic Peace Corps. Through AmeriCorps, young, college-age people do community service at the local level and earn money that can only be spent on college tuition. The New Mexico Youth Services Project worked with kids to develop their leadership skills while providing community service. The Christmas in April program, which was patterned after the Habitat for Humanity concept, recruited volunteer labor to remodel and rebuild the homes of senior citizens.

At the end of my third term, I could honestly say that New Mexico was a healthier, more child-friendly state than it was when I took office in 1991. More women were getting maternity care, more children were getting immunized against early childhood diseases, and more people were covered by health insurance than any other time in the state's history. Infant mortality rates hit an all-time low—they were well below the national average—while child support collections increased by 60 percent. The school dropout rate declined, the average length of stay of a child in foster care dropped by more than half, more families stayed together, and more women received prenatal care. Thanks to the coordinating work of the Children, Youth, and Families Department, the focus brought on by the Children's Agenda, and the tireless advocacy of my wife, Alice, I think we left New Mexico a better place when I finally turned the governor's office over.

As I had seen before when a new governor comes into office, my successor didn't choose to continue many of these programs that we had started. Fortunately, a number of them took on a life of their own. Christmas in April, Strengthening Quality in Schools, and AmeriCorps survived by becoming private, nonprofit corporations. The State Police took over the Drug Abuse Resistance Education program. It was encouraging to Alice and me that these worthy activities found enough support to carry on even without guidance and leadership from the governor's office.

᪛

One of my campaign promises in 1990 had been to boost New Mexico's economy by creating jobs in new and existing companies. I took that promise seriously. Economic development was a primary focus of my third administration, and we had great impact in that area. From an economic perspective, New Mexico still needed some work as we came out of the 1980s. We needed to get into the global marketplace. That meant bringing new investment dollars to New Mexico and creating our own wealth. I wanted to see more value-added processing, whether it was making cheese or fabricating computer microchips, so we could reverse the trend of exporting our raw materials and importing finished goods. To attract new industry to the state as well as to help our existing businesses grow, we developed several strategies: aggressively recruiting new industries, effectively promoting tourism, developing new foreign trade opportunities in Mexico and overseas, increasing our share of the movie-making business, and promoting our high-technology capabilities through partnerships among businesses, Los Alamos and Sandia National Laboratories, and our state universities.

For people who were raised and educated in New Mexico, we were creating more opportunities to stay here in good jobs rather than having to move someplace else to earn a living that matched up with their skills. Through in-plant training programs, we also provided a way for our workers to upgrade their skills on the job—that helped both the employers and the workers.

Probably our highest-profile industrial-recruiting achievement was the Intel expansion at Rio Rancho, which began in 1993 and became the largest construction project underway in North America. Bringing them here was quite a coup. We were competing heavily against Texas and California for the plant, which would make microchips for IBM-compatible computers. I wanted Intel here for several reasons. The project fit with my desire to create new wealth through value-added manufacturing. Also, we needed a large-scale, high-tech project to give New Mexico credibility as an industrial site and to demonstrate that we could accommodate the needs of a manufacturing plant of that magnitude. Intel is a big player in the high-technology arena, and their expanded presence here would help us recruit similar companies. Finally, Intel's manufacturing process was relatively clean and represented little threat to the environment.

Back in 1979, I had worked with Intel when they had approached Rio Rancho about opening their original—and much smaller—New Mexico plant. At that time, Floyd Bailey was head of AMREP, the developer of Rio Rancho since they started building houses there in the early 1960s. At first, Rio Rancho was known as a retirement community. People moved out here from the east and settled in the AMREP-built homes. The community sits on the West Mesa just above the old farming village of Corrales along the Rio Grande and a few miles northwest of Albuquerque. There was nothing out there but houses and a lot of sagebrush—one of our ranches, the Alamo, borders Rio Rancho on the north and west, and we still run cattle out there. But Rio Rancho grew steadily, and more rapidly as time passed. By the late 1970s, AMREP and the local chamber of commerce were working hard to entice new businesses to locate in Rio Rancho. They were concerned that the city had little in the way of a local economy and few jobs. Though many of the residents were still retirees who didn't have to work, it was hard on the younger people. AMREP started marketing Rio Rancho to corporate prospects, and Intel took an active interest.

When Intel first began negotiating with AMREP, Floyd Bailey asked Alice and me to meet with the top brass of Intel, including Gordon Moore, CEO and one of the company's founders. Gordon and I developed quite a friendly relationship. He had a very similar educational background to my son, Gary—both have the unusual combination of a law degree and a Ph.D. in organic chemistry—so we always had that in common. When I met with Gordon in 1979, and as my staff followed up, we pitched our inexpensive property, good tax base, mature government, cheap utilities, and available water. Intel liked what they saw and built a small plant in Rio Rancho right at the eastern edge of the West Mesa, overlooking Corrales and the river valley. The plant employed about 1,500 people in the early 1980s. Rio Rancho had already grown explosively as a bedroom community to Albuquerque, based on its inexpensive housing. Now Intel was adding a large employment base to the local economy and more people could live and work there instead of commuting in heavy traffic across the congested bridges over the Rio Grande into Albuquerque. At that time, we were pretty excited to have attracted a high-tech company that did business with IBM—we had no idea Intel was destined to become an international giant of the semiconductor industry.

When I came back to the governor's office in 1991, Intel was looking around the West for a location to build a major manufacturing facility for its new Pentium chip, which would boost the computing power of IBM PCs and compatibles. Although Intel was considering expanding the Rio Rancho plant, they were also scouting sites in California and Texas. I first heard about the project from the economic development group in Rio Rancho, which approached my office for help persuading Intel to pick their city. I thought it matched our goal of attracting clean, high-technology industry by touting our base of technical excellence associated with the national laboratories in Albuquerque and Los Alamos. So I asked Economic Development Secretary Bill Garcia to lead a team of cabinet members, legislators, county officials, and others in putting together a proposal for Intel. Bill did an excellent job coordinating all that.

We knew the other states would offer strong packages, too, and we had a number of issues to address in selling New Mexico to Intel. Putting the deal together took cooperation at several levels of government. On the legislative side, I had my son Bill work with the legislative leadership to develop legislation creating favorable tax incentives. House Speaker Raymond Sanchez and Senate President Pro Tempore Manny Aragon, both of Bernalillo County, were very supportive. We also worked closely with Sandoval County Commission Chairman Joe Lang and County Manager Debbie Hays, since the industrial revenue bond legislation that we developed would involve the county holding title to the Intel land as part of the tax abatement provision. I had worked on getting the legislation that enabled those bonds passed through the House when I was speaker in the early 1960s. Intel would gain clear title when the bonds were paid off. The legislature also passed a double-weighted sales tax law that spared Intel from paying certain corporate income taxes because it was a manufacturing facility.

These kinds of tax incentives carried weight with Intel, but there were other hurdles to clear. The microchip manufacturing process requires plenty of water and Rio Rancho is in the middle of the desert. I suggested they purchase their own water rights, which they eventually did, buying rights farther south in the state and transferring them up. I also suggested they drill wells several miles west of Rio Rancho so they wouldn't draw down the aquifer around Corrales, but they passed on that advice and wound up having disputes with the village over water.

Intel liked having the University of New Mexico and Albuquerque Technical Vocational Institute nearby to provide well educated and highly trained workers to fill their jobs, and they liked our in-plant training programs and our high school system that prepared students for the work force. They also appreciated our keen interest in bringing clean industry into the state. Bill Garcia and his group worked hard to provide information, answer questions, and work out the details needed to close the deal. He never hesitated to bring me in when he thought it would help, and of course I kept in contact with my friend Gordon Moore. We learned that Texas Governor Ann Richards had flown out to Santa Clara to visit with the Intel brass, but we felt I had already established a strong rapport with Gordon and that a special trip was unnecessary. I was right. Intel finally settled on New Mexico as the location for the Pentium plant.

In the end, I think my rapport with Gordon Moore tipped the balance in our favor. We had a very good personal, working relationship. A couple years later Gordon came to Rio Rancho to dedicate the new plant. In his speech he credited our good friendship and my office's continuing efforts to point out the positives of New Mexico as being very important in their decision to locate the new facilities here. He even kidded me a little bit, saying, "Governor, you were right in all the things you told me about the good work force and so on, but you sure mislead me on that cheap power and electricity. This is the highest price for power we pay anywhere." We had seen some rate increases, all right, but he knew that I couldn't do anything about that.

When Intel decided to bring the new project here, California in particular couldn't believe that such a small state in terms of population and gross state product could land this $1.5 billion project. It was a terrific boon to our state economy, for Albuquerque and Rio Rancho in particular. Early official estimates said it would bring in 1,000 new jobs, but the numbers have far exceeded that, with about 6,000 people working at Intel in 1997. That's a huge workforce, by New Mexico standards. Back in 1979, we never in our wildest dreams thought Intel would grow to be so big, with annual revenues exceeding $20 billion, or that they would become such a dominant player in the worldwide computer industry.

The total cost of the project reached about $2 billion, and much of that money worked its way through the New Mexico economy. However, the impact of the Intel expansion goes beyond its direct contributions. The company became a base economy of its own, spinning off other businesses in much the same way a high mountain peak creates the weather around it. A dozen firms sprang up to supply and support Intel in various supporting capacities. On top of that, the Intel plant gave us the critical mass we needed to become a credible site for high-tech industrial development and relocation. Now we had the leverage to pull in other companies in the computer and semiconductor industry, and in other sectors, as well. Sumitomo Sitex of Osaka, Japan, decided to take over an old mental hospital site in northwest Albuquerque and build a facility to manufacture silicone wafers as a supplier to Intel. They have since announced plans to expand their site. The software company Intuit came to Rio Rancho, and US West and J.C. Penney moved their credit-card processing headquarters there, too, while PepsiCo and Taco Bell brought their regional advertising offices. Medical instrument companies and others soon followed suit, all within about a four-year period, and recently America Online, the computer network company, opened a customer service center here, so the momentum for growth continued after I left office.

Our industrial recruiting and other economic development activities ranged far beyond the Albuquerque area and high-tech industries. Under Bill Garcia, the Economic Development Department worked as a catalyst for business growth and lent a hand to the various community and regional economic development teams around the state. Just as the Intel expansion came to our attention through the Rio Rancho developers, other opportunities came up from the community level. One of our strategies was to encourage economic development in rural communities. For instance, we brought in a large cardboard operation to McKinley County. They used the waste heat from the Plains Electric generating plant to manufacture containers. It was the biggest thing to come there in years, eventually hiring nearly 300 employees.

In many small communities, agriculture remains the lifeblood of their economy. Working with the U.S. Department of Agriculture, I established the Rural Development Response Council in 1992. This council assisted communities on projects ranging from marketing their agricultural products to maintaining the hospital in Santa Rosa. The council also helped to create the New Mexico Country Stores, which showcased locally produced food products at the State Fair and at the "New Mexico's Own" country store at Winrock Mall in Albuquerque. My staff also backed an effort to get grocers to stock more New Mexico products on their shelves and we obtained USDA funds to promote our pecans, chiles, and other food products in Europe and Asia.

The growth of the dairy and cheese industry on the east side of the state is a great example of how we succeeded in rural agricultural business development. My staff and I worked with the Departments of Agriculture and Economic Development to bring Leprino Foods, a cheese-making company, to Roswell. There's always some hitch in the deal, it seems. With Leprino, they needed a slightly cheaper source of power, because they use a great deal of electricity so it's a big expense. Even though it made the rural electric cooperatives out there unhappy, I worked out a deal in the legislature so Leprino could buy power from the Texas-New Mexico Electrical Company. You have to work those things fairly rapidly, and Leprino wasn't going to come without it. After we resolved that issue, they committed to New Mexico and built a milk processing plant to make cheese. Then in 1994 they started a $35 million expansion. The dairy industry is like the semi-conductor industry in a couple ways: they both need water and once you get one of them to come, others will follow. Next, Mid-America Dairymen, Inc., constructed a new milk processing plant in Portales, and soon we were ranked twelfth in the nation in milk production. In 1993, our cows were the most productive producers of milk per cow in the nation.

≋

Developing a more productive, mutually beneficial relationship with Mexico was an old goal of mine, dating back to my first administration. When I came back into office in 1991, I tried to pick up where I'd left off with our neighbor to the south, and I lobbied hard for the North American Free Trade Agreement, which I thought would open up new markets for New Mexico businesses. Mexico was a natural business partner because of our extensive shared border and our long-standing cultural connections. During my third term, we boosted exports to Mexico 144 percent, from $15.5 million in 1990 to $74.3 million in 1993. We also pursued trade with other partners that at first glance might seem less obvious than Mexico, but turned out to be important from an economic standpoint. Chief among them was Japan. We brought a new focus to overseas markets for our products and services by going to Japan and Taiwan on formal trade missions, which proved worth the effort.

The decision by Sumitomo Sitex to locate a plant in Albuquerque was just one highlight among many in our trade relationship with Japan. In the fall of 1991, the Japanese External Trade Organization placed a senior trade advisor named Akihasa Inagaki in the New Mexico Economic Development Department. His job was to help increase the volume of trade between New Mexico and Japan. Developing that relationship with the External Trade Organization really paid off. By the end of 1993, Japan was a leading foreign customer for New Mexico, buying $72 million in exports, an increase of $50 million compared with 1991. Leading the list of products that we exported were electronics, machinery, transportation—including buses from a Roswell manufacturing plant—and chemicals. Visits from Japanese tourists were also up, while they were down in the rest of the United States. I credit Mike Cerletti's Tourism Department for that, since they targeted Japan as one of the ten countries for intensively marketing New Mexico as a vacation destination.

We traveled to Japan and Taiwan in November 1993 to promote new trade relations. Along with spreading the word about our products and abilities, we wanted to emphasize that New Mexico offered an opportunity to access the Mexican market under the recently ratified North American Free Trade Agreement. They could manufacture goods in New Mexico, then use our newly opened Santa Teresa port of entry to ship them south without tariffs.

Alice and I went on this Asian trade mission, along with Bill Garcia, Ed Herrera of the Foreign Trade Division, Mike Cerletti, Richard Gilliland, who was president of the Albuquerque Convention and Visitors Bureau, and a few others. We flew into Tokyo, then took a 45-minute taxi drive and finally rode a streetcar to reach our hotel. During our week in Japan, we had a full schedule of appointments with government officials and industry representatives. Our activities were varied. We attended a lunch sponsored by the national government, where we discussed our mutual interests, and we visited manufacturing plants and other industrial facilities. All the while, we talked up our scientific and high-technology base at the national laboratories and in industry, our agricultural products, and even our world-famous art. We also set up an exhibit to display various New Mexico products, and that generated a gratifying amount of attention. By this time, Akihasa Inagaki had returned home to Japan after his stint in Santa Fe in the Economic Development Department, and even though he was no longer working for us he helped promote our interests among his countrymen.

We attended social events, too, and these presented further opportunities for cultural exchange on a more personal basis. I had experienced Japanese culture before, first in the Army after World War II and then in 1974 as governor, so I knew about the differences in protocol and etiquette. Many of their ways are pretty far-removed from my cowboy upbringing, and sometimes my naturally outgoing nature startled folks over there, who tend to be more reserved and formal. Of course, that was as true with royalty from England and office workers in Mexico City as it was with business leaders in Tokyo. I tend to view everyone as being equal, and I relate to them that way—social standing never counted for much in the homestead country where I grew up, so I never really learned to judge people based on their position. I figure the farm worker who's cutting alfalfa on the ranch deserves the same kind of basic human respect as the trade minister in Japan. I always believed in the old saying that the people you pass on your way up the ladder will be waiting there when you come back down.

Sometimes my openness went contrary to Japanese notions of prestige and maintaining "face." One example had to do with gift exchanges. When we met with senior officials, we would present a gift from New Mexico, usually a piece of artwork or some kind of craft. Often we took a piece of Nambé ware, the unique cast alloy bowls, platters, and the like that are created at the forge just a few miles north of Santa Fe. In Japan we gave a Zuni Pueblo kachina doll, which is a handcarved wooden figure about a foot tall that represents one of the tribe's ancestral spirits. As mythological characters, the kachinas occupy a prominent place in Zuni religion. The dolls themselves are carved as human figures in animated positions, with masks on their faces and actual feathers and other materials decorating their torso, arms, and legs. I thought these dolls made a great gift, and when we exchanged them with the Japanese, who likewise presented gifts to us, I was eager to explain what the kachinas were all about.

The trouble was, in Japan it's impolite to open gifts in the presence of the giver. The way they see it, the gift you receive might turn out to be of greater value than the one you give, and they don't want to embarrass you that way. Bill Garcia and his people had briefed me on all this, but on this one occasion we had just finished an informal lunch, with everyone laughing and joking. That informality suited my style, so when it came time I said, "Aw, just open it up." At my prompting, the Japanese officials unwrapped the present, while I started telling them about Zuni Pueblo and how these kachinas fit into their culture. The Japanese were shocked at first, since I was going against protocol, but then they reacted very positively and really seemed to appreciate what I was saying. I guess we found the common ground underneath all the cultural differences, and it worked out all right. It's like the fuss they made over the cowboy boots I always wore with my suits—I think they got a kick out of meeting the genuine article, a real cowboy governor.

The Japanese weren't the only ones fascinated by the cowboy boots I wore with my business suits. Here I compare footwear with a future voter. (Photograph courtesy Santa Fe *New Mexican*)

The food in Japan, however, didn't always agree with me so well. We raise beef on the ranch, and over the years I've gotten pretty used to eating a well-cooked roast or a even a steak—over in Tokyo, I just couldn't handle all that raw fish. I'd always look around for the bowl of hot oil they put on the table, then soak my fish in it as long as I could to make sure it got cooked. I wasn't too slick with those chopsticks, either, and I learned to slip a fork into my pocket before we went out to a restaurant. That made eating a whole lot easier. The other New Mexicans started asking, "Hey, Governor, where did you get that fork?" I told them I brought it with me, and pretty soon they started doing the same.

One night in Tokyo we went out to a little traditional restaurant where we all had to take off our shoes and sit on the floor. We had some big fellas in our group from New Mexico, myself included, and by Japanese standards we were a pretty out-sized bunch of tall and broad-shouldered men. I imagine we made quite a sight folding our legs under us and squeezing around the table. We got to laughing and kidding each other and had a great old time. I bet the local diners didn't forget that group of Americans anytime soon.

Another overwhelming difference between New Mexico and Japan is population density. New Mexico is still a pretty sparsely populated state, especially outside the Rio Grande corridor—a visit to Japan shows just how sparse we are. We don't have any people compared to Japan. When we went to Osaka to visit the Sumitomo Sitex plant across town from the hotel, we had an appointment for dinner at six but we had to leave at four just to fight our way through the traffic to the restaurant, then we got back about midnight, although the dinner itself didn't last more than two hours. Later, we went to catch a flight out of Osaka, and I've never seen an airport so crowded. I honestly began to wonder if we would ever get out of there. In the cities, golf was all the rage, but space was so limited that they built driving ranges on top of their high-rise buildings, with nets to keep the balls from flying onto the streets or through the windows of another building.

After a week in Tokyo, we flew on to Taiwan for a few days, where the government had offered us rent-free space for a state trade office. We had visited Taiwan before during this administration—that previous trip included showcasing New Mexico art in an exhibit at a new art museum. We had taken the work of several prominent New Mexico artists, including the land-scape painter Wilson Hurley, the world famous Navajo painter R.C. Gorman, sculptor Luis Jimenez, Glenda Goodacre, and Alan Houser.

This time we were focusing strictly on expanding our trade relationship with the Taiwanese, and they are so attuned to trade, we really got the red-carpet treatment. A limousine met us at the airport and took us to the Grand Palace, a very picturesque, luxurious hotel set high on a hill with a long sweeping driveway and tremendous views of the city and water. Inside, the Grand Palace was decorated with impressive chandeliers, ornate and vividly colored carvings, and huge vases of fresh-cut flowers arranged in the lobby every morning.

When it was time for our appointments, a limousine would pick us up at the hotel, then a police escort—with lights flashing and sirens blaring—whipped us through traffic to our destination. We met with government officials at every level and we toured through their enormous trade fair build-ing to see exhibits of the goods and services offered in Taiwan. I was very impressed with how the people of Taiwan thrived on such little land and so few resources. They were aggressive in developing new trading partners, and they wanted every state to open a trade office there. We didn't want to be left out, since I knew how New Mexico would benefit from increased busi-ness with Taiwan. On the other hand, I told them, we hadn't even opened a trade office with our neighbor, Mexico, and I felt we needed to do that first. We didn't have the money to open two trade offices, and the Taiwanese wanted us to commit to a long-term program. So we had to let that oppor-tunity pass us by.

All in all, our Asian trade mission was fruitful. We were able to firm up relations with Sumitomo Sitex and get several new industrial prospects in the pipeline, although some of them didn't come to New Mexico until after I left office. Richard Gilliland from the Albuquerque Convention and Visi-tors Bureau also managed to persuade the Japanese to bring their annual convention in the U.S. to Albuquerque for 1996. It was a huge success and turned out to be one of the largest conventions ever held in New Mexico.

Going as the governor effectively draws attention to New Mexico and ensures the trade mission meets with officials at the highest level possible. As long as you don't make it a full-time job, it's worth taking time away from all the duties of the governor to promote the state abroad.

∾∾

Promoting tourism certainly is an aspect of economic growth, but I felt that it needed more attention than it had been getting. That's why I asked the legislature to split out a separate Tourism Department from Economic Development. During my administration, and thanks in no small way to the leadership of Secretary Mike Cerletti, tourism grew to be a $2.8 billion industry.

For generations, New Mexico has enjoyed a certain mystique among travelers. Places like Taos and Santa Fe have lured visitors from the eastern United States since the mid-1800s. These days, they come from all over the country and all over the world. We have lots to offer them, including spectacular natural features—places like Carlsbad Caverns, the endless gypsum dunes of White Sands, the vast wilderness of the Gila area in the southwest, the striking mesas and canyons of Indian country, and the spectacular mountains of the Rockies in the north-central part of the state. We're far enough south to benefit from a warm winter sun, but high enough in altitude to capture plenty of snow—in the winter you can golf and ski on the same day. Summers are pleasant and long, so over the years most parts of the state have developed annual events for tourists and locals alike, whether it's the Balloon Fiesta in Albuquerque or the Deming Duck Race. It seems like there's always something going on.

We also have a unique blend of three cultures: Indian, Hispanic, and Anglo. Each culture retains much of its original identity, yet they have also stimulated each other in creative ways. That diversity and creativity is apparent in art, architecture, fine food, unique holiday traditions, annual festivals of all kinds, and so on. There's no place like New Mexico anywhere else in the United States. When people visit the historic old towns, they often comment that it's like coming to a foreign country—the adobe, pueblo-style homes are like nothing they've ever seen. With all these natural assets, it's not hard to persuade people to try us out for a vacation, then they keep coming back.

Tourism helps the economy in different ways from industry. It contributes to the tax base but doesn't strain the education system, which is 60 to 70 percent of the state budget, because out-of-state tourists spend money but don't stay and put their kids in school. Tourism also doesn't strain other aspects of the state infrastructure as heavily as industry—you don't have to build major new roads, sewer systems, communications networks, and so on. The film industry—making movies in New Mexico—brings similar benefits to the state. Typically, Hollywood production companies come to New Mexico for location shooting against the backdrop of our outstanding scenery. In the fiscal year of 1993-1994, film companies spent $63 million in the state, which generated tax revenues of $9.4 million, a three-fold increase over 1990.

All our efforts to boost the economy paid off. By the end of my third administration, New Mexico had climbed up from near the bottom to number 1 in creating new jobs—85,000 since 1991—and we were second fastest overall in personal income growth among the states. Our aggressive economic development strategies and our rapid expansion of tourism had a lot to do with that. It was a good time to live in New Mexico.

≈

Throughout all my years as governor I kept the routine of making morning rounds through the office suite, saying hello to my staff, giving everyone a hug, and catching up with the goings-on in their lives. One morning in 1992 I was walking down the hallway pretty early with my old buddy Chuck Spath, who had worked with me in the early 1970s on loan from the federal government and had come back now, 20 years later, on a similar arrangement. I could hear the phone ringing and as the people around me know, I hate to hear a phone go unanswered: it might be a constituent with a problem, and that's too important to ignore. So I ducked into the nearest office and picked up the receiver.

"Betty Starr's office," I said. She was my scheduler. "Can I help you?"

There was just the slightest pause on the other end, a chuckle, and then a familiar voice with a mild southern drawl said, "You can't fool me, Bruce. I know that's you!"

It was Bill Clinton. He was running for president, and every week he called all his governor friends to check the pulse in their states, find out what issues were hot, and brainstorm ideas about addressing them.

I met Bill Clinton in 1978 at a National Governors' Association meeting. I had just been re-elected for a second, non-consecutive term and Bill was a freshman governor. The first day, my good friend Ruben Askew of Florida was chairing an orientation session for first-time governors. Since I had been out of office four years, I sat with the other new governors in the audience. Right off, Ruben said, "I'm not going to lead this meeting with Bruce King sitting out there. I don't consider him a new governor. He's going to have to come up here and sit with us."

"But I am a new governor," I said. "I've been out for four years." Waving off my protest, Ruben insisted, so I went up to sit with the panel of veteran governors. I knew a lot about the situations that were under discussion, which allowed me to contribute right away. That impressed Bill Clinton.

A lifetime of farm and ranch chores had conditioned me to rise at the crack of dawn no matter where I was, and Bill Clinton got up early every day to jog, so the next morning when I went down for breakfast, he was already in the dining room. Recognizing Bill as one of the new governors, I went over and sat with him. From that time on, a National Governors' Association conference didn't go by without us having at least one breakfast together to talk over all kinds of political situations, and we got to be good friends. Often we were the only ones at the early breakfast table.

As we got to know each other better, Bill noticed how friendly I was to everyone. I was always shaking hands and putting my arm around folks like they were long-lost relatives, and he kidded me about it by telling a story. "The first time I met Bruce King, you know, he's got his arm around me, patting me on the shoulder and talking," he would say. "I thought he's either the warmest politician I ever met, or a pickpocket! I'm not sure which." I got a kick out of that. Of course, Bill Clinton has a natural warmth, too. When you're talking to him, he makes you feel like you're the only thing on his mind—that's a great quality in a politician.

As the years passed, Bill started setting his eyes on higher office. Even after he had lost that one race for governor, he had been looking ahead, and had wondered if he should go for national Democratic Chairman to keep his name before the public. I had told him I thought it was a dead-end because the chairman was always stuck trying to mediate among all the differing interests in the party without any authority to enforce party discipline. I said I thought Bill would be better off just hanging out his shingle as a lawyer in Little Rock and biding his time before jumping back into the game. So those of us who knew Bill Clinton weren't surprised when he emerged as a national politician in the early 1990s.

In the spring of 1991, Alice and I went off to the National Governors' Association conference at Lake Tahoe. That's a beautiful setting, with the clearest water you can imagine. One evening we went to a reception for the governors and their wives on a houseboat on the lake. We had a good time catching up with our friends from around the country, and pretty soon we hooked up with Bill and Hillary Clinton. As usual, we talked about our common interests, and they were many. We had always shared a similar philosophy as moderate Democrats. We both believed that you had to support business while maintaining social programs to benefit the less fortunate members of society. Strong business kept your tax base on solid footing and provided opportunities for people to better their own lives. But if you didn't put money into a social support system, some people would never have a chance to get ahead. They needed the best in health care and education. Government had a role in providing these things, just as it did in stimulating business growth.

After a while our conversation turned to Bill's interest in running for president. Still trying to decide whether to go for it, he was feeling out all his friends among the governors. The Clintons kicked the idea around with Alice and me for most of that dinner cruise around the lake. We talked about how the campaign would change their lives forever, and Alice warned Hillary that campaigning on the national stage can turn nasty, especially for the wife of a candidate. We knew that when it came to ripping apart Bill's past for ammo to attack him, his opponents and the press would be relentless and show no mercy, Democrats and Republicans alike. Compared to the race for president, state-level politics would look downright friendly.

Apparently nothing we or any of the other governors said permanently dampened Bill's enthusiasm—he announced his candidacy a few months later. Along with Mike Sullivan of Wyoming and John Waihi of Hawaii, I was one of the first three governors to endorse him. Later in 1991, Bill came to New Mexico to talk strategy with me. He called up and said he knew that the only way the Democrats could succeed in 1992 was to take a moderate line, addressing the concerns of business while continuing to improve the social programs that we as Democrats felt committed to.

"You've done a better job of that than anybody else I know," Bill said. "Let's get together and talk."

Since he was willing to fly out here, we met in Moriarty at El Comedor Cafe, an old Route 66 diner where a bunch of farmers get together to swap stories, compare crop yields, and dissect the events in Santa Fe, Washington, or anyplace else in the world that catches their interest. I still go there just about every morning for a cup of coffee and the chance to read the paper and catch up on the news with my old hometown friends. The day Bill Clinton stopped in, the men in suits outnumbered the fellas in feed-store caps for maybe the first and only time. We had a pretty good crowd of national and state Democratic politicians, including my brothers Sam and Don, former Carter presidential campaign coordinator Tim Kraft, Mike Anaya, Ben Alexander, and John Pound, and we hashed out ways the party could involve business while maintaining a strong social agenda. We had a good conversation and I like to think it helped the future president establish not only the successful new direction of the Democratic party but also to clarify many of his positions that eventually turned into national policy initiatives.

As Bill's campaign developed, I helped him out whenever I could. I felt he was a dynamic young leader with a good vision of where the country ought to be heading. Bill seemed to think I could help his candidacy in the West, so with about seven other governors I flew all around the region campaigning with him in 1992. It seemed like most of our time was spent traveling. The first time I got on the plane, I remember being surprised to see my name tag stuck on the seat beside his.

I asked Bill about the seating arrangements.

He kidded me a little bit and said, "Well, Bruce, I always like to sit with you because we can talk politics, we can talk government and I can pick your brain, or I can just relax and read or go to sleep or whatever and you don't mind. The others are always trying to tell me what to do." So the whole trip, that was the way we rode, though of course he'd move around and talk to the others on the plane as we traveled from state to state. I worked on that campaign for the love and enjoyment of it, and maybe my efforts contributed to Bill Clinton's success over the incumbent President Bush.

♒

Back at home, while my administration's successes in economic development made for a smooth ride, the controversies surrounding Indian gaming rubbed at me all four years like a burr under the saddle blanket. Indian gaming caused me more problems in my third administration than any other issue. It just wouldn't go away. While I was home on the ranch between terms in office, the U.S. Congress had passed the 1988 Indian Gaming Regulatory Act, which allowed Indian tribes to operate games that were already permitted under state law, but only after the tribes entered into compacts with the state. In New Mexico, fraternal organizations and the Catholic church had for years run bingo operations, so a few tribes in our state rushed to open bingo facilities in the late 1980s. Sandia Pueblo, which is next door to Albuquerque, and the Mescalero Apache tribe were the first to come forward wanting to negotiate compacts. The Apaches were eager to add gaming as an attraction for their resort, the Inn of the Mountain Gods in the Sacramento Mountains near Ruidoso in the south. Sandia was ready to jump in with bingo. Other pueblos would soon follow suit. The Navajo Nation, which is the most populous tribe in New Mexico and a representative democracy like ours, had not chosen to pursue gaming.

I oppose gambling, and Indian gaming in particular, for a few reasons. I believe that gambling isn't good for people, both morally and economically. Whether it's a state lottery or bingo on an Indian reservation, gambling tends to attract many of the people who can least afford it. Recent statistics in New Mexico have shown that in the wealthiest county, Los Alamos, people gamble the least, while in the poorest counties like Rio Arriba and Mora, people gamble most heavily. Low-income folks see it as a chance to strike it rich, but in reality gambling just slowly drains away the little money they have. That's not good for people or their families, and it's not good for the economy. Another problem with gambling is that organized crime—and *unorganized* crime—seems to follow it wherever it goes, whether it's mob connections or the casino cashier who skims a little on the side.

As economic development, gambling is a poor strategy. It doesn't add any new wealth to the economy. It just recirculates existing money, taking it from a large group and concentrating it in the hands of the few. In the case of the state lottery, those in favor tout how much money it contributes to education, but actually only about two-fifths of the proceeds go to the schools. The rest covers administration and pays the management company. As for Indian gaming, the argument that it provides sorely needed economic development for the tribes doesn't hold up. Once again, it tends to suck money right away from the people who need it most, and there's always a middle man running the casino who siphons off much of the profit. I would tell the tribes that if they wanted economic development, let's work together on bringing in some kind of base industry that will give people jobs and a productive way to make a living. For instance, the Navajo Nation, which still has not approved gambling because their people won't vote for it, operates Navajo Farms, an agricultural enterprise that benefits many people and gives the tribe a sustainable economic activity.

A few years before I was elected in 1990, public opinion and the legislature were against expanding gambling in New Mexico. Various bills to create limited casino-style gambling had died in the legislature for lack of support, but by 1991 the tide seemed to have turned the other way. Many Indian tribes had bingo and pull tabs. I agreed to that because I felt the federal law was very clear about granting the tribes permission to offer those games that were already legal in other circumstances in the state, although I felt pull tabs was stretching the law just a might. But now they wanted to offer games in all three federally regulated classes of gambling, just like Las Vegas, Nevada. I was against that. Some tribes already had video-gaming machines, like poker, and I wanted to close them down, but I didn't get very far with that idea.

Under the federal Indian Gaming Regulatory Act, each state was required to negotiate compacts with the tribes to establish the legal foundation of gaming on the reservations, and in 1991 I was ready to do that for bingo and even pull tabs. Everyone agreed we would write the compacts to cover those two activities, but when we got down to work on the deal, the Indians immediately tried to add slot machines and other Las Vegas-style games. In the spring of 1991, I sent Tourism Director Mike Cerletti down to Ruidoso to see what the Mescaleros had set up at the Inn of the Mountain Gods.

When he came back he said, "They've got a lot more than bingo and pull tabs—they've got a whole room of machines."

Although I felt they were trying to force the issue, I told the Mescaleros and other tribes that I wouldn't sign the compacts if they were adding those other games. The federal law seemed explicit on this point: the Indians could not offer games of chance that state law did not allow. Therefore, I said, I didn't have the legal authority to sign those compacts. So the Mescalero Apaches and Sandia Pueblo sued the state and me personally, claiming I hadn't negotiated in good faith. At that point, it was all out of my hands and in the lap of the U.S. Attorney and the federal courts. I couldn't close the casinos down—I didn't have the authority, either.

The lawsuit was complicated by the fact that New Mexico Attorney General Tom Udall declared he couldn't represent me against the Indians because he had a conflict of interest. His office had helped negotiate the compacts and it was conceivable that some of his people could be called to testify on whether I had dealt with the Indians in good faith. He thought I was on shaky ground and told me to find my own attorney, so I hired my 1990 primary opponent Paul Bardacke. I figured you don't know anybody any better than you know your opponents, and his qualifications were top-notch, including a term as state attorney general from 1983 to 1986. He had a sharp legal mind and he had become a national leader in Indian gambling litigation by promoting the argument that the U.S. Constitution protected states from the kinds of lawsuits filed against me.

Paul and I looked at the situation and decided that we not only had a strong defense, but that we should also countersue to shut the casinos down. He did a great job defending me as the cases made their way upward through the federal court system. He won every case but one, and as of this writing the lawsuits are still pending at the Supreme Court of the United States, where I'm confident we will prevail. By mid-1994, however, it was gubernatorial primary season. The gambling interests decided they would settle the issue by pouring money into my opponents' treasuries during the primary and general elections. I'm sure they got commitments from the others to sign those compacts, even though they were illegal. In any case, the final outcome of that governor's race made the lawsuits against me moot.

New Mexico was not alone in facing the controversies surrounding Indian gaming. About half the states signed compacts, and about half didn't. In our area, Governor Fife Symington of Arizona did and Governor Pete Wilson of California didn't. Fife later told me he wished he hadn't. Across the nation, the issue had been further complicated by a Wisconsin court ruling that essentially said if a state allows a tribe to have bingo, then the state must permit any kind of gambling that is legal under federal law. That decision went directly contrary to the interpretation of the law that many of us had followed. I felt the ruling created some difficult questions that the wording of the federal law didn't answer. For instance, could states let tribes operate games that non-Indians were prohibited by state law from operating? I couldn't see how that was fair.

When the Western Governors Conference met in Las Vegas, Nevada, in 1993, they asked me to represent their views on Indian gaming before the U.S. Senate Committee on Indian Affairs. Under the chairmanship of Senator Daniel Inouye of Hawaii, the committee was hearing testimony about revising the Indian Gaming Regulatory Act. I flew to Washington to testify, and at times I was joined by our two Senators, Pete Domenici and Jeff Bingaman. I talked about the devastating social and personal impact of gambling, and I explained why I thought it was bad for the economy, too.

At one point during all this testimony, Senator Inouye said, "Governor, you just don't like Indians."

I took exception to that. "No, I love the Indian people," I said. "But I think Indian gaming is going to be disadvantageous to the state of New Mexico."

I also testified about the lack of supervision over Indian gaming. There wasn't anyone in charge. The states didn't have jurisdiction to monitor the Indian casinos, and the federal government had only about a half-dozen people across the country to police it. In fact, I asked during the hearing how many federal agents were assigned to monitor Indian gaming, and they couldn't answer. Senator Inouye wanted to find out, too, and he told the legal counsel of the Interior Department to get an answer during the lunch break. When they came back, he called me in before we reconvened and said, "You're right, governor. This is not working well. I think we've got less than half a dozen people supervising the entire United States. I never dreamed it was that few."

Senator Inouye finally said that we had opened up problems that needed attention and he hoped we would continue to work on them, and he would try to resolve them, too. The trouble was, by this time the gaming industry was so powerful that we couldn't get the changes we wanted passed out of that committee. Without those revisions to the Act, the situation was never going to improve, and subsequent events in New Mexico proved just how ugly it could get—when the compacts finally were signed, U.S. Attorney John Kelly charged they were illegal, just as I'd said, and he threatened to close down all the casinos. It was a tense time, and I believe it could have all been avoided if the federal law had been thought out more carefully before it was enacted. In New Mexico, the issue was not resolved until the 1997 legislature finally passed a bill enabling the Indian casinos—and others, on a limited basis—to expand gambling in New Mexico to include these other games, and the industry did begin to flourish

Indian gaming has turned out to have a wider-reaching impact than I had first thought, particularly considering the influence it's had on New Mexico politics. It's difficult to operate a very professional, honest, efficient government when you have large amounts of money going into the gambling industry, which they invest in the political system to gain advantage. When all that money sways the election, it diminishes the professionalism of the people who are elected. You can end up with someone who is representing basically one interest, gaming. Those candidates may not be as concerned or knowledgeable about other issues as the people they beat. Often those incumbents who lose take away considerable experience in various aspects of running government. This is true in the smaller races as well as the statewide elections. Overall, it's devastating to government, just as it is to society.

I suffered from the influence of gambling money on campaigns, and so did several legislators across the state. I didn't lose as much of the Indian vote as some thought—the Navajo Nation stayed with me, and they make up more than half the New Mexico Indian population. Rather than lost Indian votes, I was hurt more by the financial impact of the campaign contributions from supporters of Indian gaming. I also took hits for supposedly not letting Indians exercise their rights, though I always believed I was just following the law.

≈

As Indian gaming was heating up in 1993, another problem exploded on the scene in New Mexico, coincidentally striking Indians first but widening its killer reach to include people from all walks of life in every part of the nation. In May I had been enjoying another New Mexico Amigos tour, this time in Florida, when I got a call from Secretary of Health Mike Burkhart, who told me an unknown disease had suddenly claimed five lives. The victims happened to live in remote parts of the Navajo reservation in northwestern New Mexico, and Dr. Bruce Tempest of the Gallup Medical Center had noticed a pattern and reported this outbreak to the state Health Department. Health officials had identified the disease as a virus, but they were trying to figure out exactly what it was, how people contracted it, and how to prevent its spreading. The Health Department immediately set up a crisis management center to tackle the disease.

Of course the Navajos were very upset and concerned, since most of the cases had affected their people. The disease, which came to be called the hantavirus, struck rapidly. These early victims were all young and healthy, but they died quickly and painfully. First they felt common flu-like symptoms—fever, chills, and muscle aches—which rapidly worsened into respiratory failure in just a day or so. Their lungs just filled with fluid and they died. If the disease was diagnosed accurately right away, a major hospital could treat the patient and perhaps save their life. A slow response was fatal—the hantavirus attacked just that quick. For the victims on the remote parts of the Navajo reservation, survival depended on a doctor recognizing this new and totally unfamiliar disease, then speeding the patient to the hospital. After the first few unfortunate people died, the hantavirus had generated enough publicity that doctors were on the lookout for those symptoms, and their quick responses started saving lives.

At first, the press unfairly labeled the hantavirus as an "Indian disease." The Indian people justifiably resented that portrayal, but at the same time it increased their own fears about it. Right away I got a call from Gallup Mayor George Galanis, who had served in the legislature and was a good friend of mine. He was very concerned about how the hantavirus scare was affecting the entire community. George was getting swamped by inquiries from the press, and he asked for help handling them all. I wanted to provide immediate assistance and decided to send my Press Secretary John McKean along with Mike Burkhart out to Gallup. Then I thought I'd better go along in a further show of support. I also intended to demonstrate that we didn't believe you could catch hantavirus just by being around Gallup and the Navajo Nation.

We got in a plane and flew over to Gallup, then after landing at the little airport we hurried to the municipal chambers in time for a press conference. The room was packed with reporters from the national media and the local press, along with government officials, including Navajo Nation Vice President Marshall Plummer and city officials. The tension rose up from that crowd like a heat wave. Reporters were hungry for a story, and the people of Gallup were angry about the unfair treatment they felt they'd received in the papers and on TV, which were playing up the sensational, scary aspects of the story. Even the local paper was in on the act, and the board of regents of the University of New Mexico branch at Gallup had canceled a meeting based on what they'd read in the *Gallup Independent*. Then other papers reported that the board had canceled based on a headline in the *Independent*, and pretty soon you just had reporters reporting on what was in the paper.

I got up and quickly explained to the press that printing hearsay and rumors wasn't helping our efforts to identify the disease, to diagnose its onset, and to determine how it spread. I pointed out that by this time other outbreaks had popped up around the country, and it plainly wasn't just an "Indian disease," or even a localized New Mexico disease. I came right out and told them they needed to report the facts as we learned them, and I didn't mince any words. After that press conference, we did start to see some improvement in the press coverage.

Researchers from several agencies—primarily the state Health Department, Indian Health Service, Gallup Medical Center, the Centers for Disease Control, UNM Hospital, the state Office of the Medical Investigator, and even the U.S. Department of Defense—worked closely together and made some quick breakthroughs, both in determining the cause and figuring out the treatment. They handled it like the Pony Express, handing off the investigation in relay fashion to the next investigator, depending on their expertise.

It turned out that hantavirus spread through the droppings of deer mice, which are quite common in rural areas all over. Victims caught the disease by inhaling dust from the droppings, and often that dust was kicked up when someone was sweeping, for instance.

I think our prompt appearance in Gallup went a long way toward alleviating fears and preventing hysteria about a hantavirus epidemic. Beyond the

incalculable impact on families and others of losing a loved one to the disease, it also had a significant economic impact on the state. All that national
publicity and those false rumors gave the impression that traveling to New
Mexico was unsafe. In Santa Fe, our top tourist destination, some of the
hotels were experiencing a cancellation rate of up to one-third. And it was
all based on misinformation and unfounded hysteria.

More than a dozen people died during that outbreak of the hantavirus
in 1993, and within a year, more than 70 cases were reported nationwide.
Despite these grim numbers, I'm proud of our health workers' rapid success
in determining the diagnosis, treatment, and prevention of the disease. Their
brilliant work may well have staved off an epidemic and halted the spread of
tragedy to untold numbers of additional victims.

≋

When you're in politics, you can't always be certain which issues are going to
kill you with the voters, and which will sail past the public unnoticed. I'll
always be amazed how often your opponents could fabricate a case against
you when the facts clearly told a different story than theirs. A classic case
was the 1993 gasoline tax. During the legislature that year, the leaders of the
House, Senate, and Democratic party all thought it was a good idea to create a 6-cent a gallon tax on gasoline, then use those revenues to jack up the
education budget. Over the years, pay for teachers had lagged behind inflation. By 1993, teachers' salaries in New Mexico ranked lower nationally than
I liked. We were working hard to upgrade our educational system, but we
knew we couldn't attract, keep, or even motivate the best teachers without
giving them more realistic compensation. In places like Santa Fe, teachers
could hardly afford to live in the same town where they taught. Unfortunately, the current revenue projections didn't show enough growth to cover
a pay raise.

Senate President Pro Tempore Manny Aragon, House Speaker Raymond
Sanchez, and others came up to my office during the last week of the session
to make their case. Because we had a lower gas tax than neighboring states
and tourists would bear about one-third the burden, they argued it was a
smart way to solve the problem of teacher pay, but I thought it was a bad

idea to use tax money raised from the highway system to fund educational improvements. My position was that those monies ought to be spent on highways, and we should look for other revenue sources to support education. The legislative leaders weren't seeing things my way this time, and they made it clear that some of our programs for children and families wouldn't fare too well if I didn't come around. In the closing days of the legislature, everything gets a little sticky, and I was looking to maintain harmony.

I wanted to get some more input from my trusted advisors on this matter, so I turned to my son Bill, who was once again working as my unpaid legislative liaison. He knew the politics of the situation as intimately as anybody. Well, Bill just about came unglued, which went contrary to his usual quiet counsel—but this time, he wasn't holding back.

"Daddy," he said, "you'll lose the election if you support this gas tax! We can get that money other ways." Even though the primary was still a year away, we had been at this game long enough to know the early maneuvering was already taking place among the hopefuls. Every step we took now would get a new spin in the upcoming campaign. Still, I couldn't see how such a small tax—maybe $75 per family in a year—could be such a big deal. After I convinced the legislators to put a penny of it into the road fund, I went along with the 6-cent gas tax. The legislature passed the bill, I signed it, and nobody in the press or public paid it too much attention.

Then, just a few days after the close of the legislative session, we got some new revenue projections, which turned out significantly higher than the numbers we had used to make the state budget. Now we could cover the raises for teachers without the gas tax. Right away, I wanted to bring the legislature back to Santa Fe for a special session to repeal the tax—nothing goes over so well with the public as rolling back a tax. Since we didn't need the revenues now, it would be a fiscally prudent and politically smart move for us Democrats. I called all the key legislators, and I had a hard time reaching them, since everyone was still recuperating from the session. To the person, every one of them said no. They refused to come. Even Lieutenant Governor Casey Luna, the presiding officer of the Senate, strongly opposed the special session. He said we could deal with it in the regular session next year. Despite having this chance to help me kill the tax before it even went into effect, Casey would later use the gas tax against me in the 1994 primary campaign.

Maybe I had a different perspective. I remembered all the way back to the 1950s, when Republican Lilburn Holman of Torrance County and my old friend Calvin Horn, who was a leading Democrat, had pushed through about a 3-cent gas tax and then they got beat in the next election. Sometimes a few pennies could turn into high stakes.

For their part, the legislators wondered why the state revenue projections had changed in such a short time, and they wanted a chance to study the matter. I understood that point. These projections are compiled by various groups—the Department of Finance and Administration, the Legislative Counsel, the Bureau of Business and Economic Research at the University of New Mexico, and others. It seems like they are always in dispute or being kidnapped for political purposes. They're either too high, if you're a fiscal conservative, or too low, if you're a liberal. When the liberal Mama Lucy Democrats were running things, they would overproject, and that kept me busy corralling their excessive appropriations, but then the conservative coalition that came into power in the late 1970s kept underprojecting revenues so they could justify under-appropriating. The pendulum would just swing back and forth according to the power structure in the House. It was all in a day's work for me, and I adapted to whoever was there.

In the midst of this wrangling in 1993, Press Secretary John McKean told a reporter that there would be a special session, even though it hadn't come together, and Speaker Raymond Sanchez and Senate President Manny Aragon were furious. That didn't help matters any, and I think John feels bad to this day about that slip. I always gave John a lot of leeway—he did an excellent job—so he knew from our morning meetings that I was planning to call a special session. The trouble was, I still had to make a few calls to the legislative leadership, and a number of them didn't want to come, so I changed my plans. I could have gone ahead and called the special session. In retrospect, it would have helped me politically, but I didn't want to start a feud with the legislature by forcing them to convene. If I had brought them back, everyone would have known I was against the tax, but a governor has to work with the legislature and I didn't want them up there unless I thought we could reach a solution. I wasn't interested in grandstanding simply for my own political gain. Calling a special session is something like using the veto—it's most effective in moderation. Plus I knew the money would just sit there untouched, since we now had the regular revenues to cover the budget, and I thought we could put it into the road fund at a later date, which I suggested for the remaining 4 cents during the next campaign. So I let the tax ride until the 1994 session, when the legislature returned for that year's session and did take back 2 cents of the tax.

The way things worked out, I ran into lots of political trouble over a minor issue. That 6-cent gas tax was going to generate something like $45 million dollars a year, just barely a blip in the $2.5 billion state budget. On the other hand, people are extremely sensitive about gasoline prices, and resistance to that tax kept building as the press rode the topic for all it was worth. I began to think my son Bill was right about the consequences of letting that tax slip through.

∿

When it comes to electing the governor and lieutenant governor, the New Mexico system is flawed by a built-in fallacy. Candidates for each position run independently during the primary, then the two winning the party nominations join forces as the governor/lieutenant governor ticket in the general election. The fallacy is that the gubernatorial candidate doesn't get to pick his running mate: you're stuck with the luck of the draw. In my case, I'd felt I'd been lucky each time. Roberto Mondragon and I worked well together in my first two terms. The position had been part-time at best before then, but Roberto wanted to expand his role, even though the duties of lieutenant governor are limited in the constitution. They include presiding over the Senate, where he can vote to break ties, acting as governor when the governor leaves the state or is somehow incapacitated, and being on hand to succeed a governor who dies or otherwise vacates the office. However, since Bob was fired up to do some work, I let him be an ombudsman so he could handle citizens' inquiries. I also gave him the responsibility for running the state's programs for senior citizens. With these duties, the job justified greater operational status, so I introduced legislation, which passed, to make it a full-time job. Bob set up an office and went to work.

When Casey Luna won the nomination for lieutenant governor in 1990, I thought we'd make a good team. Casey and I were friends and I thought we were quite compatible. We worked hard together to win the election, and once in office I always included him in cabinet meetings and asked him to express his views on whatever we were discussing. Like Mondragon before him, Casey and his staff took on the role of ombudsman. If a citizen called, I gave Casey and his people full authority to call the appropriate state agency and ask them to resolve the situation. Most administrations don't give the lieutenant governor that kind of latitude. I also made Casey chairman of the state Border Commission and the Space Commission, which was working on developing a spaceport for shuttle landings in the White Sands area.

As happens to any team, Casey and I had our occasional flare-ups, and between my staff and his. Once when I left the state, I gave my staff people the authority to call out the National Guard to provide relief to Navajos caught in a winter storm. I guess Casey took offense at that, feeling he should have taken that action, or at least been notified in advance. Other incidents began to pile up, and before you know it Casey was campaigning against me in the 1994 primary, using information about the trouble spots in government that he'd learned from sitting-in on all my cabinet meetings. I really resented how he turned that privilege against me. I felt he should have been working to resolve those problems, not using them to build a negative campaign against me. The bottom line was that he just wanted to be governor. I had thought we'd be running together again as a team. Obviously that wasn't going to happen.

Things just got worse as we moved toward 1994. In late January, President Clinton invited Alice and me to come stay in the Lincoln Bedroom at the White House. Casey asked if he could use the Governor's Conference Room, which is a formal meeting room dominated by an impressive marble roundtable that seats probably 30 people. It's a good place for special occasions. Word went around that Casey was going to announce his campaign for governor, and I didn't want him using my conference room to kick off his campaign while I was gone. So I had about decided not to go to Washington, when Casey assured me that I had nothing to worry about from him back home.

"You know I'm not the kind of guy who would announce while you're gone," he said. "I wouldn't do that."

He didn't use the conference room, but he did announce while I was in Washington. Still, we had a pleasant stay at the White House—Alice and I were excited and honored. In the evening, the president visited with us, then the next morning, which was Sunday, we had coffee and rolls early and chatted just like we always did at those National Governors' Association conferences.

During that weekend, we got some bad news from home. While we were enjoying the historical ambiance of the Lincoln Bedroom, our son Gary was in a terrible crash driving from Moriarty to Santa Fe for an early-morning legislative committee meeting. He wrecked his car and was seriously injured. His pelvis was crushed and he broke several other bones. For a while, the doctors thought he might never walk again—we thank God he has since made a great recovery and is able to walk with a cane, and he continues to improve. When Alice and I got news of the accident, we hurried home from Washington to be at Gary's side.

My son, Gary, shown here with his wife, Yolanda, served for many years as a representative in the New Mexico Legislature.

≋

As we geared up in the winter of 1994 for the June primary election, I felt we had a very strong record to stand on. I had managed to at least hold off the expansion of Indian gaming, which I thought had the potential of tearing up communities around New Mexico. In the area of economic development, we had brought in thousands of new jobs and new businesses, capped by the crown jewel of the Intel expansion. Splitting the Tourism Department from the Economic Development Department had paid off in a great upswing in state revenues from tourist activity within our state. Balancing this focus on business was our emphasis on social programs. We had created the innovative Children, Youth, and Families Department and gotten the ball rolling on significantly reforming our educational system.

I always loved campaigning. We had fun and met thousands of people across the state.

To spotlight environmental concerns around the state, we had created the cabinet-level Environment Department. That had gone well, despite a few hiccups in the financial management of that department. It also came under fire from businesses for its aggressive approach to inspecting underground gasoline storage tanks, but we had great success in passing a stricter mining reclamation bill, which was introduced in the House by my son Gary. The Department put a statewide solid waste management plan into place and developed the first environmental response plan for our border with Mexico. We were also protecting our interests regarding the Waste Isolation Pilot Plant that the U.S. Department of Energy was developing in the underground salt beds near Carlsbad in far southeastern New Mexico. The DOE wanted to bury low-level nuclear waste at WIPP from its facilities all around the country. Many New Mexico environmentalists were strongly opposed to WIPP, but the Carlsbad area saw it as a great way to boost the local economy. Most of the controversy, which had been building for a decade or so, centered on whether WIPP would be safe or the contaminated materials might someday leak out into the surrounding earth. Environment Secretary Judy Espinosa felt the feds hadn't researched the issue adequately, while I was working with Washington to make sure our state would be involved in the decision-making process concerning WIPP.

The Health Department and Human Services Department had worked together to push through a major health care reform package while toning down the radical liberal proposals that would have bankrupted the state. I signed the bill in 1994. It brought health coverage to more New Mexicans than ever before by expanding Medicaid coverage, creating a voluntary Health Insurance Alliance for small businesses, expanding the voluntary low-cost insurance plan, and providing subsidized premiums for low-income people in the state's high-risk pool. In a related measure, the state increased funding for rural health clinics and for training health care professionals. We also created incentives for professionals to serve in rural areas that weren't well served by doctors, nurses, or physicians' assistants.

Despite my record of successes in this term and the rest of my career in office, as the primary campaign got underway I could see stiff competition within my own party. Casey Luna's candidacy was just the beginning of my problems. My opponents would use every tactic they could get away with to unseat me. 1994 would turn out to be another one of those years when the Democratic party tripped itself over its own fancy footwork. Nobody was happy with the results, except the Republicans.

15

The Greatest Accomplishment

In the first few months of 1994, the primary field for governor began to shape up. It was a group of familiar faces. Of course, Casey Luna had tossed his hat into the ring. Then my old liquor director, Jim Baca, jumped in. Since working for me in my second administration, he had been elected state Land Commissioner, then Bill Clinton appointed him director of the federal Bureau of Land Management in the Interior Department. That last position hadn't quite worked out, and now he had come home to get active in state politics again. On the Republican side, a trio of similarly old-line Republicans and a total newcomer to politics were squaring off against each other. My old sparring partner Dave Cargo was running yet again—hardly an election goes by without Candidate Cargo entering the race—as were Dick Cheney and John Dendahl, both longtime Republican leaders. The new boy was Gary Johnson, a 40-year-old Albuquerque entrepreneur who had built his own construction company from a remodeling business—much of that, somewhat ironically for me, based on large contracts with Intel.

I couldn't begrudge Jim Baca his chance at the governor's seat, but I was a lot less happy about Casey Luna's candidacy, or his tactics. He tried to smear me in a negative campaign, using information that he had been privy to as a participant in my cabinet meetings over the years. It cramped my style running against an opponent who worked right inside my own office suite—imagine the president running against his own vice president! I really had to watch my flanks. He had pulled together all the dissident Democrats who were unhappy with me, usually because I hadn't rewarded them with patronage or somehow done them a favor. Casey managed to convince a lot of people they would get a better deal if he was governor.

On the issues, Casey also supported Indian gaming—and his campaign benefited from gaming money, I'm sure—while I had spent much of my time actively opposing it. In fact, the lawsuits against me and my countersuits were still making their way through the courts. And sure enough, Casey also brought up the gas tax. I had a hard time throughout the campaign getting my position on it across to the public—I couldn't ever get out from under that one. Still, I campaigned hard and emphasized everything we had accomplished in my administration in the areas of economic development, education, health care, children and family programs, and the environment.

I must have made my case well, because when the primary votes were tallied, I beat Casey Luna by several thousand—not the margin I was hoping for, but still a win. Jim Baca trailed a distant third. Former district court judge and Albuquerque lawyer Patricia Madrid won the nomination for lieutenant governor, so she would be my running mate this time. Since Patricia had been on friendly terms with the Luna camp, I was hoping she would bring them over to my side. The biggest surprise of the primary was the Republican nominee: political neophyte Gary Johnson used a high-tech campaign marked by simple but apparently effective television advertising to squeak past veteran Dick Cheney by barely 1,000 votes. Dendahl trailed Cheney, and Cargo finished dead last. Walter Bradley won the Republican nomination for lieutenant governor.

I can't say I was thrilled to face Johnson as an opponent, although I felt confident my experience would carry the day. Running against an unknown like that is a bit like climbing onto the back of a green colt the first time. You don't know if he's going to tuck his head and set to bucking, rear over backwards on top of you, or just freeze up. The trouble was, a candidate without a record can say anything and get away with it, because the press can't hold him to his political past if he hasn't got one. His ideas are untested. Johnson used that to his advantage throughout the campaign.

For instance, Johnson kept saying he'd repeal the gas tax. Well, it's one thing to make that claim during a campaign, and quite another to get it through the legislature, especially if you're a political outsider. There's a lot to consider besides the politics, too, including having a grasp of the overall state revenue picture and weighing the various needs of such a diverse citizen population. But the public loved to hear it. I countered that we should spend the tax on improving the highways—they needed it—and it turned out in the next legislature that the Republicans wanted to do that, too. So I was right on the issue, but wrong with the voters.

Often, the press would ask Johnson some technical question about running government, and he'd answer that he had no idea and he'd have to research the matter before answering fully. He didn't even know all the counties of the state when quizzed on it. Yet these gaps of knowledge and experience didn't seem to matter. His nomination definitely reflected the anti-incumbent sentiment that was sweeping the country. You could see it in the 1992 Ross Perot presidential campaign and all the proposed term-limitation amendments. I had never campaigned against someone like this.

Unfortunately for me, Gary Johnson's dark horse victory wasn't the last surprise hurdle I had to clear in that election. Lurking in the background during the spring was my old lieutenant governor, Roberto Mondragon. I had thought Roberto and I were still on good terms. We had always worked together in office, and other than a few minor incidents we had gotten along well. Then when I ran in 1990, Roberto wanted to work for me on contract during the primary, handling public relations. I didn't have the money to put him on full time, and he said, "Don't feel bad if I feel like I have to earn a livelihood." Then about a month later, the story was going around that my primary opponent, Paul Bardacke, had a secret weapon, and it came out that Roberto had endorsed him. In fact, Bardacke had employed Mondragon. But after I beat Bardacke, there still weren't any hard feelings, and they both endorsed me.

In 1994, Mondragon had endorsed Casey in the primary. You expect that kind of thing, and I didn't let it bother me—that's how politics works. But now Mondragon made an unexpected move, and it would prove catastrophic for the Democrats. After teasing the press with his possible candidacy, he filed as a Green party candidate for governor in July. It was bad news for the Democratic party, since Mondragon had a strong following of his own in the Santa Fe area and the Democratic strongholds of north-central New Mexico. Also, I have no doubt that Casey Luna was encouraging Mondragon's candidacy, as well, just to get back at me. So here I was, facing yet another former lieutenant governor of mine, a long-time Democrat turned defector who had the support of the man I just narrowly beat in the primary election.

I was more upset that Mondragon had jumped parties than I was about him leading the dissident Democrats with Casey Luna—disharmony is common in just about every election, especially in a party as large and diverse as ours. You can't be everything to everyone, and you can't create a position for everyone who works for you politically, even though I've been accused of that. There's only so much money and you need cohesiveness in your organization, so you end up making some decisions that put a few people off. In 1994, these dissidents realized they weren't going to fit in my organization and they went with Casey Luna after the primary, even though many of them had backed Patricia Madrid. Again, no hard feelings. Usually the dissidents will come back over in the general election, when your primary opponents endorse you for the sake of party unity. After all, where else can they go?

This time, however, they had an alternative. Mondragon's defection to the Greens was a brand new power play. I didn't think that was quite fair and we had to scramble in the backfield. Patricia Madrid filed a lawsuit on my behalf claiming that Mondragon couldn't run as a Green because he had been registered as a Democrat when the election proclamation went out in January. We didn't see how he could change horses in midstream that way. We had Gene Gallegos representing us for free in this case and he thought it was a lead-pipe cinch. On the other side, Attorney General Tom Udall was representing the secretary of state, who wanted to leave Mondragon on the ballot. Udall sent his best lawyers to represent Mondragon, which I didn't appreciate very much.

We lost the case, and I still can't figure out why. Besides leaving Mondragon in the race to put the squeeze on me, the outcome was a public relations fiasco for my campaign. Everyone was saying that I was afraid he was going to beat me. It was worse than before we filed the suit, and I was the one that got us into all that trouble.

≈

I spent my political life leading government down the middle path because I believe a moderate philosophy brings the greatest good to the most people. I also built my career on fostering unity and forging compromises among groups with often radically opposing views, again for the common good. The three-way race for governor in 1994 made it very difficult for me to highlight the virtues of that philosophy. Gary Johnson was pretty far to the right on the political spectrum, a promoter of downsizing government, eliminating social programs, building new prisons as a means of preventing crime, and loosening the reins on government regulation of business, regardless of the environmental or social consequences.

Then on the other side I had Roberto Mondragon. A very liberal former Democrat, he was now leaning farther left and singing from the Green party hymnal, which in its more radical expression tended to be anti-growth and anti-business, with an emphasis on environmental and social programs that we probably couldn't afford, in my opinion. Even so, parts of their platform overlapped with mine. I probably would have had the Green vote if Roberto had not entered the race, since I was on good terms with the environmentalists and they sure didn't see much to like in Gary Johnson. And despite their opposite views on every other issue, both my opponents favored Indian gaming. In fact, the gaming interests were pouring money into both Mondragon's and Johnson's campaigns. The gaming people didn't care who won, so long as it wasn't me.

Having the Greens on my left often backed me into a corner throughout the race. I had trouble separating out my positions from some of theirs. It was especially challenging at the many joint appearances and television debates that all three of us made together. The art of politics is to convince people of all interests that they're going to get fair treatment from you, that you're going to take care of them. Unfortunately, whenever you have a very conservative candidate running against you with no record and making all kinds of promises, it's hard to say, "Look, business is doing quite well right now, and I've done this, that, and the other." It made me look defensive. At the same time, I'd have to be careful not to make statements in favor of business that would alienate the environmentalists, since now they had another option besides me. Competition from the Greens completely negated my ability to run a strong, public-oriented campaign like I always did.

Gary Johnson campaigned heavily on being tough on crime. He pointed out how high the crime rate was, and played up the public's fear over the rising number of drive-by shootings, gang murders, and drug-related crimes, particularly in the Albuquerque area. Naturally, I wasn't happy about those problems, either, but I thought he misunderstood the basic issues underlying crime. Johnson seemed to believe that all problems could be solved simply by building more prisons. Alice and I had a more compassionate view, favoring community-based approaches for straightening out the offenders who weren't dangerous to society. For more than 20 years Alice and I had worked to create programs that would help wayward youth get back on the right path. Many of them could be rehabilitated with education, work opportunities, family counseling, and so forth.

On the other hand, no one was any harder on the habitual offender than I was, and I had pushed through new prisons to accommodate those hardened criminals. We also believed that you had to have a good classification system to separate those who were obviously going to continue a life of crime from those who had committed lesser crimes and needed help getting back into society. You can't lock them all up forever. I was worried that at the rate we were going, we would have two classes of people, the ones who were locked up and the ones watching them. Johnson never did make a case against me on this.

≋

I always took great care to keep my business dealings completely separate from my political work. Sometimes that wasn't easy, since through the years we had a lot of business activity going on: the main ranch at Stanley, the York Ranch near Grants, the Alamo Ranch northwest of Rio Rancho, King Brothers Butane in Moriarty, and a land-development venture under South Mountain by Edgewood. I had also served on the board of Sunwest Bank in Albuquerque. I always knew you had to keep all that activity far-removed from your work as a public official or the press and your opponents would crawl all over you. So it was ironic that one of the biggest problems I had in the 1994 was defending my involvement in a land trade that the federal government forced on the King Brothers, never even giving us a choice in the matter.

Back in 1969, we—the King Brothers—had bought the 221,000-acre York Ranch southwest of Grants, New Mexico, which is about 100 miles west of Albuquerque. Like so many ranches in New Mexico, it was a mix of fee-simple deeded land and government-lease grazing land held by the Bureau of Land Management. The deeded land took in the open water and other high-value areas—some previous owner had cherry-picked the best parts for private ownership—and the BLM lease surrounded those private parcels.

The York is a beautiful place. I loved sneaking out there from the governor's office in the early 1970s to work cattle on horseback, maybe helping out the cowboys with the branding or whatever other chores needed doing. The ranch covers a rugged spread of mesas and canyons and a scattering of piñon trees and ponderosa pines, with cottonwoods growing where the water collects. Towering on the northern horizon is Mt. Taylor, a cone-shaped, 11,000-foot peak you can see from Albuquerque. Cutting through the tract is the *malpais,* Spanish for "badlands," which are lava beds so jagged and broken-up you can't even cross them on a horse. Otherwise it's good cattle country, and we bought it from the York family of Odessa, Texas, to run as a yearling ranch and maintain a cow-calf herd. We would pasture a yearling herd out there, then bring them into the feedlot at our Stanley ranch to fatten them up for market.

For a while in the 1970s and 1980s, the BLM had wanted to create a wilderness area around the *malpais* to preserve the beauty of that geologic feature, as well as some historical homesteads and more ancient ruins around there. In 1987, Congress created the 137,000-acre El Malpais National Monument, which included about 33,000 acres of our federal grazing allotment and a few thousand acres of our deeded land. Another 60,000 acres were designated as wilderness, again including our land. Part of the Act empowered the BLM to acquire those deeded lands within the area that were considered key to maintaining the wilderness character of the monument. I strongly opposed the wilderness areas because I didn't want our ranch taken away. I testified before Congress on the matter and sent letters to all the right people, but the feds weren't backing down. The conservationists were stronger than I was this time. When our lease expired in 1986 on the federal lands, the BLM just took them back. They also had the right to condemn our private land and buy us out.

However, instead of forcing the matter through condemnation, they proposed a trade for about 22,000 acres of our land, including the key acreage that had water. Without water, you couldn't ranch in that country, so naturally I was very reluctant to part with it. They came back and said they would purchase it through condemnation if I didn't agree, so they were giving us a chance to trade for property of similar value. Either way, we were going to lose our ranch.

It was looking like a shotgun deal, and being somewhat of a land trader anyway, I said, "Well, okay, but what land do you have to transfer?"

They pulled out their maps and showed me some tracts in the open country west of Santa Fe. Knowing how high property values in Santa Fe could be, I agreed to consider it. The government sent appraisers to come up with a value, but I didn't think their appraisal was a fair one, so I turned them down. Now it was getting along into the late 1980s when they came back again, saying they would exchange more land and pay us more for ours, so again we all hired special appraisers to determine the value and this time we made a better deal. Consummating the exchange dragged out, though, and I was elected governor again in the meantime. In 1992, we finally dotted all the Is and crossed all the Ts: the BLM acquired about 21,000 deeded acres, water rights, and six wells from King Brothers, and in return we received 800 acres near Santa Fe and another 697 acres near Stanley.

The Santa Fe land we traded for had been ranched for some 50 years by a man named Antonio Baca, who held a grazing allotment on that land just like we did out at the York. He probably wasn't any happier about losing his lease than we were about ours, even though it was only a part of his holdings. When the trading began in 1991, Baca went downtown to the Santa Fe *New Mexican* and told them his version of the story. The paper didn't even call me, but ran a front-page story about Baca losing his ranch to the *gringo* politician, with a big picture of him standing by a stock tank. Obviously, my side was not well-represented by the article. That really ticked me off. I went down to the *New Mexican* office and met with publisher Bob McKinney, editor Billie Blair, and others. I knew them all pretty well. Shoot, I'd been dealing with newspaper controversies at the *New Mexican* for almost 40 years by now.

"Look guys," I said, "if you don't want me to make the trade, then we'll just forget it."

"That's not for us to decide," they told me.

"I know that," I said, "but if you're going to make a big to-do about it I don't even want to deal with it."

The staff of the *New Mexican* finally saw my point. They agreed the

BLM needed to make the exchange and this was a legitimate deal. They also agreed to back off the story and not write any more about it. Things settled down for a couple years after that. Then about a year before the 1994 election, Baca went and hired an attorney to sue the government over the deal. Again he went to the *New Mexican* with his story. The first I heard about the lawsuit was what I read in the paper. I got on the phone and called the reporter, Mark Oswald.

"What's all this?" I asked him.

He said, "Well, you know, they leaked the story to us."

"Why didn't you call me for my side of the story?" I asked him.

Then I called the editor, Billie Blair, and asked her why they were riding this story when they had said during our previous meeting they would lay off it.

"Mark Oswald wasn't with us when we had that meeting," she said.

Baca contended the land been grossly undervalued by the appraisers because I was a powerful politician. At first, even presiding Judge Conway, an old friend of mine, agreed with that view and called it a "sweetheart deal." The papers splashed that all over the place. When he learned the facts of the case, though, he changed his mind and eventually ruled in our favor.

I never felt Baca had a leg to stand on. The BLM forced the trade on us, threatened to condemn our land if we didn't cooperate, and suggested the Santa Fe parcel in the first place. The whole deal had been initiated by New Mexico's former Republican Congressman Manuel Lujan, who at the time was Secretary of the Interior. Regardless of the facts, 1994 was an election year, and the lawsuit made great press in my opponents' smear campaign against me. They painted it to look like I'd pressured the federal government to trade a worthless ranch for some high-dollar Santa Fe real estate. In truth, part of that Santa Fe land was an illegal dump that would take considerable resources to clean up and make marketable, while on the other hand, our total ranching operations in the state had been deeply cut. The deal didn't smell very sweet to me.

That episode illustrates a couple things. Anybody can sue anyone else for anything, regardless of the facts, and until the case is ruled on by a judge, those facts are in dispute. If you're a politician, the press will jump on any lawsuit against you, and the plaintiffs' claims are quoted as if they *are* the facts. The reporters who have known me for many years are probably more likely to approach a story like that with caution than the newcomers who haven't been in the state too long and aren't familiar with my character. But once a story reaches the papers, it can be awfully hard to live down. As often happens in politics, it was the public's perception that counted, not the truth. The lawsuit dragged on all the way through the election and my opponents were able to use it to their advantage. The case and all its appeals were finally settled in 1996—in our favor, of course, but far too late to do me any good in the governor's race. It was one of those times when you're awfully glad you've got title insurance, since the title company paid all the legal fees.

≈

Without Mondragon in the race, Gary Johnson and I would have run in a dead heat. One factor beyond my control was the nationwide resurgence of the Republican party. I got caught trying to defend Bill Clinton, which wasn't so easy in 1994, especially in the West. That was a dark time for the Clinton administration—after the health care fiasco and conflicts with western states over logging, grazing, and the like, it seemed nothing was going right. It looked like Newt Gingrich had long coattails that were reaching into every state. My ties to the president were a political liability this time around, even though he and Al Gore tried to help me out.

Another aspect of this race that put me at a disadvantage was the rising influence of political consultants on campaigning. They just muddy the waters. Alice and I had always felt that when we ran the campaign on our own with just our family, we could beat anybody—and we did. I had been criticized for being a simple cowboy who thought you could win elections by just getting out and campaigning one on one. Even my friends among the other governors would rib me about my folksy style. Of course, that worked well in the early days, but by 1990 I let people convince me to hire an out-of-state consultant. It worked out all right, since I won, but I think I would have run strong that year anyhow. Then in 1994, my friend Ben Alexander of Lea County, who had helped raise money for Clinton and served on the national committee, told me, "I'm not even going to help you unless you hire a consultant. I'll help you raise the money for him." Times change, and you've to got change with them. You have to keep moving. So I agreed again.

The down side of working with consultants is that they fall into a formula of what's worked other places, and they don't follow the changes in your state. Often they want you to take positions you don't really believe in because they think it'll get votes. They're hard to control, they start to make mistakes, and they rely too heavily on polling. You get to where you're chasing after poll results at too fine a level of detail. It's like cutting alfalfa with your pocket knife: you might get every stalk in one acre, but you miss the other ninety-nine acres altogether.

If I was to do it again, and I know this will never happen, I would just say, "Look guys, we'll poll them on election day, and that's soon enough. I can walk down the street in Albuquerque, Santa Fe, and Las Cruces and tell you if we're winning or losing." That's what I did in 1970 against Pete Domenici—we didn't conduct a single poll. But then, I knew two-thirds of the people in the state back then, and there's been so much immigration that I don't anymore. Much of our population is from somewhere else and they don't have a long-term perspective on New Mexico politics.

When I started in politics, New Mexico had such a great grapevine that you could deal with some issues by simply putting the word out through a few key people. It was a great way to get your position across to the public. These days, with so many people in the state, the grapevine doesn't work anymore. Politics has completely changed from a person-to-person, local basis to "your consultants against my consultants." They figure out how to package your message and which niches you should try to fill. I had always thought I did that pretty well on my own, and I reached out to various groups because I believed we had common interests, not just because I thought it would help my campaign. Once, a consultant pointed out that I was the only candidate he knew who could get endorsements from labor and the Farm Bureau, even though they tended to be on opposite sides politically. No consultant would ever have told me to go after those two voting blocs, but I was able to work with both sides on my own, and no one told me how to do it. My success came from understanding the needs of both groups and finding ways to address them without harming the other side.

The way consultants hammer an issue before the public can either backfire or it can work just like selling soap. If you go on TV and say this brand of soap is the best there is, and repeat it over and over, then people will go buy that bar in the store, just like they will pull the little lever in the voting booth. But that kind of voting doesn't make for good government, and there's no guarantee to the voters that the message generated by the consultants is true. I think there will be a trend away from this kind of campaign in the coming years because the consultants are misleading some candidates as well as the public. We need a truth-in-consulting law and a campaign fund limit. If candidates couldn't afford consultants, they'd spend a lot more time getting out to the people with their own messages, and they would be more responsive to the needs of voters.

∼

As the fall of 1994 came on, all the negative campaigning against me began taking its toll, and Patricia Madrid hurt the effort by making some unfortunate comments about Gary Johnson, implying that he'd hire only Anglos and other "newcomers" who didn't appreciate Hispanics. Although she was trying to help, those words backfired. Meanwhile, Johnson started gaining momentum. I think even the Republicans were surprised—after all, he was an outsider in their own party without established ties to the Republican leadership. Even so, his simple message was sounding good to many voters.

On election night, I gathered with my family and close friends at the Classic Hotel in Albuquerque. As the precinct reports rolled in, I saw we weren't doing well. Even my old home base of Santa Fe County and the north-central part of the state was going to the other side—Mondragon was yanking those votes out from under me, while Johnson was hauling in the Republican strongholds in Albuquerque and precincts on the east side. The race had slipped away from me, and for the first time in my life, I lost a general election. When all the votes were in, Gary Johnson won 49 percent of the vote, while I had 40 percent and Mondragon eked out 10 percent— with his votes, I would have won, or at least pulled even with Johnson. But this time, it wasn't meant to be.

I lost that election for a lot of reasons, starting with Casey Luna's attacks all the way through the issues like the land trade and Indian gaming and Roberto Mondragon's surprise Green party candidacy. Timing had something to do with it, too. I can see the impact of changes in campaigning and the very nature of politics, and I think that maybe the newspaper headlines were right when they described my defeat as the "end of an era." Some said it signaled the death of the old *patrón* system of political patronage, and while I did know how to work the community-level structure of the Democratic party, I had really built my career on personal, face-to-face politics. The way New Mexico has grown, far more than doubling its population during my 40-year career, it's no longer possible to have that kind of personal contact with the voters. For their part, many of them don't want such close involvement with their leaders. Society doesn't work that way anymore.

In hindsight, I can also see how over the decades, I probably gained a new enemy every year. After awhile, the numbers build up. As I grew older, I eased up my defenses and stopped watching my flanks as carefully as I had in the past. Partly that was because the 1994 race was the first time I ran for governor while serving as governor. I was so busy running state government that I couldn't mount the kind of aggressive campaign I had waged so successfully against Frank Bond in 1990. He even told me, "Bruce, if you campaigned against Johnson the way you did against me, he wouldn't have had a chance!"

℥

At the end of December, we cleaned out the office, kept the papers we thought we might want later, and packed up our personal things at the mansion. We were moving home again. There were tears among the staff at the Christmas party—I guess we all knew this was our last stint in the Roundhouse. I wouldn't be coming back. It was time for me to retire from politics and get back to my ranch and helping my brothers Don and Sam and my son Bill with all our business ventures. I had no intention of running for office again.

It wasn't so hard getting back into the swing of things on the ranch. Winter is a slow time, anyhow. We hadn't really lived in Stanley for four years, so we took some time settling back in the house, unpacking boxes and establishing our routine around the old home place. Nowadays, we lead a simple life, starting ranch work at seven in the morning like always, running our businesses, getting involved in community and church work, and traveling to speaking engagements, where I can share my experience with people from all kinds of backgrounds. I stay active in the legislative process by lobbying for bills that I believe we need, at both the state and federal level. I still have a world of friends in key positions, and I can influence the direction of legislation that I feel is important. Alice continues her role as an advocate for children and families as chair of the New Mexico Children's Foundation, which she helped set up. I also keep my hand in Democratic politics, trying to maintain the party's strength and supporting my son Gary's career—maybe we'll get him elected governor someday.

Try as we might, Alice and I will probably never get out of public life entirely, even though the day-to-day job is over. When you're in politics, you have to enjoy it, and enjoy helping people, which I did. Even after "retiring," I've found there are still so many things to do, and people to help. If they have a problem or they don't know who to call, they start with me. The first time you see something that needs some attention, you go trying to be helpful. Now when I see Gary Johnson at a function, he'll say, "You know, I really appreciate you a lot more now than when I started. I realize how hard all this is." Of course, he might be saying that just to be nice. As my old friend Franklin Jones once told me, "The trouble with you, governor, is you have a tendency to believe people."

"Well," I told him, "I believe them till they cross me up."

Looking back over my 40-year career, I like to think I've left a legacy of good government. Naturally, I see the highlights—things like the port of entry at Santa Teresa, which took years to complete, along with sound management of state revenues, expansion in the private economy, professionalizing government, and so on. I also see a smooth flow, starting with my work as a county commissioner in 1955, when the future was just waiting to happen. Frankly, I think that future has turned out well, and I'm proud of my role in creating it.

People who are around me know there's only one side to Bruce King, and I won't ever deviate from that. I have always applied myself to doing what's best for people at all times. It's a great philosophy. I figured out through the years that you have to try to lift up all areas and give everyone an opportunity. I am genuinely concerned about all parts of New Mexico, and I have wanted to see every area grow and prosper—I wasn't interested in just enhancing my own image and getting re-elected. That kind of strategy will backfire in the long run anyhow. Instead, you go to work every day and try to be responsible, acting in the interests of the greatest good. I never had any other motive. I did the best I could every day. Nearly every action a governor takes has an impact on the average citizen, so it's a responsibility you can't take lightly. History will show whether I was able to improve the quality of life for all New Mexicans, but I like to think I did.

My friend Governor Ned McWhorter of Tennessee liked to say that I worked very hard to make my mark on history and to go down as being an excellent public official who made great accomplishments in the state of New Mexico. "Well," he would say, "I've got news for Bruce King. How many people come to his funeral will depend a great deal more on the weather that day than what he's done." There's quite a bit of truth in that. On the other hand, a whole lot more people know who Bruce King is now than if I had just run the ranch. Once you've been governor a while, they may not like you but they know who you are.

Back around 1960 or so, when my legislative career was really starting to take off, my brothers and I were looking to acquire more ranch land. My old good friend George Savage handled the sales, so we spent a great deal of time riding around with him, looking over the properties like the Alamo Ranch and the pastures up in the Valle Grande in the Jeméz Mountains. We had a great old time. George liked to string it out, and we did too. We'd be riding along in the car, and pretty soon talk would turn to politics. People were already saying that I ought to run for governor. George was a Republican and he had a great ability to focus ideas. One time he turned to me and said, "Now, Bruce, here you've been in the legislature all these years. What have you really accomplished?"

"Well, I'll tell you, George, I've accomplished one thing in my five or six years in the legislature. I've at least proved the fact that I'm honest." I just said it as a quick off-the-cuff shot.

We rode along home, then I saw George after a week or so, and he told me, "You know, Bruce, I got to thinking about what you said. If you can convince people that you're totally honest, I guess that's about the greatest accomplishment anyone can claim."

I think he was right.

"Out on the ranch, when you get things moving
in the right direction, that's when the work really starts.
I've found government is pretty much the same.

As much as we have accomplished, there is plenty
to be done and there are lots of ways to get it done.

The best time is always now."

Bruce King

Index

A

B

C

Pie Town, water situation in, 140
Pittinger, Hershell, 178
Plummer, Marshall, 329
political consultants, 36, 224, 347
Poole, Bob, 97
Popejoy, Tom, 71
Portillo, López, 264, 266, 269
Pound, John, 322
Powell, Pat, 241
Powell, Ray, 159–160, 281
Powell, Wayne, 299
Prentice, Larry, 196
pre-primary nominating convention, bill to
    create, 73
presidential campaign, 1972, 180
Price, Jesse, 7
prison riot. *See* State penitentiary riot
Public Works Committee, 27

Q

Quality in Schools, 306
Quinn, Anthony, 144
Quintana, Santos, 23, 29

R

Racing Commission, 172–173
Ramming, John, 222
Rampton, Cal, 126, 215
Rankin, Noel, 97
Re:Learning New Mexico, 305
Reagan, Ronald, 222, 224, 269
reapportionment, 71–72, 82, 174, 185–187
Reapportionment Bill, 1982, 185
Red Ribbon Campaign against drugs, 302
Republican party, 78, 82, 182, 347
Reynolds, Steve, 128, 286–288
    death of, 289
Richards, Ann, 278, 310
Richardson, Bill, 271, 273, 275–276, *275*,
    278
right-to-work, 45–46, 70, 80, 82, 146, 218–
    222, 230, 232
right-to-work bill, 236
Riley, Richard, 304
Rio Arriba County, politics of, 283
Rio Rancho, Intel expansion, 308
Robb, Dean, 139

Roberts, Austin, 60, 68–71, 73, 80, 137
Rodriguez, Felix, 113, 169–171, 192, 246–
    250, 252, 255
Rodriguez, Reuben, 91
Romero, Al, 42, 161
Romero, Boleslo, 95
Romero, Isidro, 57
Romero, Mercedes, 102
Romney, George, 99
Rosa, Al, 173
Rothrock, Howard, 147
Roundhouse, 76, *121*, 123, 232, *235*, 350
Rowley, Marshall, 111
Roybal, Ben, 139
Ruidoso Downs, 172–173
Runnels, Harold, 116, 265
Rural Development Response Council, 311

S

Saavedra, Louis, 133
Saenz, Adolph, 244, 253–255
Sahd, S. P., 96
Salazar, Dennis, 97
Salazar, John, 113, 171
Salazar, Victor, 113
Salinas (President), 273–276, 278
Salman, David, 144–145
Salvo, John, 234
Salyer, Jo, 110
Samberson, Gene, 234, 253
Sanchez, Maurice, 171
Sanchez, Raymond, 94–96, 102, 104, 106,
    144–145, 298, 309, 330, 332
Sanderoff, Brian, 187, 204, 209–210, 230,
    238
Sandia National Laboratories, 307
    King visited with Bill Clinton, 277
Sandoval, Mr. (neighbor), 210
Santa Fe city police, 245
Santa Fe County
    airport, 30
    convention of county officials, 31
Santa Fe County Central Democratic
    Committee, 161
Santa Fe County Commission, 17, 91, 147
Santa Fe County, roads, 24, 33
Santa Fe grand jury report on penal institu-
    tions, 170